Identity, Motivation and Autonomy
in Language Learning

D0782997

MIX
Paper from
responsible sources
FSC® C014540

FSC
www.fsc.org

SECOND LANGUAGE ACQUISITION
Series Editor: Professor David Singleton, *Trinity College, Dublin, Ireland*

This series brings together titles dealing with a variety of aspects of language acquisition and processing in situations where a language or languages other than the native language is involved. Second language is thus interpreted in its broadest possible sense. The volumes included in the series all offer in their different ways, on the one hand, exposition and discussion of empirical findings and, on the other, some degree of theoretical reflection. In this latter connection, no particular theoretical stance is privileged in the series; nor is any relevant perspective – sociolinguistic, psycholinguistic, neurolinguistic, etc. – deemed out of place. The intended readership of the series includes final-year undergraduates working on second language acquisition projects, postgraduate students involved in second language acquisition research, and researchers and teachers in general whose interests include a second language acquisition component.

Full details of all the books in this series and of all our other publications can be found on http://www.multilingual-matters.com, or by writing to Multilingual Matters, St Nicholas House, 31–34 High Street, Bristol BS1 2AW, UK.

SECOND LANGUAGE ACQUISITION
Series Editor: David Singleton, *Trinity College, Dublin, Ireland*

Identity, Motivation and Autonomy in Language Learning

Edited by
Garold Murray, Xuesong (Andy) Gao
and Terry Lamb

MULTILINGUAL MATTERS
Bristol • Buffalo • Toronto

Library of Congress Cataloging in Publication Data
A catalog record for this book is available from the Library of Congress.
Identity, Motivation and Autonomy in Language Learning/Edited by
Garold Murray, Xuesong (Andy) Gao and Terry Lamb.
Second Language Acquisition: 54
Includes bibliographical references and index.
1. Second language acquisition. 2. Language and languages–Study and teaching.
I. Murray, Garold, 1952- II. Gao, Xuesong. III. Lamb, Terry (Terry E.)
P118.2.I34 2011
418.0071–dc22 2011000718

British Library Cataloguing in Publication Data
A catalogue entry for this book is available from the British Library.

ISBN-13: 978-1-84769-373-0 (hbk)
ISBN-13: 978-1-84769-372-3 (pbk)

Multilingual Matters
UK: St Nicholas House, 31–34 High Street, Bristol BS1 2AW, UK.
USA: UTP, 2250 Military Road, Tonawanda, NY 14150, USA.
Canada: UTP, 5201 Dufferin Street, North York, Ontario M3H 5T8, Canada.

The policy of Multilingual Matters/Channel View Publications is to use papers that are natural, renewable and recyclable products, made from wood grown in sustainable forests. In the manufacturing process of our books, and to further support our policy, preference is given to printers that have FSC and PEFC Chain of Custody certification. The FSC and/or PEFC logos will appear on those books where full certification has been granted to the printer concerned.

Typeset by Datapage International Ltd.
Printed and bound in Great Britain by Short Run Press Ltd.

Contents

Part 3: Cultures and Contexts

Contributors

Stephan Breidbach received his PhD in EFL from Bremen University, Germany. He is an experienced teacher in EFL, Social Studies, History and Drama. He is currently working at Humboldt-Universität zu Berlin as Full Professor of EFL/Foreign Language Education. He publishes on content and language integrated learning, European language policies, and foreign language learning and education.

E. Desirée Castillo Zaragoza is an Assistant Professor at the Foreign Language Department of the Universidad de Sonora, Mexico. She received her PhD in Language Sciences at the Université Nancy 2, France. Her main research interests and publications are related to self-access centres, self-directed learning and advising, and she is currently exploring the multilingualism of learners working in Mexican SACs. She is also the review editor of *Innovation in Language Learning and Teaching*.

Alice Chik's main research areas include language learning histories, English for young learners and popular culture in language education. She is currently working as an Assistant Professor at the Department of English, City University of Hong Kong.

Neil Cowie has taught English in the Language Education Center of Okayama University in Japan since 2004. Prior to that, he taught in various universities, language schools and businesses in Japan and the UK. His research interests include teacher development, student resistance and exploring the connection between emotions and language learning and teaching.

Xuesong (Andy) Gao is an Assistant Professor in the Department of English at the Hong Kong Institute of Education. His research and teaching interests are in the areas of sociolinguistics, vocabulary studies, language learner narratives, language teacher education and higher education.

Jing Huang received his PhD in Applied Linguistics from the University of Hong Kong. He is currently Assistant Professor in the Department of Education Studies at Hong Kong Baptist University. His research interests include autonomy in language learning, TESOL teacher education and second language learner identity. He has published extensively in both Chinese and international journals.

Terry Lamb is a Senior Lecturer at the University of Sheffield. Until recently, he was Director of Initial Teacher Education, where he introduced the PGCE in Mandarin, Japanese and Urdu. He is now Director of Teaching and Learning and Director of the MA in Applied Professional Studies in Education, a programme designed to support teachers at all stages in their careers. He also teaches on the Singapore Distance Learning Programme as well as the EdD in Language Learning and Teaching. In addition, he supervises ten doctoral students.

Martin Lamb is a Senior Lecturer at the University of Leeds, where he teaches undergraduate and postgraduate courses in TESOL for experienced and novice teachers. His main research interest is language learning motivation, both as a traditional psychological construct and as a dynamic, contingent social phenomenon closely related to identity. He previously taught English in Sweden, Indonesia and Bulgaria.

Noemí Lázaro, PhD, is currently researcher at the Center for Autonomous Language Learning in Navarre (CNAI), where she is project manager in innovation programmes for ESP, technology-assisted language learning, staff development and action research in education. Her research interests are in autonomous language learning and self-access centres and she has published widely in these areas. She is also a lecturer at the Spanish Distance University (UNED) in the Doctoral Program for Applied Linguistics.

Diane Malcolm heads the English Language Unit at the Arabian Gulf University, Manama, Bahrain, where she has taught English to first-year Arabic-speaking medical students for many years. The difficulties faced by these students in reading English for their medical studies was the subject of her recently completed doctorate in applied linguistics from Macquarie University, Sydney.

Vera Lúcia Menezes de Oliveira e Paiva, PhD in Linguistics and former president of the Brazilian Association of Applied Linguistics, is a Full

Professor of Applied Linguistics at Universidade Federal de Minas Gerais and a researcher sponsored by CNPq, a Brazilian research agency. She is the editor of the *Brazilian Applied Linguistics Journal* and the coordinator of AMFALE, an international research project on language learning histories. She has edited several books and published papers in Brazil and abroad.

Sarah Mercer teaches English at the University of Graz, Austria, where she has been working for over 10 years. Her PhD, which she completed at the University of Lancaster, investigated the self-concept of tertiary-level EFL learners. Her research interests include all aspects of the psychology surrounding the foreign language learning experience. She is particularly interested in learner beliefs, self-concept, motivation, attributions and mindsets.

Linda Murphy is a Senior Lecturer in the Department of Languages at the Open University, UK, based in Oxford. Apart from her regional work supporting distance language learners and tutors, she has worked on the production of German, French and English courses for distance study. Her research and publications focus on learner strategies, motivation, self-direction and autonomy, as well as tutor skills in the distance language learning context.

Garold Murray is Associate Professor in the Language Education Center at Okayama University, Japan. His research employs narrative inquiry to explore learner autonomy in language learning in classroom, out-of-class and self access contexts. His recent publications examine metacognition, communities of practice and pop culture in relation to out-of-class and self-access language learning.

Hayo Reinders (www.innovationinteaching.org) is Head of Learner Development at Middlesex University in London and Adjunct Professor at the University of Groningen, the Netherlands. He is also editor of *Innovation in Language Learning and Teaching*, and Convenor of the AILA Research Network for CALL and the Learner. Hayo's interests are in CALL, autonomy and out-of-class learning. He is a speaker for the Royal Society of New Zealand. His most recent books are on teacher autonomy, teaching methodologies and second language acquisition, and he edits a book series on *New Language Learning and Teaching Environments* for Palgrave Macmillan.

Stephen Ryan is Associate Professor in the School of Economics at Senshu University, Tokyo. He has been involved in language education for more than 20 years, spending more than 15 years teaching and researching in Japan. His main areas of interest concern issues relating to the motivation to learn a second language.

Liliane Assis Sade received her PhD from the Federal University of Minas Gerais, Brazil. She is Associate Professor of English and Applied Linguistics in the Department of Languages, Arts and Culture at the Federal University of São João del-Rei, Brazil, where she teaches undergraduate students and is in charge of English teaching practice. Her research interests centre on the interface between complexity theory, identity issues and second language learning. They also revolve around discourse analysis and narrative research.

Keiko Sakui is Associate Professor at Kobe Shoin Women's University, Japan. She teaches EFL classes as well as teacher education courses. She has taught Japanese and English in Japan, New Zealand and the USA. Her research interests include teacher and learner beliefs, motivation and critical pedagogy.

Ema Ushioda is an Associate Professor at the Centre for Applied Linguistics, University of Warwick. Her research interests include language learning motivation, autonomy, sociocultural theory and teacher development. Publications include *Teaching and Researching Motivation* (Pearson, 2011, 2nd edition, co-authored by Zoltán Dörnyei), *Motivation, Language Identity and the L2 Self* (Multilingual Matters, 2009, co-edited by Zoltán Dörnyei) and *Learner Autonomy 5: The Role of Motivation* (Authentik, 1996).

Lawrence Jun Zhang, PhD, is Associate Professor at Nanyang Technological University, Singapore. His interests span psycholinguistics, language acquisition and teacher-education. His publications appear in *Applied Linguistics, Perceptual & Motor Skills, Journal of Psycholinguistic Research, British Journal of Educational Psychology, Instructional Science* and *TESOL Quarterly*. He is on the editorial boards of *Metacognition and Learning* and *TESOL Quarterly*.

Chapter 1

Exploring Links between Identity, Motivation and Autonomy

XUESONG GAO and TERRY LAMB

Introduction

Motivation, identity and autonomy have been subjects of intensive research in recent years. In autonomy research, it has been acknowledged that motivation is crucial in learners' autonomous learning, while identity is also seen as a goal or a product of their autonomous learning (Benson, 2007). As researchers increasingly see motivation, identity and autonomy as interrelated, a more convergent approach to exploring these issues may help 'lend some coherence to an increasingly fractious research agenda' caused by 'a proliferation of concepts' (Van Lier, 2010: xvi). To this end, in this edited volume we aim to synergise findings from the three distinctive areas into a concerted pursuit of a better understanding of the role that motivation, identity and autonomy plays in the language learning process.

This book is divided into three sections and includes studies from a variety of contexts, including Brazil, China, Germany, Hong Kong, Indonesia, Japan, Mexico, the Middle East, and the UK. The first section has four chapters, advancing different theoretical perspectives that could be used to explore the links between motivation, identity and autonomy. The second section contains a selection of empirical research conducted in self-access centres (SACs) and distance education contexts, while studies in the third section are primarily concerned with autonomous language learning in particular cultural contexts. In section 2 and 3, we include studies related to the professional development of in-service and pre-service English language teachers or manager-teachers in SACs so that the teachers' side of the story can also be presented.

Emerging Theoretical Perspectives

The first section starts with Ema Ushioda's chapter, entitled 'Motivating Learners to Speak as Themselves'. In this chapter, Ushioda contends that insights from autonomy theory and practice can usefully inform our analysis of motivation, theory and practice. In particular, she explores how processes of engaging, constructing and negotiating identities are central to this analysis. Theorising language learners as fully rounded persons with social identities situated in particular contexts, she argues that such conceptualisation of language learners contrasts sharply with those projected in writings underpinned by psychometric traditions of 'individual difference' research, which ironically rather overlooks learner individuality. She further notices that such motivation research, in pursuing rule-governed patterns linking thought and behaviour, has depersonalised learners. For this reason, she maintains that motivation theory and practice must address the individuality of learners as self-reflective agents, who bring unique identities, personalities, histories, motives and intentions to the social learning context (Ushioda, 2009).

Xuesong (Andy) Gao and Lawrence Jun Zhang's chapter draws attention to the debate over the role of agency and metacognition in autonomy research, which often sees the two concepts as two worlds apart (see Palfreyman, 2003; Wenden, 2002). As the field of autonomy research expands, they believe in the necessity to explore the interrelatedness of the two concepts. In the chapter, they argue that the division of agency as a sociological/sociocultural construct and metacognition as a cognitive construct is unnecessary as each strand of research leads to findings concerning different aspects of learners' autonomous learning. Therefore, research into learner autonomy can capitalise on both areas in order to synergise our understanding of learners' autonomous learning and inform our support for their learning efforts. To illustrate this convergent approach towards agency and metacognition, they analyse a set of data from a longitudinal enquiry into mainland Chinese undergraduates' language learning in Hong Kong. Through interpretations of the data from both perspectives, they advance a view that metacognition and agency be considered complementary to each other in revealing the process and goals of autonomous learning.

In the third chapter, Liliane Assis Sade notes that the increasing interaction among individuals and societies in the contemporary world, and the ever-growing access to new discourses have been contributing to generate a fluid, dynamic, unstable and unpredictable character to human relations. Consequently, certain phenomena, be they physical, biological or social, can no longer be attributed to general laws and simple cause/effect explanations. The positivist paradigm is also no longer appropriate to deal with the complexity of today's world. To achieve a better understanding of such interrelationships, Sade argues that a new paradigm is needed to offer new ways of seeing the same phenomena through a different lens. This new paradigm, as argued by the chapter, focuses on dynamicity and change, not on stability; and on emergence, not on single fixed elements. In this direction, the theoretical framework provided by complexity theory has proved to be useful for a deeper understanding of the complexity that characterises human relations in the global society (Holland, 1995; Larsen-Freeman & Cameron, 2008). This chapter also contends that the participation of the individual in social practices contributes to a process of 'fractalisation' of the self, and at the same time it constructs a sense of wholeness that is achieved from the interactions established among the several emergent social selves. This process, in turn, affects and is affected by language learning.

Vera Lúcia Menezes de Oliveira e Paiva's chapter further develops the argument that theories of dynamic systems and complexity offer better understandings of language learning. In this chapter, language is understood as a non-linear dynamic system, made up of interrelated bio-cognitive, sociocultural, historical and political elements, which enable us to think and act in society. As a consequence, second language acquisition (SLA) will also be treated as a dynamic system, made up of several elements, including identity, motivation and autonomy. In this new theoretical perspective, any change in an element of the SLA system can affect all the other elements. Having these assumptions as starting points, Menezes examines a *corpus* of language learning narratives written by Japanese and Brazilian English learners. She compares the 'initial conditions' of their language learning to see what motivates the SLA system's set-up processes, and how identity construction and autonomy influence their trajectories and changes. In the analysis, she places special emphasis on identity, motivation and autonomy as interconnected agents in the process of language acquisition. In her view, minimal differences in identity, motivation and autonomy, among other factors, can cause very different results in the acquisition outcomes.

Independent Learning Settings

The second section has four chapters about language learners and teachers in independent learning settings, such as SACs, and distance education. Garold Murray's chapter explores the potential of second language (L2) pedagogies that foster the development and realisation of learners' ideal L2 selves (see Dörnyei, 2005, 2009; Ushioda, 2009) by reporting on a research project investigating the experiences of Japanese first-year university students studying English in a self-directed learning course. In accordance with Holec's (1981) model, the learners in the course determined their own goals and subsequently devised and carried out learning plans designed to help them meet these goals. In a preliminary analysis of the data, Murray identified the role that imagination played in the participants' language learning experiences. Employing the combined theoretical perspectives of possible selves and imagined communities, this chapter illustrates how imagination mediated the role of possible selves and imagined communities in the daily learning experiences of the participants in this study, thereby demonstrating the potential of this mode of learning as a pedagogical intervention capable of fostering learners' visions of L2 selves and enabling them to work towards the realisation of this ideal self.

Desirée Castillo Zaragoza's chapter examines the relationship between multilingualism and learners in SACs. In this chapter, SACs are considered multilingual by virtue of the languages they offer, thereby providing opportunities for researchers to explore the link between multilingualism/plurilingualism and language learner autonomy. Castillo Zaragoza notes that the research literature on SACs usually takes a monolingual posture even though language learners usually have access to a variety of resources, such as materials, advisors, other learners and native speakers as well as other languages. To address this missing link in autonomy research, Castillo Zaragoza reports on a study on Mexican learners who learn up to five languages using the classroom and/or SACs, despite the fact that Mexico is a *de facto* monolingual country and has no explicit policy on multilingualism. Based on 33 interviews in two Mexican public universities, this exploratory inquiry reveals how learners have seen the importance of developing their plurilingual identity, have high intrinsic motivation and use their agency in a context that does not explicitly encourage multilingualism.

Linda Murphy's chapter deals with a critical question concerning distance language learners who are generally responsible for scheduling their study time and are increasingly expected to manage their own learning progress and maintain their motivation within a programme framework that may offer more or less guidance and structure. Given that self-motivation is crucial in distance learning, how do these language learners keep going when the going gets tough? After outlining the key issues in relation to autonomy and motivation within the context of distance language learning, this chapter considers how theories play out in practice by examining the experiences of adult distance learners of French, German and Spanish, who logged anything that negatively affected their motivation, how they handled setbacks and what inspired or motivated them during a period of seven months while studying with the Open University (UK). This chapter reports on the findings emerging from the analysis of these language learners' experiences in light of research on self-regulation, autonomy and Dörnyei's (2005) motivational self-system. It also concludes by suggesting how these experiences could be used to enhance distance language learning programmes.

The fourth chapter by Hayo Reinders and Noemí Lázaro reports on a large-scale investigation that delved into teachers' roles as agents in the learning process and, in particular, their roles as facilitators of autonomous learning in SACs. The study, in which extensive interviews were held with manager-teachers of 46 SACs in five countries, aimed to (1) elicit teachers' beliefs about learner autonomy in self-access contexts, (2) identify conflicts between teachers' beliefs about autonomy and students' (self-access) language learning behaviour, and (3) identify conflicts between teachers' beliefs and institutional constraints. As reported in this chapter, the inquiry revealed a complex and sometimes conflicting interaction between the managers' beliefs and their everyday roles, which shows that the concept of agency cannot be separated from those of motivation and identity. A particular area of tension emerged (both negatively as frustration and positively as challenge) from the relationship between teachers' beliefs and learners' beliefs about autonomy and the roles of teachers and learners in the learning process, as well as the perceived need to reconcile those beliefs.

Cultures and Contexts

Following the chapters on language learners and teachers in independent learning settings, the third section contains six chapters, four concerning language learners' experiences in various contexts and two concerning teachers' perspectives on classroom motivation practices and pre-service teachers' autonomy development.

In their chapter, Alice Chik and Stephan Breidbach report on a comparative study on two groups of language learners' language learning experiences (German postgraduates in Berlin and Chinese undergraduates in Hong Kong). Both groups of learners are learning English as a second language with the Hong Kong students majoring in English while their German counterparts are preparing for their future careers as English teachers. In the study, these learners wrote and shared their multimodal language learning histories through course wikis, and asynchronous responses were also posted. By doing so, learners from both countries would initiate conversations on the process of second and foreign language learning and raise awareness on experiences of foreign language learning in different cultural and educational contexts. Drawing on the autobiographical narratives written by six learners, three from Hong Kong and three from Germany, Chik and Breidbach explore their life-long development of language learning. Despite a lack of sustained English-speaking environments, in the analysis the six learners were found to have exhibited high levels of motivation and mediated their identities through specific individual practices. In light of the growing body of academic work on the L2 self, the narratives examined in this chapter illuminate popular culture as the overarching link in identity, motivation and autonomy cultivation.

Stephen Ryan and Sarah Mercer's chapter considers language learners' mental constructions of 'abroad' and their impact on individual agency and identity. The ideas discussed in this chapter have emerged from the authors' reflections on a series of studies into language learners' ideas about the place of innate talent in the language learning process and it is these studies that provide the chapter's theoretical foundations. In the chapter, the authors contend that learners' implicit theories of language learning, in particular their evaluations of the relative roles of talent and effort in successful language learning, are a key, under-researched aspect of a sense of agency. However, within educational psychology, there is a rich body of literature dealing with implicit theories of learning in fields as diverse as music and sport. This chapter is an attempt to apply this line of research to the field of language learning. Although primarily conceptual in nature, the chapter draws on data obtained from attitudinal questionnaires, language learning histories and interviews. The data suggest that for many learners, 'study abroad' exists as a constant background presence in their language learning. In many respects, learners' constructions of abroad serve as a powerful motivating force, yet they may also undermine their learning efforts. Learners' use of 'abroad' as a reference point for validation of their identities as language users and the emphasis that this affords to language learning as a natural, effortless process appears to diminish their sense of agency as learners.

Martin Lamb' s chapter aims to contribute to the development of research relating 'future self-guides' to the learning of a second/foreign language (Dörnyei & Ushioda, 2009) by considering how stable they are over the long term, and how far they do, as hypothesised, promote autonomous learning of the L2. In the chapter, Lamb reports on the results of a follow-up study into the evolving motivation of provincial Indonesian junior high school learners to learn English. In the study,

Lamb associates the significant gains that the participants had made in oral proficiency in English with both strong future self-guides and sustained autonomous language learning. The chapter draws out the implications of these findings for the elaboration of theories linking L2 motivation and autonomy to future-related learner identities.

Diane Malcolm's chapter reports on a small-scale exploratory study that drew on interviews from four Arabic-speaking medical students in different years of studying through the medium of English at a medical college in Bahrain. In the chapter, Malcolm describes how they dealt with the experience of failing as an incentive to develop greater autonomy in language learning both for immediate gains, to improve their English language skills for study purposes, and for their imagined future selves as globalised English-language competent medical specialists. With the help of competent and experienced others and through such actions as summer study semesters in English-speaking countries, these learners were also found to have exercised their agency to improve their English ability. Malcolm argues that the development of these students' identities from unsuccessful to competent users of English in the medical school setting is related to educational and cultural factors in the immediate Gulf Arab context, as well as personal factors such as self-efficacy beliefs.

Neil Cowie and Keiko Sakui's chapter addresses the lack of research on English as a foreign language teachers' perspective on learner motivation. The study reported in the chapter aimed to examine teacher cognition and strategies for motivation in a culturally and socio-politically specific context and reveal teachers' insights that bridge motivational theories and classroom practices. Thirty-two teachers from six countries (UK, USA, Australia, Canada, Japan and China) responded to an initial e-mail survey and follow-up interviews were conducted with four of these participants. As concluded by Cowie and Sakui, the teachers' views seem to reflect recent theories on motivation, particularly from a psychological perspective (Dörnyei, 2005; Williams & Burden, 1997) and adds important pedagogical evidence to the motivation literature, which has relatively little to say about teacher beliefs and practices in the area of learner motivation.

The final chapter by Huang Jing provides empirical evidence for Benson's (2007: 30) contention that 'agency can perhaps be viewed as a point of origin for the development of autonomy, while identity might be viewed as one of its more important outcomes'. In this chapter, Huang conceptualises autonomy and agency (and identity) as interrelated but distinct concepts. Drawing on learner autobiographies, life history interviews and participant observation, Huang's chapter explores the long-term development of autonomy among students in a particular Chinese social and institutional context (a non-prestigious teacher-education university in mainland China). Following an interpretative-qualitative paradigm, and foregrounding insider perspectives, the chapter gives particular attention to the role of agency and identity in the long-term development of autonomy in language learning.

As mentioned earlier, this book is a collection of attempts to explore the links between identity, motivation and autonomy. A volume of collected studies such as this one is by no means exhaustive and further efforts are still needed to deepen our understanding of these crucial concepts. Nevertheless, we hope that this collection of studies, using a whole spectrum of new theoretical perspectives and reporting freshly collected research evidence in a variety of contexts, will further the research on autonomy, identity and motivation as interrelated concepts.

References

Benson, P. (2007) Autonomy in language teaching and learning. *Language Teaching* 40 (1), 21–40.

Dörnyei, Z. (2005) *The Psychology of the Language Learner: Individual Differences in Second Language Acquisition*. Mahwah, NJ: Lawrence Erlbaum.

Dörnyei, Z. (2009) The L2 motivational self system. In Z. Dörnyei and E. Ushioda (eds) *Motivation, Language Identity and the L2 Self* (pp. 9–42). Bristol: Multilingual Matters.

Dörnyei, Z. and Ushioda, E. (eds) (2009) *Motivation, Language Identity and the L2 Self*. Bristol: Multilingual Matters.

Holec, H. (1981) *Autonomy and Foreign Language Learning*. Oxford: Pergamon Press.

Holland, J.H. (1995) *Hidden Order: How Adaptation Builds Complexity*. Reading, MA: Addison-Wesley.

Larsen-Freeman, D. and Cameron, L. (2008) *Complex Systems and Applied Linguistics*. Oxford: Oxford University Press.

Palfreyman, D. (2003) Expanding the discourse on learner development: A reply to Anita Wenden. *Applied Linguistics* 24, 243–248.

Ushioda, E. (2009) A person-in-context relational view of emergent motivation, self and identity. In Z. Dörnyei and E. Ushioda (eds) *Motivation, Language Identity and the L2 Self* (pp. 215–228). Bristol: Multilingual Matters.

Van Lier, L. (2010) Foreword: Agency, self and identity in language learning. In B. O'Rourke and L. Carson (eds) *Language Learner Autonomy: Policy, Curriculum, Classroom* (pp. ix–xviii). Bern: Peter Lang.

Wenden, A. (2002) Learner development in language learning. *Applied Linguistics* 23, 32–55.

Williams, M. and Burden, R. (1997) *Psychology for Language Teachers*. Cambridge: Cambridge University Press.

Part 1

Emerging Theoretical Perspectives

Chapter 2

Motivating Learners to Speak as Themselves

EMA USHIODA

Introduction

For over a dozen years now, I have been interested in the twin areas of motivation and autonomy in language learning and their interactions. By interactions, I mean interactions in a *practical* sense, in terms of how motivation and autonomy interact in learner behaviours and classroom practices; and I also mean interactions in a *conceptual* sense, in terms of how these two constructs of motivation and autonomy have been theorised and developed in somewhat different traditions of inquiry, reflecting different literature bases, philosophies and research paradigms, and yet clearly these constructs share much in common. To put it simply, we might say that motivation theory has broadly developed in a positivist cognitive paradigm, which is characterised by psychometric measurement and the development of abstract computational models of mental processes and learning outcomes and behaviours. This is true for both mainstream motivational psychology as well as the specific field of language learning motivation research. Autonomy theory, on the other hand, originated in the very different domain of political and moral philosophy; and autonomy theory in language education has broadly developed in a constructivist paradigm, grounded in specific contexts of practice and the needs and concerns of particular learners.

Within the language learning motivation field, which has a rich history of over 40 years of research, I am regarded as representing something of an 'alternative' perspective, since I bring to the analysis of motivation a particularised, contextually grounded and qualitative angle of inquiry, influenced in no small measure by my engagement with the autonomy literature. This 'alternative' perspective goes against the grain of much mainstream language learning motivation theory to date, which has been concerned more with the general than the particular, with statistical averages and relations rather than rich descriptive analysis. As

I will argue in this chapter, if our pedagogical concern is to engage the motivation of particular (rather than generalised) learners, then we need a theoretical perspective that addresses its uniquely personal and contextually grounded nature. In this regard, I will further argue that insights from autonomy theory and practice can usefully inform our analysis of motivation, and in particular, I will discuss how processes of engaging, constructing and negotiating identities are central to this analysis.

Motivation Theory and Practice: Abstract Models, not People

Motivation has traditionally been characterised as an individual difference (ID) variable that is implicated in learning success, alongside other ID variables such as aptitude, personality, anxiety or cognitive style (for a recent overview of ID research in second language acquisition (SLA), see Ellis, 2008: 643–723). Dörnyei (2005: 4) describes ID constructs as 'dimensions of enduring personal characteristics that are assumed to apply to everybody and on which people differ by degree'. Ironically, however, despite its theoretical focus on how people 'differ' from one another or from some kind of normative standard, ID research concerns itself not with the unique characteristics of particular individuals, but with the shared characteristics of particular types of individuals. Anchored in psychometric approaches to the measurement of personal traits, ID research deploys measurement techniques and statistical procedures that make certain assumptions about the normal distribution of particular traits in a given population. As I have argued elsewhere (Ushioda, 2009: 215–216), one might say that ID research focuses not on differences between individuals, but on averages and aggregates that lump together people who share certain characteristics such as high intrinsic motivation or low self-efficacy. In pursuing rule-governed patterns linking cognition, motivation and behaviour, such research depersonalises learners, who are treated simply as abstract bundles of variables so that, as Bandura (2001: 2) wryly notes, 'it is not people but their componentized subpersonal parts that are orchestrating courses of action'.

Thus, in Ushioda (2009), I have argued instead for what I call a 'person-in-context relational view' of motivation. By this, I mean a focus on real persons, rather than on learners as theoretical abstractions; a focus on the agency of the individual person as a thinking, feeling human being, with an identity, a personality, a unique history and background, with goals, motives and intentions; a focus on the interaction between this self-reflective agent, and the fluid and complex web of social relations, activities, experiences and multiple micro- and macro-contexts in which the person is embedded, moves and is inherently part of. My argument is that we need to take a relational (rather than linear) view of these multiple contextual elements, and see motivation as an organic process that emerges through the complex system of interrelations.

This focus on the individuality of the person and on the contextually grounded and relational nature of motivation does not reflect a purely theoretical interest in how we conceptualise motivation. As I indicated in the Introduction, if our pedagogical concern is to engage the motivation of particular (rather than generalised) learners, then we need a theoretical perspective that addresses its uniquely personal and contextually grounded nature. A problem with the traditional computational models of motivation that have dominated the field is that they seek to make generalisable predictions about what kinds of motivation might lead to what kinds of learning behaviour in what kinds of context, and thus to identify what kinds of pedagogical intervention might be needed to change maladaptive patterns of motivation and so improve learning behaviours and outcomes (Ushioda, 2009: 218). Translated into classroom practice, such models thus promote a view of motivation as essentially controlled by the teacher through various techniques and strategies, rather than as actively shaped through personal meaning-making, intentionality and reflexivity. Moreover, such models focus teachers' attention on generalised types of learner behaviour and attitude and how to deal with them, rather than on how to engage with the complex and uniquely individual people in their classrooms: people who bring particular identities, histories, goals and motives; people for whom learning a language is just one small part of their lives; people who are not just 'language learners' and who perhaps do not see themselves in these terms.

Autonomy Theory and Practice: People, not Abstract Models

In contrast to the literature on language learning motivation, as Riley (2003: 239) observes, a key characteristic of writing on autonomy is its concern with the learner as a fully rounded person, with a social identity, situated in a particular context. In language classrooms that seek to promote autonomous learning, it seems that this concern is translated into pedagogical practices that encourage students to develop and express their own identities through the language they are learning – that is, to be and to become themselves, so that as Little (2004: 106) puts it, 'what they learn becomes part of what they are'.

This is vividly demonstrated in Legenhausen's (1999) comparative analysis of English conversation practice among 12-year-old German and Danish children learning English in different kinds of classroom environment. Socialised in traditional textbook-based communicative classrooms in Gymnasium and comprehensive schools, the German children seem somehow unable or unwilling 'to speak as themselves' (Legenhausen, 1999: 181) when invited to converse in English with one another in pairs. Invariably, they fall back instead on memorised routines and content from textbook dialogues, such as asking one another how old they are, where they live and what their favourite subjects are at school, and thus engage in a kind of pseudo-communication where the emphasis is on practising language rather than expressing personal meanings and identities (see Example 1).

Example 1

S: Ehm, how old is your father?
I: My father is forty years old. And how old is your father?
S: Fifteen years old. How old is your mother?
I: My mother is thirty-nine years old.
S: How old are you?
I: I'm twelve. How old are you?
S: I'm eleven. What are your foreign languages?
I: My foreign languages are *Sport, Textil*. What are your foreign languages?
S: My foreign languages are *Biologie, Textil* and German.
I: Ehm.
S: Oh, ah how ah how *ne*, what is the name of your father?
I: The name of my father is Felix. And what is the name of your father?
S: Ehm, the name of my father is ah Bernd, ah.
I: What's the name of your mother?
S: Ehm, ah, my mother's name is Maria. And your mother's name? (Legenhausen, 1999: 166–167)

On the other hand, the Danish children have been exposed to a different kind of classroom culture that promotes autonomous learning, where they pursue activities of their own choice and according to their own needs and interests, and 'do not construe a contrast between authentic and didactic tasks' (Legenhausen, 1999: 181). Thus, when asked to talk in pairs, they engage their own motivations, identities and personal interests in their conversations, since this is how they have been socialised to use and think of English, i.e. as a means of developing and expressing their own identities and engaging with the world. Their conversations also proceed in a far more natural and organic fashion and exhibit the interactional features of authentic communication (see Example 2).

Example 2

> L: What should we talk about, Claus?
> C: I don't know, we could talk about our music group 'Big Engine'.
> L: Yeah, that's a good idea –
> C: I think it's fun. Now we have to play, ah, record our tape.
> L: Yeah, the first time.
> C: Yeah, it's very exciting. I have made a cover to our tape at home.
> L: That one you showed me?
> C: Yes.
> L: The only thing it's beautiful.
> C: Beautiful?
> L: Yes
> C: It's lovely. (Laughing)
> L: I think it's good, too.
> C: Yes.
> (Legenhausen, 1999: 167)

Analysing the contrasts between the German and Danish children's conversations, Legenhausen draws attention to the critical relationship between the language classroom and the world of the children's lives outside the classroom. As he argues, whether the classroom is seen as an integrative constituent part of the life surrounding it, or is seen as separate from real life, will have a major impact on the kinds of target language communication that take place in the classroom, and on the degree to which those learning the language are enabled to 'speak as themselves' instead of merely behaving as 'language learners' practising language (Legenhausen, 1999: 171).

Speaking as Themselves: Motivation and Transportable Identities

What happens then to *motivation* when students are encouraged to 'speak as themselves' and to express and engage their identities through the language they are learning? I will refer here to another interesting analysis of conversations in the language classroom that, though not explicitly focused on motivation, certainly sheds light on the motivational dimension.

Richards (2006) sets out to explore whether 'real conversations' are possible in the institutionalised setting of the language classroom, particularly in the context of teacher–student interaction in whole-class teaching, where teacher-controlled patterns of initiation–response–follow-up (IRF) invariably dominate. He argues that in order to understand whether and how 'real conversations' may occasionally permeate teacher–student classroom talk, the analytical lens needs to focus on aspects of identity as these are dynamically constructed in the developing discourse. Adopting Zimmerman's (1998) model of discoursal and social identities, Richards makes a distinction between three aspects of identity:

- Firstly, there are *situated identities*, which are explicitly conferred by the particular context of communication, such as doctor–patient identities in the context of a health clinic, or teacher–student identities in the context of a classroom.
- Secondly, there are associated *discourse identities*, as participants orient themselves to particular discourse roles in the moment-by-moment organisation of the interaction (e.g. initiator, listener, questioner, challenger).
- Thirdly, and most importantly, there are *transportable identities*, which are latent or implicit but can be invoked during the interaction for particular reasons. For example, during an English lesson, a teacher might allude to the fact that she is a mother of two, a keen tennis player or an avid science fiction fan.

It is this notion of transportable identities, and students' transportable identities in particular, which seems key to the analysis of motivation. In his paper, Richards analyses samples of classroom talk between teachers and students in different language classrooms. Through a careful line-by-line analysis of interactional moves in these samples, he shows very convincingly the powerful motivational impact of invoking and orienting to students' own transportable identities in the classroom talk. Engaging students' transportable identities (e.g. as football fan, amateur photographer, art lover, film buff) can stimulate a much higher level of personal involvement, effort and investment from them than traditional teacher–student talk, where students are invariably positioned as language learners who are merely practising or demonstrating knowledge of the language, rather than expressing their identities and speaking as themselves through the language.

The notion of transportable identities connects strongly with Legenhausen's (1999) emphasis on bridging the worlds inside and outside the classroom, since transportable identities by definition extend beyond the physical boundaries of the classroom and beyond teacher–student roles and relationships. However, an important critical issue raised by Richards (2006: 72) towards the end of his paper is that engaging students' (and teachers') transportable identities in the language classroom will necessarily involve an investment of self, with all the emotional, relational and moral considerations that this entails. One can imagine classroom contexts where such an investment of self may be perceived or experienced as uncomfortable or threatening, and where students may prefer not to invoke particular transportable identities in their talk. Here too, I would argue that insights from autonomy theory and practice are relevant: essentially, a key pedagogical principle in this regard is one of enabling students to exercise autonomy or choice in terms of which aspects of their identity they wish to engage and are motivated to express.

By contrast, the motivational consequences of *not orienting* to students' transportable identities when they try to give expression to these seem potentially rather detrimental, as is implicit in this telling example of teacher feedback and error correction from Scrivener (1994: 19):

> Student: I am feeling bad. My grandfather he die last week and I am . . .
> Teacher: No – not die – say died because it's in the past.

In short, to the extent that we as teachers invoke and orient to students' transportable identities in the classroom and engage with them as 'people' rather than as simply 'language learners'; to the extent that we encourage and create opportunities for them to 'speak as themselves' and engage and express their own preferred meanings, interests and identities through the medium of the target language; the more likely that students will feel involved and motivated to communicate and thus to engage themselves in the process of learning and using the language.

Of course, the argument I am developing will hardly seem new to many classroom practitioners. The notion of engaging our students' identities is something that many experienced language teachers have intuitively recognised as important, and is a principle that has often found its way into the language teacher training literature in the shape of buzzwords like *learner-centred teaching*, *authentic communication*, *personalisation* and so on. In fact, without wishing to sound too provocative, I believe that this is very much a case where practice leads and where motivation theory has rather lagged behind. In other words, it is only now that motivation theory is catching up with what many effective teachers have long been doing in their classrooms, and finding ways of analysing and theorising this practice. As I argued earlier, a basic limitation of language learning motivation theory to date is that it has been primarily concerned with abstract models and with learners as theoretical bundles of variables, and not with language learners as people who bring uniquely individual identities, histories, goals and intentions and who inhabit complex dynamic social realities.

Current Perspectives: Towards Motivation as Value-based and Identity-oriented

However, perhaps it is not surprising that language learning motivation theory is only now beginning to look beyond traditional abstract frameworks and models and take a more contextually grounded and identity-oriented perspective, since it is only within the last decade that such perspectives have begun to inform motivation theory in education in general (e.g. Volet & Järvelä, 2001). Broadly speaking, much of the history of motivation in educational psychology over the past 40 years has revolved around the central notion of 'achievement', building on the early classic model of achievement motivation developed by John Atkinson in 1964, and the associated concepts of need for achievement, achievement orientation, expectancy of success or fear of failure. Of course, motivation researchers in education have also recognised the importance of non-achievement-related personal goals in the classroom, such as need for affiliation, need for power or various social and peer-related goals (e.g. Wentzel, 2000, 2007). However, theories of motivation in education have struggled to accommodate the idea of goal multiplicity, and have inevitably tended to focus attention primarily on achievement-related goals and on motivation behaviours and cognitions revolving around, for example, success or failure, mastery or performance orientations, competence, self-efficacy (see, e.g. Elliot & Dweck, 2007; Pintrich & Schunk, 2002).

But there are signs that things are now changing, and that theories of motivation in education are beginning to shift away from achievement-oriented frameworks, as reflected in a recent special issue of the journal *Educational Psychologist* edited by Kaplan and Flum (2009), which focuses on motivation and identity. As Brophy (2009) argues in his commentary paper in this special issue, many of the key constructs defined as *achievement based* (i.e. focused on success) in achievement motivation theories are, in fact, *value based* and *identity oriented*. Of course, at a very general level, it seems a rather obvious thing to say that motivation and identity are linked in this way, i.e. that there is an intimate connection between our goal-directed behaviours and the identities we pursue; between the activities we engage in and the social groups we want to identify with; between what we do and the kind of person we see ourselves as or want to become. However, as Kaplan and Flum (2009) point out, it is only fairly recently that motivation researchers have really begun to explore these connections and to re-theorise motivation in education in terms of socially grounded value-based and identity-oriented frameworks, and to reframe existing motivational theories such as self-determination theory (La Guardia, 2009) and expectancy-value theory (Eccles, 2009) in relation to constructs of identity.

In the language education field too, we have begun to re-theorise motivation in relation to concepts of self and identity, particularly in terms of one's aspirations towards certain kinds of linguistic or cultural identity, or towards valued personal or professional identities that are defined, in part, by proficiency in particular languages (Dörnyei, 2005, 2009; Dörnyei & Ushioda, 2009). This push to re-theorise language learning motivation in relation to self and identity has not just been prompted by developments in the mainstream motivational literature in education. It has also been shaped by growing critical debates within the SLA field about the relevance of Gardner's (1985) notion of integrative motivation in the modern globalised world, particularly where the learning of English as the target language is concerned, given the status of English as an international language and, increasingly, as a basic educational skill in many curricula (e.g. Ushioda, 2006), and given the complex sociolinguistic realities of language use and identity in postcolonial world Englishes contexts (Coetzee-Van Rooy, 2006).

This re-theorising of language motivation in relation to self and identity has been spearheaded in particular by Dörnyei, who conducted a large-scale longitudinal survey of Hungarian teenagers' language learning attitudes and motivation (Dörnyei & Csizér, 2002; Dörnyei *et al.*, 2006), spanning the period from 1993 (just after the fall of Communism) to 2004 (on the eve of Hungary's membership of the European Union) and comprising data from over 13,000 learners. Although an integrative motivation factor emerged consistently strongly in the longitudinal analysis, this factor was underpinned by both practical instrumental motivation as well as positive attitudes to target language speakers. This composite finding led Dörnyei and Csizér (2002) to speculate that the process of identification theorised to define integrative motivation might be better conceived as an *internal process* of identification *within the person's self concept*, rather than identification with an external reference group.

Dörnyei (2005, 2009) subsequently develops this speculation further by drawing on the psychological theory of *possible selves*. According to Markus and Nurius (1986), possible selves represent individuals' ideas of what they might become, what they would like to become and what they are afraid of becoming, and so provide an important conceptual link between the self-concept and motivation. Building on this theory, Dörnyei (2005, 2009) has developed a new conceptualisation of language motivation, which he calls the 'L2 Motivational Self System'. The central concept in the L2 Motivational Self System is the *ideal self*. This refers to the attributes that we would ideally like to possess, i.e. our personal hopes, aspirations or wishes. A complementary concept is the *ought-to self*. This refers to the attributes that we believe we ought to possess, i.e. attributes that are perhaps foisted on us by others (e.g. parents, teachers, social pressures). A basic assumption in Dörnyei's theory is that if proficiency in the target language is part and parcel of one's ideal or ought-to self, this will serve as a powerful motivator to learn the language because of our psychological desire to reduce the discrepancy between our current self and possible future selves.

Autonomy, Identity and Personal Motivational Trajectories

As Dörnyei (2009) argues, these future self-states can have strong psychological reality in the *current* imaginative experiences of learners, as they try to envision themselves projected into the future as competent second language (L2) users. In other words, these future self representations are entirely continuous with their current selves. Thus, to the extent that language learners engage (or are enabled to engage) their current selves in their L2 interactions in the classroom now and to 'speak as themselves' with their 'transportable identities', one can argue that they are also enabled to engage directly with their future possible selves as users of the target language, but within the scope and security of their current communicative abilities.

This integral connection between current and future motivational self-states is one that has been similarly highlighted in the shift towards value-based and identity-oriented frameworks in motivation in education. While achievement motivation theories have focused primarily on proximal short-term outcomes of choice, engagement and performance, as Kaplan and Flum (2009) explain, by linking motivation with identity goals and identity formation, we bring into focus more long-term developmental processes and personal trajectories that contribute to and are shaped by current situated motivational processes. Students' engagement in school, their choices, struggles and negotiations are clearly affected by and in turn influence who they think they are, who they think they want to be and who they actually become (Kaplan & Flum, 2009: 76). Moreover, as McCaslin (2009) explains, who I am or want to be is also defined in terms of who I am not or do not want to become.

As Brophy (2009) emphasises, this perspective on the developmental trajectories of motivation and identity underlines the critical importance of socialisation in promoting motivation towards adaptive values and identities, and away from those that are less desirable. Identities grow and change, partly in response to encouragement and pressure from the culture at large, or from socialisers, peers and significant others within one's social circle; and these emerging motivational dispositions and identities can solidify and develop into core values and more long-term stable identities (Brophy, 2009: 155).

In this connection, involving students in making relevant choices and decisions about their learning may facilitate this process of alignment towards culturally valued adaptive values and identities (Ryan *et al.*, 1992; Ushioda, 2003). However, as McCaslin (2009: 138) points out, in many educational settings, involving students in making meaningful choices is not always a possibility and opportunities for learning to make choices are not equitably distributed. Nor is *choice* necessarily the prime expression of individual motivation and identity. McCaslin suggests that *struggle* and *negotiation* may also guide the emerging dispositions and identities of students, since struggle and negotiation promote particular response patterns (e.g. striving, compliance, resistance, adaptation), which express and inform motivation and identity. When students are enabled to voice opinions, preferences and values, align themselves with those of others, engage in discussion, struggle, resist, negotiate, compromise or adapt, their motivational dispositions and identities evolve and are given expression. As McCaslin (2009: 139) argues, these motivations and identities are shaped, in part, by the social relationships that support and validate them; or as she writes: 'What we do and in connection with whom inform who we might become' (McCaslin, 2009: 137–138). Thus, she regards *participation* in opportunity and interpersonal validation as crucially important in the development, socialisation and *co-regulation* of students' motivation and identities. In other words, it is through social participation in opportunities, negotiations and activities that people's motivations and identities develop and emerge as dynamically co-constructed processes.

The identity perspective on motivation thus brings into sharp relief the socially mediated nature of motivation as emergent through complex interactions among social, individual and contextual processes (Ushioda, 2009). It also brings into sharp relief the intimate connections between motivation and autonomy, particularly those between motivation and what Little (2007) calls *language learner autonomy*, as opposed to learner autonomy in general. By this, I mean that the identity perspective highlights a psychological dimension of student motivation that is concerned not just with personal agency or self-determination, which can apply equally to autonomy and learning in any subject or skill domain (e.g. Deci & Ryan, 2002). The identity perspective also highlights a dimension of student motivation that is specifically concerned with *self-expression*, which has unique relevance, of course, when the object of learning is a language. By enabling students to 'speak as themselves' in the target language with their preferred 'transportable identities', as they negotiate, struggle, participate, share ideas and experiences and evaluate these, classroom practices that promote autonomy are likely to contribute to socialising and consolidating adaptive values, identities and motivational trajectories in terms of how students relate to the target language and use it to develop and express themselves. Such classroom practices contrast sharply with those that seek to regulate students' language learning and language use behaviours in a controlled way.

Thus, by promoting autonomy and motivating learners to speak as themselves now, we may enable them to fulfil their potential to be the persons they want to become or grow to value, and to use the language to do the things they want or grow to value, in a healthy and adaptive way that is internally consistent with their own motivation and sense of self.

References

Atkinson, J.W. (1964) *An Introduction to Motivation*. Princeton, NJ: Van Nostrand.

Bandura, A. (2001) Social cognitive theory: An agentic perspective. *Annual Review of Psychology* 52, 1–26.

Brophy, J. (2009) Connecting with the big picture. *Educational Psychologist* 44 (2), 147–157.

Coetzee-Van Rooy, S. (2006) Integrativeness: Untenable for world Englishes learners? *World Englishes* 25 (3/4), 437–450.

Deci, E.L. and Ryan, R.M. (eds) (2002) *Handbook of Self-Determination Research*. Rochester, NY: The University of Rochester Press.

Dörnyei, Z. (2005) *The Psychology of the Language Learner: Individual Differences in Second Language Acquisition*. Mahwah, NJ: Lawrence Erlbaum.

Dörnyei, Z. (2009) The L2 Motivational Self System. In Z. Dörnyei and E. Ushioda (eds) *Motivation, Language Identity and the L2 Self* (pp. 9–42). Bristol: Multilingual Matters.

Dörnyei, Z. and Csizér, K. (2002) Some dynamics of language attitudes and motivation: Results of a longitudinal nationwide survey. *Applied Linguistics* 23, 421–462.

Dörnyei, Z., Csizér, K. and Németh, N. (2006) *Motivation, Language Attitudes and Globalisation: A Hungarian Perspective*. Clevedon: Multilingual Matters.

Dörnyei, Z. and Ushioda, E. (eds) (2009) *Motivation, Language Identity and the L2 Self*. Bristol: Multilingual Matters.

Eccles, J. (2009) Who am I and what am I going to do with my life? Personal and collective identities as motivators of action. *Educational Psychologist* 44 (2), 78–89.

Elliot, A.J. and Dweck, C.S. (eds) (2007) *Handbook of Competence and Motivation*. New York: The Guilford Press.

Ellis, R. (2008) *The Study of Second Language Acquisition* (2nd edn). Oxford: Oxford University Press.

Gardner, R.C. (1985) *Social Psychology and Second Language Learning: The Role of Attitudes and Motivation*. London: Edward Arnold.

Kaplan, A. and Flum, H. (2009) Motivation and identity: The relations of action and development in educational contexts – An introduction to the special issue. *Educational Psychologist* 44 (2), 73–77.

La Guardia, J.G. (2009) Developing who I am: A self-determination theory approach to the establishment of healthy identities. *Educational Psychologist* 44 (2), 90–104.

Legenhausen, L. (1999) Autonomous and traditional learners compared: The impact of classroom culture on attitudes and communicative behaviour. In C. Edelhoff and R. Weskamp (eds) *Autonomes Fremdsprachenlernen* (pp. 166–182). Ismaning: Hueber.

Little, D. (2004) Democracy, discourse and learner autonomy in the foreign language classroom. *Utbildning & Demokrati* 13 (3), 106–126.

Little, D. (2007) Language learner autonomy: Some fundamental considerations revisited. *Innovation in Language Learning and Teaching* 1 (1), 14–29.

Markus, H. and Nurius, P. (1986) Possible selves. *American Psychologist* 41, 954–969.

McCaslin, M. (2009) Co-regulation of student motivation and emergent identity. *Educational Psychologist* 44 (2), 137–146.

Pintrich, P.R. and Schunk, D.H. (2002) *Motivation in Education: Theory, Research, and Applications* (2nd edn). Upper Saddle River, NJ: Merrill Prentice Hall.

Richards, K. (2006) 'Being the teacher': Identity and classroom conversation. *Applied Linguistics* 27 (1), 51–77.

Riley, P. (2003) Drawing the threads together. In D. Little, J. Ridley and E. Ushioda (eds) *Learner Autonomy in the Foreign Language Classroom: Teacher, Learner, Curriculum and Assessment* (pp. 237–252). Dublin: Authentik.

Ryan, R.M., Connell, J.P. and Grolnick, W.S. (1992) When achievement is *not* intrinsically motivated: A theory of internalization and self-regulation in school. In A. Boggiano and T.S. Pittman (eds) *Achievement and Motivation: A Social-Developmental Perspective* (pp. 167–188). Cambridge: Cambridge University Press.

Scrivener, J. (1994) *Learning Teaching*. Oxford: Heinemann.

Ushioda, E. (2003) Motivation as a socially mediated process. In D. Little, J. Ridley and E. Ushioda (eds) *Learner Autonomy in the Foreign Language Classroom: Teacher, Learner, Curriculum and Assessment* (pp. 90–102). Dublin: Authentik.

Ushioda, E. (2006) Language motivation in a reconfigured Europe: Access, identity and autonomy. *Journal of Multilingual and Multicultural Development* 27 (2), 148–161.

Ushioda, E. (2009) A person-in-context relational view of emergent motivation, self and identity. In Z. Dörnyei and E. Ushioda (eds) *Motivation, Language Identity and the L2 Self* (pp. 215–228). Bristol: Multilingual Matters.

Volet, S. and Järvelä, S. (2001) *Motivation in Learning Contexts: Theoretical Advances and Methodological Implications*. Amsterdam: Pergamon-Elsevier.

Wentzel, K.R. (2000) What is it that I'm trying to achieve? Classroom goals from a content perspective. *Contemporary Educational Psychology* 25, 105–115.

Wentzel, K.R. (2007) Peer relationships, motivation, and academic performance at school. In A.J. Elliot and C.S. Dweck (eds) *Handbook of Competence and Motivation* (pp. 279–296). New York/London: The Guilford Press.

Zimmerman, D.H. (1998) Discoursal identities and social identities. In C. Antaki and S. Widdicombe (eds) *Identities in Talk* (pp. 87–106). London: Sage.

Chapter 3

Joining Forces for Synergy: Agency and Metacognition as Interrelated Theoretical Perspectives on Learner Autonomy

XUESONG GAO and LAWRENCE JUN ZHANG

Introduction

In the last two decades, the emergence of sociocultural perspectives on language learning has challenged the domination of cognitive theories in language learning research (Block, 2003; Sealey & Carter, 2004; Zuengler & Miller, 2006). Researchers endorsing sociocultural perspectives contend that language learning is also a social act related to learners' identity formation in addition to the cognitive process taking place in the learner's mind (Donato & McCormick, 1994; Norton & Toohey, 2001; Zuengler & Miller, 2006). In such research, context or real-world situations are considered 'fundamental, not ancillary, to learning' (Zuengler & Miller, 2006: 37), while in research endorsing cognitive perspectives, context may be treated as a variable modifying the internal acquisition process occurring in individual minds.

Due to the increasing popularity of sociocultural perspectives, the current debate on autonomy in the field has begun to expand its research horizon by incorporating these new perspectives and new concepts, such as identity and agency (Palfreyman, 2003; Ushioda, 2009). As indicated by Zungler and Miller (2006), there is some rising tension among researchers as to whether or not the two paradigms, namely, socio-cultural and cognitive, should be regarded as two worlds parallel or complementary to each other. Likewise, in learner autonomy research, agency as a sociological/sociocultural construct and metacognition as a cognitive construct have often been viewed as two worlds apart. In a debate between Palfreyman (2003) and Wenden (2002), Wenden's (2002) proposal to theorize metacognition as the core of language learner development has met with Palfreyman's (2003: 244) rebuttal, arguing that by placing such emphasis on metacognition, there is a danger of reinforcing the 'cognitive individual' and presenting an impoverished view of language learners. Given such tensions, little effort has been made to see the interrelatedness of agency and metacognition or reconcile the two paradigms in research. In our view, this division is unnecessary, as each strand of research leads to findings concerning different aspects of learners' autonomous learning or similar components of learner autonomy from different perspectives.

In this chapter, we argue that metacognition and agency be conceptualized as prerequisites for learners' autonomous learning, both contributing to our understanding of the processes underlying their autonomous learning and enabling us to offer informed support to their learning efforts. To advance this proposal, we will analyze a set of data from a longitudinal enquiry into mainland Chinese undergraduates' language learning experiences, with a focus on their strategic learning efforts in Hong Kong (Gao, 2010). In the chapter, we also see language learners' strategic learning or use of language learning strategies (LLSs) as one of the most important aspects of autonomous learning (e.g. Oxford, 2003, 2008; Palfreyman, 2003; Phakiti, 2003; Tseng et al., 2006). For this reason, we shall first discuss the connections among agency, metacognition and strategic language learning.

Agency, Metacognition and Strategic Language Learning

Strategic language learning is considered to involve the use of LLSs, defined by Wenden (1987: 6) 'as language learning behaviors learners actually engage in to learn and regulate the learning of a second language'. So far, an enormous body of research on language learners' strategy use has documented its crucial contributions to learners' linguistic development (see McDonough, 1999; Cohen & Macaro, 2007; Zhang, 2001, 2003). However, despite its popularity among researchers, LLS research has also been subjected to critical examination in recent studies (see Cohen & Macaro, 2007; Dörnyei, 2005; Zhang, 2008). For instance, as noted by Ellis (1994: 553), '[d]efinitions of learning strategies have tended to be *ad hoc* and atheoretical', and the concept of LLS is often conflated with terms such as *tactics*, *skills*, *techniques* and *moves* (also see Macaro, 2006; Tseng et al., 2006; Zhang, 2003). Arguing that LLSs can only be defined in relation to particular learners' intentions and creative efforts, Tseng *et al.* (2006: 81) propose that there should be a 'shift from focusing on the product – the actual techniques employed – to the self-regulatory process itself and the specific learner capacity underlying it'. In line with this proposed shift, strategy researchers are also cognizant of the problem that LLS research tends to present a decontextualized and static picture of learners' strategy use (Donato & McCormick, 1994; Macaro, 2006; Parks & Raymond, 2004; Phakiti, 2003).

Various solutions to these problems in LLS research have been suggested. One solution, limited in size but increasingly significant in the field, echoes the sociocultural 'turn' in language learning research (Block, 2003). In a sociocultural perspective, language learners' strategy use is not only seen as a result of their individual cognitive choices; it is also viewed as related to the mediation of particular learning communities (Donato & McCormick, 1994; Gao, 2006, 2008; Norton & Toohey, 2001; Parks & Raymond, 2004). It reflects learners' exercise of agency, often regarded as a defining quality of being human and revealed within a continuous flow of human conduct involving the use of power or the will and capacity to act otherwise (Giddens, 1984). In other words, agency can be seen as 'a point of origin for the development of autonomy' and also a starting point for learners' strategic learning efforts in the learning process (Benson, 2007: 30). Moreover, if learners' strategic behavior is theorized as learners' exercise of agency to 'open up access within power structures and cultural alternatives' for learning (Oxford, 2003: 79), an inquiry into language learners' strategic learning can reveal the dynamic interaction between language learners' agency and social structure and it will also deepen our understanding of learners' strategic learning as shaped by interaction (Gao, 2007). This may present an alternative perspective for researchers to examine the connection between learners' actual strategy use and its underlying processes in particular contexts.

Another important construct, metacognition, is theorized as a critical process in language learning. It consists of metacognitive knowledge, metacognitive experiences and use of metacognitive strategies (Wenden, 1998, 2002). Successful learners can almost always be distinguished from novices not only in terms of the metacognitive knowledge they possess, but also in terms of their strategic decision making in the learning process. In accordance with the Flavellian framework (Flavell, 1979), language learners' metacognitive knowledge comprises knowledge about themselves as learners (person knowledge), the learning task (task knowledge) and strategies to be used for tackling the learning task (strategy knowledge). Wenden (1998: 519) states clearly that metacognitive strategies are 'general skills through which learners manage, direct, regulate, [and] guide their learning, i.e. planning, monitoring, and evaluation'. In light of such theorization, metacognition can be understood in terms of the monitoring and regulation mechanisms that play a significant role in learning (Azvedo *et al.*, 2004; Zhang, 2008; Zimmerman, 2001). In Schunk's (1991: 267) view, learning is 'deliberate attention to some aspects of one's behavior'. Such theorization addresses learners' self-determination in learning, particularly with regard to how to chart their learning journeys and make adjustments along the way when and where any need arises for doing so. Winne and Hadwin (1998) also pointed out that metacognitive monitoring and cognitive monitoring are two closely related aspects pertaining to successful learning. Generally, the former engages the learner in evaluating learning and the entire learning process; and the latter refers to processes that are more specific when autonomous behaviors are manifest (Azvedo, 2009; Azvedo *et al.*, 2004; Winne & Hadwin, 1998).

However, the emphasis on the concept of metacognition does not exclude the social context in which cognition takes place. In the words of Nelson *et al.*:

> The social world requires that we make a staggering number of decisions about the extent and the nature of our own knowledge and beliefs as well as decisions about the extent and nature of other people's knowledge and beliefs [...] Human action and interaction depend in crucial aspects upon our general success in these rough metacognitive waters. (Nelson *et al.*, 1998: 69)

Therefore, instead of treating metacognition purely as a cognitive construct, it can be viewed in conjunction with its conceptual overlap with the sociocultural view of strategic learning. In many ways, metacognition is, in fact, closely tied to learners' exercise of agency when they attempt to take control of their learning (cf. Palfreyman, 2003). Strategic language learning efforts, indicative of agency, cannot occur without learners' metacognitive operations, and autonomy is a hollow concept for learners, if they are incapable of undertaking such metacognitive operations. Having elaborated on these key concepts, we shall now illustrate the mutual complementarity of metacognition and agency in understanding learners' strategic learning with the data taken from a longitudinal study on mainland Chinese undergraduates in Hong Kong.

An Overview of the Inquiry

The longitudinal ethnographic study examined mainland Chinese undergraduates' language learning experiences with a focus on the contextual mediation of the participants' strategic language learning efforts in Hong Kong (Gao, 2010). With an aim to capture and interpret the participants' shifting strategic learning, the inquiry also explored the following question:

How do mainland Chinese undergraduates' accounts of shifting strategic language learning efforts reveal interactions between their agency and contextual mediation?

The inquiry also noted that these mainland Chinese students encountered obstacles in accessing linguistic resources and language learning opportunities like their counterparts in other parts of the world after they came to Hong Kong's English-medium tertiary institutions with an aspiration for better tertiary education and English competence (Gao, 2006; Parks & Raymond, 2004).

First of all, Cantonese is the dominant language in daily life and the favored language for most social, cultural and political occasions. English is widely used in the business and professional sectors and constantly promoted as an important asset for individuals' career and social development as well as a crucial means for Hong Kong to retain its international standing. The status of Putonghua (often known as Mandarin Chinese), the national dialect shared by millions on the Chinese mainland, has been rising in its importance since the handover of the sovereignty of Hong Kong to the Central Government in 1997. Most mainland Chinese students speak Putonghua and are unable to communicate in Cantonese. Apart from the linguistic barrier, mainland Chinese and Hong Kong Chinese have had dramatically different social, cultural, historical and political experiences since Hong Kong was ceded to the British in the 19th century. For instance, when the Chinese mainland was still in a state of political turmoil, Hong Kong had already achieved enviable economic success in the region. These differences constitute a significant cultural gap differentiating the two Chinese groups despite the fact that they share the same ethnicity and a similar cultural heritage, problematizing any homogenous view of Chinese learners (Schack & Schack, 2005). Although the differences between mainland Chinese and local Chinese in Hong Kong are gradually diminishing, remaining vestiges of these differences still create potential problems in the socialization process for mainland Chinese students in Hong Kong.

The inquiry had three research stages and lasted 20 months (two academic years). In the first stage, 22 mainland Chinese students were interviewed about their language learning experiences on the Chinese mainland. In the second stage, follow-up research was done among four students for two academic years, using a variety of means to collect data, including regular conversations, checklist, observation, field notes and email correspondence. In the third stage, 15 out of the 22 participants who had been interviewed two years previously were interviewed about their language learning experiences in Hong Kong. Through an extended engagement with the participants, the study aimed to obtain a 'thick description' and holistic understanding of the phenomenon under research (Geertz, 1973). The data set for re-interpretation, the narratives of a case study participant with the pseudonym of 'Liu', a business studies student, was taken from the longitudinal follow-up phase of the inquiry.

The Case Study Participant's Narratives

Liu was born into a middle-class family on the Chinese mainland. Her parents were highly educated and well-respected professionals and were closely involved in her educational progress and language learning. Throughout her academic studies on the Chinese mainland, her family not only provided her with learning resources, but also advised her on academic choices and language learning. For instance, her father read many publications related to language learning and helped her become a good English learner. Her mother had a decisive influence in encouraging her to study in Hong Kong. Liu herself also displayed a strong desire to be successful. During her preparatory year on the Chinese mainland, she started using various strategies to improve her listening and speaking. She was pleased to find that her English was actually better than that of many others and even better than that of some of the English teachers at the university on the Chinese mainland. Her superb English changed other students' perception that those students who went to study abroad were those who were not intelligent enough to go to the best universities on the Chinese mainland. Therefore, she found that her English was critical to her self-perception as an 'elite' student on the Chinese mainland. She was also determined to be an 'elite' student in Hong Kong.

Liu's language learning experiences in Hong Kong were intertwined with her persistent search for more learning opportunities and regular setbacks that frustrated her strategic learning initiatives. In the following, two biographical episodes will be presented to illustrate how she utilized the available learning resources and what decisions she made in response to emerging language learning opportunities. The first episode depicts her efforts to manage her integration with local students, critical to the creation and sustenance of a facilitative social learning environment for her learning of English and Cantonese. The second episode shows how she adopted strategy use similar to that of other mainland Chinese students following a gradual process of psychological distancing from local students.

Episode 1: Seizing emerging learning opportunities

As reflected in Liu's early learning narratives after her arrival in Hong Kong, the university provided a better learning environment for her to learn English than institutions on the Chinese mainland. It has more international students and local students with high English proficiency than other local universities in Hong Kong. It also recruits high-caliber mainland Chinese students whose English is likely to be more proficient than their counterparts on the Chinese mainland. In other words, there were many material resources and proficient English users for Liu to utilize in her efforts to improve her English. In the inquiry, she was found to have progressively adopted a variety of strategic behaviors to increase her exposure to English and to use English in Hong Kong. In her first semester at the university, she established an English-speaking partnership with another mainland Chinese student; she also regularly listened to English radio or watched English TV programs; she tried to implement a rule to ensure that she would use English for all academic matters including discussions and tutorials, where her peers were likely to use Cantonese and even Putonghua. Apart from these strategic moves, she invested her time and energy in socializing with local students at her hall and in her faculty, which helped expand her access to local student groups to improve her Cantonese competence. Consequently, she also had more opportunities to use English through social interaction. The following interview extract shows how she started a language-exchange partnership with a local student and how the partnership evolved into a scheme involving the use of three languages in the end:

> One day, I got a message from an Arts student, a girl. She said that she was interested in learning Putonghua. She asked me whether I was interested in language exchange with her. At that time, my Cantonese was poor. So I agreed. For the first time meeting, both of us talked in Putonghua because I could not express myself in Cantonese. Last night, both of us were speaking in Cantonese

(laughter). Do you think it funny? Hong Kong people could not change their human nature. Whenever they could speak Cantonese, they would speak Cantonese. Because her Putonghua was not too good, sometimes she would use a lot of English to explain herself. Once she started speaking English to me, I would switch to English. But when she switched back to Putonghua, I would try to speak in Cantonese. If I failed in my attempt, I would use Putonghua. It was just like that. In the beginning, I would ask her about basic terms in Cantonese. In the middle, we spoke more English because she found my English was good. So she was interested in practicing English with me. In the end, both of us switched to Cantonese. I think that it is funny. They could not change their human nature of speaking Cantonese. (3 September 2004)

As indicated in the extract, Liu was ready to embrace possible language learning opportunities arising from her exchanges with local students. The interview extract is also indicative of various contextual constraints, in particular, linguistic complexity, which she had to cope with in her efforts to use more English. For example, as she skillfully maneuvered the language exchange scheme to benefit her Cantonese and English learning, she needed to avoid a common phenomenon shared by many mainland Chinese students, that is, their opportunities to use English significantly decreased when they were identified as able speakers of Cantonese. Therefore, it became a strategic move for Liu to use the evolving relationships among three languages (Cantonese, English and Putonghua) in the wider social context for achieving her own language learning objectives.

However, despite Liu's active strategy use to carve out a supportive social network for her language learning, her efforts to use more English and strive for acceptance in the learning community were also constrained by contextual conditions. Although her integration into the students' community was quite successful, the data also recorded her feelings of alienation from local students at the same time. As revealed in her narratives, the differences she had with local students gradually became more, not less, apparent in ongoing social exchanges. Unhappy incidents that she experienced in socializing with her local counterparts for quite a long period of time discouraged her from using more English with them. In addition, as she spent more time interacting with her mainland Chinese peers, speaking more Putonghua and less English, she began to feel the influences of her mainland Chinese peers on her language learning.

Episode 2: Assert control of learning by any means

In the inquiry, many mainland Chinese students were found to have regarded achieving good academic results, receiving a doctoral scholarship from an American university, or getting a job offer from a prestigious company in Hong Kong as the pinnacle of success for their educational endeavors. The inquiry also recorded that these mainland Chinese students undertook strenuous efforts to achieve these objectives. For instance, at least three of the four longitudinal case study participants reported memorizing the Graduate Record Exam (GRE) vocabulary list, a crucial part of the preparation for the GRE a gate-keeper examination for graduate studies in North American universities. Some of the participants in the inquiry did consider Hong Kong's English-medium tertiary education as a stepping stone for them to pursue postgraduate studies in countries like the USA and Great Britain. Others might initially have intended to seek employment in Hong Kong, but they also felt obliged to prepare for undertaking postgraduate studies elsewhere on graduation – plan B – as the linguistic and sociocultural differences they had with local students added to their insecurity and uncertainty as non-local residents in Hong Kong. As a result, Liu felt compelled to memorize the GRE vocabulary even though she did not actually believe in the long-term impact of memorization on her acquisition of English vocabulary.

The most popular vocabulary book had 51 sub-lists (6000 words in total). As advised by the book, one needs to memorize three sub-lists of new words in the vocabulary list and review all the sub-lists previously memorized every day until each word has been reviewed seven times. This was obviously a daunting learning task for Liu. Nevertheless, even though she once disliked rote memorization of English words, she did spend some time memorizing and reviewing the GRE wordlists to acquire more vocabulary in a modified way:

> I could not do it myself. It was terrible. But I decided to review two lists a week, after a semester, I can finish forty lists. From the beginning of the semester, I have completed 8 lists. It is not that bad. The problem is whether I will persist. I think that my way is much better. Because in the 17-days way, people just look at or stare at the words, they do not know how to read, they do not know how to use. They do not care. (21 September 2005)

Though Liu's decision to memorize the GRE words was visibly influenced by her mainland Chinese peers, she appreciated the importance of having a large vocabulary. Meanwhile, she also realized that it was extremely difficult for her to sustain her memorization effort. The problem was that she could not find meanings and discourses that could motivate her learning efforts. Although she probably shared some of these motives with her mainland Chinese peers, she did not find the image of successful students in the dominant discourse of success among them inspiring and wanted to have her own voice in learning English. In other words, she was in search of reasons or paths alternative to the popular ones among her mainland Chinese peers:

> There is always a voice inside me, telling me to come back to China. But after I came to Hong Kong, everybody is talking about going abroad, going overseas, PhD, finding a good job, staying in Hong Kong, making a lot of money. My own voice is becoming less and less audible. I cannot say it. I need to have my own voice. [...] Now because I found studying English, if you have some good knowledge of English, it really means something, [...] if I have a good knowledge of English, if I go back, it is OK just for me to be an English teacher, it does not matter. [...] Even if I do not have to be a PHD, I can still help other people. (21 September 2005)

She found an unusual way to maintain the momentum in learning English. In a series of conversations, she recounted how she became a fan of a nationwide *Super Girl* competition winner in the summer of 2005 and found new meanings in learning English. The *Super Girl* competition is like a Chinese version of *American Idol* except that all the contestants are female (Jacks, 2005; Keane, 2006). One of the winners emerging from this hugely popular event became a superstar overnight and she was widely seen as an iconoclastic figure, who possesses 'attitude, originality and a proud androgyny that defied Chinese norms' (Jacks, 2005: 56). The message mediated through this new cultural icon to Liu as well as thousands of fans was clear, that is, it is wonderful to be different.

> Maybe in the bottom of my heart, I feel that I was a little bit like Li Yu Chun, when I was in high school. If I did something like her, it would be perfect. If I was a Li Yu Chun, [...] I will not do what I am doing now. I am not dreaming a star life. Now she is a superstar. But before that, she was just a common girl like everybody. A common girl. But I did not choose to be like her. I focused on my academic studies instead. (21 September 2005)

While watching her idol progress in the contest, Liu found that her idol could not pronounce English words properly. For this reason, she decided to write a letter trying to teach her how to pronounce them properly. In return, she received a photo with her idol's signature. An apparently insignificant incident empowered her with her own voice in learning English as she became aware that her English competence could be truly meaningful to her even if she returned to the Chinese mainland. As a result, she realized that learning English could have many other meanings. Like her idol, she could remain 'a common girl' but also a 'superstar' empowered by her English competence and tertiary education. Also like her idol, she could always pursue a life path, 'alternative' to those who view successful life in terms of receiving a good job offer in Hong Kong or doing doctoral studies in the USA.

Interpretations

The two biographical episodes from Liu's language learning experiences demonstrate how contextual conditions interact with learner agency in the strategic language learning process. The biographical episodes also reveal how Liu utilized contextual resources and used her strategic learning knowledge to regulate her own cognitive and metacognitive processes in learning languages. The interpretations from the two different perspectives, in our view, converge to deepen our understanding of Liu's strategic learning efforts. To this end, we shall proceed to present the two readings of the same biographical episodes in the following sections.

A sociocultural interpretation

Liu's narratives of strategic language learning can be interpreted from a sociocultural perspective. When elite students like Liu came to Hong Kong in pursuit of linguistic competence and academic qualification, they had to deal with complex linguistic issues and sociocultural barriers in their socialization with local and non-local students at the contextual level. As captured in the narratives of many other participants who were interviewed in the inquiry (Gao, 2010), these students also experienced many cultural differences in their socialization with local students (Schack & Schack, 2005). Therefore, while well supported by material conditions, it was particularly challenging for these participants to broaden their strategic learning efforts in pursuit of English competence. Also in the new institutional setting, the dominance of Cantonese in daily and academic socialization obliged mainland Chinese students like Liu to acquire Cantonese in order to integrate into the community of local students. At the same time, the English-medium instruction of the university also compelled them to improve their English.

As demonstrated in the first episode, Liu was ingenious in manipulating the complex linguistic situation to enhance her language learning and academic socialization. Her active efforts to turn linguistic constraints into a facilitative learning environment revealed her agency in taking control of her own language learning and participating in the local student community (Norton & Toohey, 2001; Oxford, 2003). However, the constraints at the contextual and institutional levels can still be seen in the second episode, which took place after she had experienced setbacks in her socialization with local students. For this reason, it is particularly important to see how Liu sustained her control of learning after these setbacks. As can be seen in the second episode, Liu began to be much influenced by her mainland Chinese peers, who were determined to find ways to do further studies and secure good job offers. Against these powerful popular discourses among her mainland Chinese peers, Liu decided to regain control of her own language learning after becoming a fan of a Chinese pop idol, which helped her see the importance of learning English within the Chinese mainland and the importance of holding beliefs 'alternative' to the discourses of 'success' dominant among her peers. Her reflections on the meaning of learning English on the Chinese mainland gave her a sense of ownership in her language learning, which made memorization efforts relatively pleasant and enjoyable for her. The whole episode shows that Liu, as a social agent, could reflexively and purposefully transform a series of strenuous memorization efforts into something meaningful to pursue her idealized life and social relationships by drawing inspiration from her own life experiences. However, this does not negate the fact that Liu adopted memorization strategies because she was almost obliged to do so by peers from her social group and the situation she found herself in after discovering the enduring gap between local students and herself. Thus, her strategy use could be seen as a product of the interplay between her agency and contextual realities, both having mediated her language learning (Gao, 2007, 2010).

A metacognitive interpretation

Apart from the above sociocultural interpretation of the data, Liu's language learning experiences can also be interpreted using the concept of metacognition. For instance, her decision to participate or not to participate in collaborative learning with her local peers is not only a sociocultural enterprise, but also a metacognitive one. As is evident in

Liu's narrative, her strategic language learning initiatives were often explicitly or implicitly undergirded by her metacognitive decision making.

Given that autonomous learning entails the learner showing her capacity in defining what the task of language learning is, setting and planning for its goals, enacting and adapting the learning process as well as evaluating learning effectiveness, cognitive monitoring and regulation are essential (Wenden, 1998, 2002). As can be seen in Liu's narratives, she appears to have been effective in controlling the language learning process and displayed great metacognitive capacity. Her realization that the new learning context was rich in terms of social learning resources (i.e. peers proficient in English) was followed by her moves to actively take this advantage in learning English. These moves were indicative of her attempts to redefine the task of learning English to appropriate English competence through socializing with peers proficient in English. Such goal setting and planning in the language learning process show her capacity for autonomous learning, which is part and parcel of developing into autonomous learners (Palfreyman, 2003; Zhang, 2008). Indeed, her persistence in looking for opportunities to use English socially as a means to achieving high levels of competence not only illustrates her clear understanding of the purpose of language learning, but also reflects her awareness of the differences between the Chinese mainland and an English-medium university in Hong Kong as contexts for learning the language. Acting on such understandings, she deployed her strategic learning efforts appropriately as recorded in the first episode. For instance, in the first episode, she monitored the collaborative learning process she had with the local student and adapted her learning efforts in response to emerging situations. She made efforts to transform the language exchange partnership into a scheme involving the use of three languages so that she could ensure the use of English in the process.

Having said that, however, we have to be cautious in interpreting the second episode, in which she made systematic efforts to memorize the GRE wordlist. Her adoption of such a strategy was surely instrumental to her passing the required test, in the first place. In the long run, this practice can be said to be based on an inappropriate belief of language learning. Were she to continue to learn English vocabulary in this way, she would be feeling bored and the learning process would be decontextualized and socially devoid of meaning. Such negative metacognitive experiences would potentially impede her language learning effort. Nonetheless, it is apparent that Liu did all this with a clear purpose. The clear goal in Liu's thinking and behavior is worthy of being advocated because learner autonomy and strategic learning build on the assumption that learners have to take initiatives for making smooth progress toward becoming autonomous or strategic learners (Azvedo, 2009; Azvedo *et al.*, 2004; Winne & Hadwin, 1998). As can be seen from the second episode, Liu's initiatives in memorizing the GRE vocabulary reflect her understanding of who she wanted to be, what she learnt English for, what resources were available for her learning of English and what she could do to achieve her goals. It is most likely that she had made one of the best available metacognitive decisions concerning her strategic learning efforts based on such understandings.

Conclusion

It must be noted that, no matter how critical and insightful learners' understanding of contextual conditions, such understanding serves no purpose if learners do not translate it into action through metacognitive operations. Therefore, the learning episodes of Liu as presented in this chapter can be a starting point for teachers to encourage language learners to reflect on how contextual conditions have been mediating their autonomous and strategic language learning efforts and what alternatives are available for them in their pursuit of linguistic competence. Through such reflections, they may also find out how they can improve their metacognitive management of the language learning task.

Therefore, we contend that metacognition and agency be considered complementary to each other in revealing the process and goals of autonomous learning. We have done so by presenting an analysis of a language learner's experiences, including her realizations of who she was and what she was, the various but selective learning opportunities she encountered, and her deployment of learning strategies for academic success. We have also analyzed and interpreted the data using the concepts of agency from a sociocultural perspective and metacognition from a cognitive perspective. While a sociocultural perspective helps us see the complex processes that mediate and engender language learners' strategic learning behaviors, a cognitive perspective helps us identify possible solutions that teachers can adopt to support language learners' efforts in coping with contextual mediations and the cognitive process of language learning effectively. Therefore, we think that it is both possible and necessary that both perspectives be adopted to understand the processes underlying language learners' strategic and autonomous learning efforts. Doing so will help us adopt a broadened learner development scheme, which enables learners with both capacities to optimize the cognitive and metacognitive processes within their brains, as well as to utilize any resources within the immediate settings and broad sociocultural contexts.

References

Azevedo, R. (2009) Theoretical, conceptual, methodological, and instructional issues in research on metacognition and self-regulated learning: A discussion. *Learning and Metacognition* 4, 87–95.

Azevedo, R., Cromley, J.G., Winters, F.I., Moos, D.C. and Greene, J.A. (2005) Adaptive human scaffolding facilitates adolescents' self-regulated learning with hypermedia. *Instructional Science* 33, 381–412.

Benson, P. (2007) Autonomy in language teaching and learning. *Language Teaching* 40, 21–40.

Block, D. (2003) *The Social Turn in Second Language Acquisition.* Edinburgh: Edinburgh University.

Cohen, A.D. and Macaro, E. (eds) (2007) *Language Learner Strategies: 30 years of Research and Practice.* Oxford: Oxford University Press.

Donato, R. and McCormick, D. (1994) A sociocultural perspective on language learning strategies: The role of mediation. *The Modern Language Journal* 78, 453–464.

Dörnyei, Z. (2005) *The Psychology of the Language Learner: Individual Differences in Second Language Acquisition.* Mahwah, NJ: Lawrence Erlbaum.

Ellis, R. (1994) *The Study of Second Language Acquisition.* Oxford: Oxford University Press.

Flavell, J.H. (1979) Metacognition and cognitive monitoring: A new area of cognitive developmental inquiry. *American Psychologist* 34, 906–911.

Gao, X. (2006) Understanding changes in Chinese students' uses of learning strategies in China and Britain: A socio-cultural re-interpretation. *System* 34, 55–67.

Gao, X. (2007) Has language learning strategy research come to an end? A response to Tseng *et al.* (2006). *Applied Linguistics* 28, 615–620.

Gao, X. (2008) You had to work hard 'cause you didn't know whether you were going to wear shoes or straw sandals! *Journal of Language, Identity and Education* 8, 169–187.

Gao, X. (2010) *Strategic Language Learning: The Roles of Agency and Context.* Bristol: Multilingual Matters.

Geertz, C. (1973) *The Interpretation of Cultures: Selected Essays.* New York: Basic Books.

Giddens, A. (1984) *The Constitution of Society: Outline of Theory of Structuration.* Berkeley, CA: University of California Press.

Jacks, S. (2005) Li Yu Chun loved for being herself. *Time (International Edition)* 166 (15), 56.

Keane, M. (2006) From made in China to created in China. *International Journal of Cultural Studies* 9, 285–296.

Macaro, E. (2006). Strategies for language learning and for language use: Revising the theoretical framework. *Modern Language Journal* 90, 320–337.

McDonough, S.H. (1999) Learner strategies. *Language Teaching* 32, 1–18.

McDonough, K. (2006) Interaction and syntactic priming: English L2 speakers' production of dative constructions. *Studies in Second Language Acquisition* 28, 179–207.

Nelson, T.O., Kruglanski, A.W. and Jost, J.T. (1998) Knowing thyself and others: Progress in metacognitive social psychology. In V.Y. Yzerbyt, G. Lories and B. Darnne (eds) *Metacogntion: Cognitive and Social Dimensions* (pp. 69–79). Thousand Oaks, CA: Sage.

Norton, B. and Toohey, K. (2001) Changing perspectives on good language learners. *TESOL Quarterly* 35, 307–321.

Oxford, R.L. (2003) Towards a more systematic model of L2 learner autonomy. In D. Palfreyman and R.C. Smith (eds) *Learner Autonomy across Cultures: Language Education Perspectives* (pp. 75–92). Basingstoke: Palgrave Macmillan.

Oxford, R.L. (2008) Hero with a thousand faces: Learner autonomy, learning strategies and learning tactics in independent language learning. In S. Hurd and T. Lewis (eds) *Language Learning Strategies in Independent Learning Settings* (pp. 41–63). Bristol: Multilingual Matters.

Palfreyman, D. (2003) Expanding the discourse on learner development: A reply to Anita Wenden. *Applied Linguistics* 24, 243–248.

Parks, S. and Raymond, P.M. (2004) Strategy use by non-native English speaking students in an MBA program: Not business as usual. *Modern Language Journal* 88 (3), 374–389.

Phakiti, A. (2003) A closer look at gender and strategy use in L2 reading. *Language Learning* 53, 649–702.

Schack, T. and Schack, E. (2005) In- and outgroup representation in a dynamic society: Hong Kong after 1997. *Asian Journal of Social Psychology* 8, 123–137.

Schunk, D.H. (1991) *Learning Theories: An Educational Perspective*. New York: Merrill/Macmillan.

Sealey, A. and Carter, B. (2004) *Applied Linguistics as Social Science*. London: Continuum.

Tseng, W., Dörnyei, Z. and Schmitt, N. (2006) A new approach to assess strategic learning: The case of self-regulation in vocabulary acquisition. *Applied Linguistics* 27, 78–102.

Ushioda, E. (2009) A person-in-context relational view of emergent motivation, self and identity. In Z. Dörnyei and E. Ushioda (eds) *Motivation, Language Identity and the L2 Self* (pp. 215–228). Bristol: Multilingual Matters.

Wenden, A. (1987) *Learner Strategies in Language Learning*. London: Prentice-Hall International.

Wenden, A. (1998) Metacognitive knowledge and language learning. *Applied Linguistics* 19, 515–537.

Wenden, A. (2002) Learner development in language learning. *Applied Linguistics* 23, 32–55.

Winne, P.H. and Hadwin, A.F. (1998) Studying as self-regulated learning. In D.J. Hacker, J. Dunlosky and A. Graesser (eds) *Metacognition in Educational Theory and Practice* (pp. 277–304). Hillsdale, NJ: Lawrence Erlbaum.

Zhang, L.J. (2001) Awareness in reading: EFL students' metacognitive knowledge of reading strategies in an acquisition-poor environment. *Language Awareness* 10, 268–288.

Zhang, L.J. (2003) Research into Chinese EFL learner strategies: Methods, findings and instructional issues. *RELC Journal* 34, 284–322.

Zhang, L.J. (2008) Constructivist pedagogy in strategic reading instruction: Exploring pathways to learner development in the English as a second language (ESL) classroom. *Instructional Science* 36, 89–116.

Zimmerman, B.J. (2001) Theories of self-regulated learning and academic achievement: An overview and analysis. In B.J. Zimmerman and D. Schunk (eds) *Self-regulated Learning and Academic Achievement: Theoretical Perspectives* (pp. 1–38). Mahwah, NJ: Lawrence Erlbaum.

Zuengler, J. and Miller, E.R. (2006) Cognitive and sociocultural perspectives: Two parallel SLA worlds. *TESOL Quarterly* 40, 35–58.

Chapter 4

Emerging Selves, Language Learning and Motivation through the Lens of Chaos

LILIANE ASSIS SADE

Introduction

These days, individuals are able to choose among different paths and courses of action due to the increasing options of discourses and opportunities available in the globalized world. This dynamicity and plurality leads us to think about new ways of seeing the same phenomena within a broader perspective, which is able to account for the fluid, unpredictable and ever-changing character of human relations. In this direction, this chapter reflects on the motivation to learn a second language from a social perspective, which views motivation as an experience of belonging rather than a personal trait. In order to do this, it examines motivation in relation to processes of identity emergence and (re)construction. To reflect on social identity and motivation as belonging, this study adopts the concept of communities of practice (Wenger, 1998, 2000) and the conceptual framework of complexity theory. Among the several theories labeled under the term 'complexity theory', two theories – chaos theory and the theory of complex adaptive systems – will inform the reflections developed here. To simplify matters, however, I will use the term 'complexity theory' throughout the chapter to refer to both theories.

The theoretical framework of complexity theory has informed the work of several researchers in the field of applied linguistics (see Kramsch, 2002; Larsen-Freeman & Cameron, 2008; Menezes, this volume; Paiva & Nascimento, 2009). This chapter adds to this growing body of work by reflecting on emergent social identities and language learning motivation through the lens of complexity theory. Researchers' interest in complexity theory stems from the need to recognize that, nowadays, social phenomena can no longer be seen as isolated and stable entities. Human beings are positioned in webs of social relations that not only mediate their actions, but also contribute to processes of identity emergence and social belonging.

I begin my discussion by presenting some key concepts related to complexity theory that I believe will shed new light on identity issues and their implications for the motivation to learn a second language. I then illustrate the points that I have made by presenting and analyzing excerpts from the language learning narrative of a young Brazilian male. While learner autonomy is not a focal point of the following theoretical discussion, it emerges as a salient feature of this learner's language learning experience, demonstrating how the interrelationship between identity emergence and motivation can lead to autonomous learning – or, perhaps we could say that it is the autonomous learning that leads to increasing motivation, mindful that, as Ushioda (2007: 4) remarks, 'we can never say which comes first, autonomy or motivation', since both come together when effective learning processes are at work. Before discussing this young man's learning, I will outline the theoretical concepts that inform my analysis.

Why Complexity?

Complexity theory presents itself as a paradigm that is able to look at dynamicity, rather than stability; emergence, rather than linearity; and interaction rather than isolation; thereby enabling a deeper understanding of the nature of the transformation processes regarding issues of identity and motivation in language learning.

Moreover, according to Larsen-Freeman and Cameron (2008), in complexity theory the context is seen as part of the system and not merely as a background on which the action is enacted. As I wish to demonstrate later, the social context is integrated as part of one's identity system, and therefore, has a strong influence on language learning motivation. It is important to mention that context in the present chapter refers both to the physical surroundings in which the individual is located as well as the sociohistorical context in which the individual was brought up.

Finally, this theoretical framework deals with the characteristics of non-linear systems: those that are sensitive to environmental changes, whose behaviors cannot be predicted based on previous behaviors or single causes. As complexity theory deals with non-linear systems, it presents useful tools to reflect on the non-linearity that characterizes human beings and to understand the unpredictable nature of language learning.

In the next section, I argue for a new view of motivation based on the understanding of social identity as a complex system. Therefore, I will also present some concepts of complexity theory and apply them to identity issues.

Theoretical Background

Dörnyei (2001: 8) defines motivation as 'the choice of a particular action, the persistence with it, and the effort expended on it'. Studies in the field of psychology have identified different kinds of motivation, such as intrinsic and extrinsic (Deci & Ryan, 1985), instrumental and integrative (Gardner & Lambert, 1972), and interactive, as I proposed elsewhere (Sade, 2003).[1]

Although some of those studies consider the influence of the social aspect on language learning motivation (see Dörnyei, 2001 and Sade, 2003), they still split the being into two dimensions: the individual and the social. The assumption in this chapter, however, is that the social aspect is an integrated part of the individual. In this view, motivation is inextricably intertwined with complex social processes; bringing it in line with Ushioda (this volume), who sees motivation as 'emergent through complex interactions among social, individual and contextual processes'. This perspective on motivation demands an understanding of the close interrelation between motivation and the emergence of social identities, which take place via processes of social belonging to multiple communities of practice. By the same token, language learning is seen in this discussion as a phenomenon that emerges from participation in communities of practice in which learners develop their learning out of experience.

To shed light on this issue, I propose a theoretical review on identity issues, borrowing the dialogic character of language (Bakhtin, 1981) and relating it to complexity theory. This provides the basis for the discussion developed in the final sections of this chapter, which will show the implications of the view of social identity as a complex system in matters relating to language learning and motivation as an experience of social belonging.

Bakhtin (1981) observes that the speakers of a language, when emitting an utterance, appropriate language constructions full of ideologies that precede them and were given to them through language and participation in discursive practices. Therefore, our thoughts, actions and, ultimately, our own identity are constrained by those 'other voices' that speak to, in and through us. Bakhtin (1981: 270–271) called the voices from the discursive genres[2] 'the centripetal forces of language', noting that they act toward unification and verbal-ideological centralization.

Turning now to complexity theory, we can relate these centripetal forces to the concept of 'attractor'. *Attractors* are patterns of movement that are repeated continually, and in which the system stabilizes (Stewart, 1991: 121). This pattern of movement 'attracts' any element put in an area next to it. This area is called the *basin of the attractor*.

Associating this concept to the dialogic character of language, we can say that the centripetal forces exerted by the discursive genres act as the attractors, that is, they help create a pattern of movement, understanding movement here as a set of actions and behaviors prescribed for a specific society. Any individual who is born in such a society is compelled to act in accordance to this set of prescribed and stabilized values. Therefore, I propose here the term *discursive attractors* to refer to the linguistic and non-linguistic patterns of behavior established in a given society, which are created by the centripetal forces of language that act through the discursive genres and carry the ideological values of that society. As for language learning, we can observe that, many times, individuals engage in this enterprise because this knowledge is considered cultural capital in a specific society. Other times, the knowledge of a second language is a necessary condition to achieve a desired social identity and, consequently, belong to specific social practices. In other words, the motivation is not individual, but is mediated by the desire for social belonging to the discursive attractors of a particular social group or institution.

The participation of the individual in the social institutions requires him/her to act in accordance with the discursive attractors established by the discourses of those institutions. For each social institution in which one participates, a social identity emerges. We can refer to this process as the 'fractalization of identities'.[3] The emergence of a social identity, which I will call here 'identity fractal', will demand a set of 'appropriate' linguistic and non-linguistic patterns of behaviors – discursive attractors – that will constrain the individual's actions while operating within a particular identity fractal.

Alongside these centripetal forces that work for stabilization and centralization, Bakhtin (2003) also states there are other forces – the centrifugal ones – which act toward destabilization and decentralization. They can be understood as the several voices from different discourses that appeal to the individual, contributing to the emergence of new social identities.

In the face of those discourses, the individual may choose among different courses of action, in the same way that complex systems choose among alternative trajectories at bifurcation points. When the system bifurcates, new attractors come into being and the system keeps oscillating among those several patterns of movements. By the same token, whenever the identity system bifurcates, the individual keeps oscillating among different discursive attractors.

Within the perspective of complexity theory, those appealing discourses work as a mechanism called *tagging*: a mechanism through which single elements get together, attracted by similar properties, and form a highly adaptive aggregate (Holland, 1995: 12). In the same way, the appealing discourses 'attract' individuals with similar interests and help create large ideological groups of people. Wenger (1998) calls those social configurations of practice 'communities of practice'. Affiliation to those communities requires a shared repertoire of linguistic and non-linguistic resources, artifacts, ideologies and practices. As I observed elsewhere (Sade, 2009a, 2009b), several students report that their motivation to learn English was due to their affiliation to different communities of practice, such as the 'rock' n' roll', 'skaters' and 'Internet users' communities, to name some.

Identity has a central role in this model. Whenever one cedes to the appeal of a new discourse and affiliates to a new community of practice, we can say that there is a bifurcation in the identity system of that person; new identities emerge and with them, new discursive attractors. The identity system of such a person will keep oscillating among those different discursive patterns. To exemplify, consider the case of a mother who, while in the family, will act in a specific way that is the 'natural way' of acting as a mother in that society. When this same mother goes to work, her social identity will change and she will act in accordance to the social norms prescribed to that other identity fractal. An infinite number of social identities may emerge throughout a life span and the identity system will be ever moving from one discursive attractor to another, tracing a pattern of movement that is typical of chaotic systems.

A *chaotic system* is one that is very sensitive to environmental conditions and a simple change in those conditions makes the system bifurcate and develop new attractors. Because such systems are very sensitive to small changes in the environment, it is difficult to predict their final behavior. Small changes in the conditions may cause huge effects. This is what is known as the *butterfly effect*.

When considering one's identity system as a chaotic system, one must be aware that one cannot predict future actions based on a set of initial conditions. Nobody can say, for example, which situations will motivate or demotivate different individuals, with different life histories.

To understand the identity system from a complexity perspective, we must focus on the interrelations established between the whole and its component parts. In order to apply those matters to the process of identity emergence, I borrow the concept of *fractal*, which is the geometric representation of chaos.

The fractal has two properties: infinite possibilities of internal subdivisions, limited by an external area, and self-similarity. Applying those properties to identity matters, we can say that the identity system also has infinite possibilities of internal subdivisions. To each community of practice a person affiliates, a new social identity emerges. This process is infinite in one's life span. However, it is also limited by 'external conditions': the biological closure of the individuals and their socio-historical contexts. The latter refers to the semiotic options available to the individuals, which constrain their choices. Our choices are made in the face of discourses, ideologies, artifacts and affordances available to us in the sociohistorical environment.

The second property of the fractals – self-similarity – is also observed. When a new social identity emerges, the others do not cease to exist. They influence and are influenced by the one that emerges. The gestaltic property of Figure and Ground is illustrative of the arguments proposed here. Note in Figure 4.1 how we can see the picture with two different perspectives: as a vase or as two faces meeting each other.

Observing Figure 4.1, we can notice that from any perspective we choose to view the object, it only emerges if we take the background as a component part of the figure on the fore. The same way we could argue in relation to the emergent social identities. When one of those social identities comes to the fore, the others stay in the background giving

Figure 4.1 Figure/Ground – a gestaltic property

support to the one that is at the front. For example, the way I think and act as a teacher is influenced by the way I am/was a daughter, a mother, a student and so on. If all these identities interact with each other, influence and are influenced by each other, we can also say that they are self-similar. This second feature of fractals also evokes the notion of the whole. When a new identity emerges, it also influences the others, causing them to be reconstructed. This process contributes to making each individual distinct from the others. As no one has lived exactly the same experiences, nobody has exactly the same identity fractals as others. In this way, we can say, as Morin (2008: 124) has stated, that 'each one of us is a society of several characters', making us unique and multiple at the same time. It is this view brought by complexity theory that compels me to suggest the term *identity fractalization*, instead of identity fragmentation. The latter evokes the idea of breaking into isolated pieces. The former, on the other hand, evokes the properties of fractals, and is able to bring to the concept the idea of the whole, which is emergent, ever changing, complex and achieved from the interactions established by the component parts.

The reflections developed so far have some striking implications for the understanding of the learning process, especially regarding the motivation to learn and this is what I will discuss next.

The Study

This discussion is part of a broader study that was conducted using narrative research methodology (Lieblich *et al.*, 1998). Twenty autobiographic narratives, written by Brazilian, Japanese and Finnish university students, were selected from the *corpus* of AMFALE[4] project. This project, developed at the Federal University of Minas Gerais (UFMG), Brazil, aims at gathering narratives from speakers and learners of a foreign language in order to study their processes of language acquisition. The narratives selected were analyzed using the properties of complexity theory. In this chapter, I analyze some excerpts of one of those narratives, written by a young Brazilian male, who is a university student at UFMG. The aim is to show how the understanding of social identity as a complex system can lead to a view of motivation as a process of social belonging. Although the excerpts analyzed here were written by a Brazilian, the evidence observed in this study is not limited to Brazilian experiences, and many aspects mentioned here are also observed in the life histories of learners from other countries (see Sade, 2009a, 2009b).

Data Analysis and Discussion

Excerpt 1

It was in 1992. I was thirteen. When I heard for the first time the question: "What is your name?" Jesus Christ, I couldn't pronounce that! And also I didn't know why we were having English class. I didn't want that! For me it was all right to speak only Portuguese. But of course I didn't have much choice, so I had to study English like everybody else. [...] Nobody in my class was comfortable with the idea of studying English. It was not part of our universe. We were just teenagers that went to school to make friends and play soccer. [...] I was a good student, but for some reason my first experience with the English language didn't make me fall in love with it at all. Of course I did not pass! (...)But after that something happened with me. I was so ashamed of my situation, because other students that were called "less intelligent" than me had passed. So I decided to learn English. It was now a question of honor.

The narrator starts his narrative by locating himself in a coordinate of time and space: the year 1992, at Junior High School.[5] This description makes the identity fractal of a student emerge in his discourse. He clearly states his demotivation toward learning a foreign language. The first thing to observe is that his studies of English were not motivated by inner reasons, but by social forces that compelled him to attend those classes at school. English learning is part of the discursive attractors developed at the institution 'Junior High School' in Brazil; it is understood as a necessary competence to be part of that community of practice.

As argued before, any element that is put next to the attractor is incorporated by its pattern of movement. In the present excerpt, we can see that once the student was admitted to Junior High School, he was 'captured' by the discursive attractors of that institution, and although it was against his personal will, he had to undertake the social patterns developed there 'like everybody else', quoting his own words.

That group of students, as many others, did not identify themselves with the formal teaching of English at school: it was not part of their communities of practice or, in the narrator's words, it was not part of their 'universe'. This fact caused their demotivation. We should observe how the situated meaning given to 'school' by the learner differed from the cultural model constructed for this social institution. While the school for him was a place to meet friends and play soccer, the discursive attractors constructed toward its cultural model prescribed the formal teaching of different subjects and kept the students' values out of the formal setting. As a result, some conflicts were established throughout this learner's adaptation process. We could argue that the student's demotivation was socially motivated since it was caused by the student's sense that he did not belong in the practices of that community.

When the narrator uses the pronoun 'we' and the noun 'teenagers' in: *We were just teenagers*, he evokes a generation and a social group – adolescents. Football, a sport that is typical in Brazil, when brought to the fore in the discourse of this narrator, evokes his 'Brazilian self'. Many boys of that age in Brazil like football.[6] I do not have the intention to generalize this observation. Probably, many Brazilian boys also hate football, but we cannot deny that it is taken for granted that football is part of the routine of a great number of Brazilian boys. So, when mentioning his expectations related to school life, the narrator makes the identity fractals of 'adolescent', 'boy' and 'Brazilian', and the discursive practices commonly associated with them, emerge in his discourse. However, the conflict established among these identity fractals with the identity fractal of 'student' contributed to his lack of motivation to learn English at school. As observed by Ushioda (2007: 3), students feel demotivated when 'language does not connect with them in any personal sense. It is not part of who they are or want to be'.

The problems faced by the student led him to fail. The amazing fact to observe here is that the student's failure was what, in fact, triggered his motivation to learn English. The first consideration to be taken into account regards the non-linearity of complex systems. Many would predict that a failure would demotivate and upset the student, as indeed often happens. However, with this particular student the unsuccessful experience was reverted into motivation. Here we can see the butterfly effect – similar initial conditions lead to different results.

Another consideration concerns the fact that the narrated episode meant an important bifurcation point in the narrator's identity system. The fractal identity of 'less intelligent student' was undesirable – a fact that impelled the narrator to make efforts to overcome it. He wished to recover his identity fractal of a 'good student', and in doing so, prove to himself and to the others he was capable: *It was now a question of honor*. His motivation in this situation emerged in the face of a desirable identity; of a possible self, as stated by Ushioda (this volume).

Excerpt 2

I was really interested in learning English, but then my father decided that we should move to Espirito Santo. Unfortunately, there they did not have English. So it seemed like I was not going to be able to learn English this time. [...] But then I met some people and I became involved with rock music. Then I really started to enjoy the idea of learning English. I wanted to know what I was listening. Every time I had the opportunity to read lyrics with the translation I became fascinated, I started to copy sentences and then to try to change words and create my own sentence in English. [...]I did not have a teacher, no money to attend an English course, but I really wanted to learn this language. [...] I had some friends, and one of them could play guitar and sometimes we got together to drink (yes it was beer although I was only 16), talk and as one of us played guitar we were supposed to sing songs that we liked. But as these songs were in English and as I was the one who studied English (using lyrics of songs), I was supposed to sing. Well I was not a good singer, but that exercise of sing helped me to learn how to pronounce many words in English. [...]As I was involved with music, I decided to learn to play guitar, so that I could sing everyday. This friend who played the guitar was my first teacher. He decided to taught me a very easy song (according to him), it was a Bob Dylan song played at that time by Guns 'n Roses: Knocking on heavens door. Well I was not exactly An English teacher but I taught him to not pronounce the "k" when he was singing Knocking on Heavens door. [...] We used to play and that helped me with my English. Let's say as a vocalist/ guitarist I was/I am a good English teacher. [...] On May 1997 my family, except my father moved to Belo Horizonte and I went to live with them. [...] I finished my high school in 1998. The English was absolutely easy for me. I never learnt anything in class. Everything I learnt alone. [...] By the way I haven't learnt how to be a good singer, but I still do it and I still study English doing that, I mean the learning process never ends for real. There's always something new as language is an unfinished process.

Some bifurcation points can be traced in this excerpt. The first one is when the narrator's family moved to Espírito Santo – a Brazilian state. There, the narrator did not have access to the formal teaching of English. However, he could learn the language through participation in another community of practice. The participation in the community of rock 'n' roll contributed to the fractalization of his identity system – there is the emergence of the identity fractal of a rock enthusiast. The competence demanded to be a member of this community required knowledge of the lyrics (which were in English), and it was this demanded competence that motivated the narrator to learn the language. The narrator developed his own learning strategies, mainly through translation. The wish to sing the songs contributed to the development of oral skills. Through participation in the discursive practices of a community whose aim is not 'to teach English', the narrator learned much more than he learned at school, where we expect students to learn. The explanation for this fact is that the desire to belong to the community of rock enthusiasts motivated the student to search for the necessary resources to improve learning in an autonomous way; while at school, the English learning process was imposed on him by a community he did not identify with.

A common social practice described by the narrator in relation to his rock 'n' roll community of practice was the meetings in bars to drink and to sing. From the interactions with and within those environments, other identity fractals emerge: 'a musician' and 'a guitarist'. Once he knew a little English, he could teach the language to his peers, therefore the fractal identity of 'an English teacher' emerges. We can argue that the emergence of his identity fractals of a rock enthusiast, guitarist and musician contributed to his learning process in two ways. First, the desire to belong to the communities of practice associated with those identity fractals motivated the narrator to learn English. Meanwhile, the same reason led the narrator to develop autonomous practices that helped him improve his knowledge of the language.

Another bifurcation point is when the narrator moves back to Belo Horizonte (his birth city), and he returns to school. This time, he mentions the easy way he could deal with English. However, he strongly states he did not learn at school. Although he said he learned 'alone', his narrative shows us that he, in fact, learned through belonging to another community of practice. He was able to reutilize the knowledge acquired in the community of rock 'n' roll in another – the school – thereby maximizing his learning. He was also able to reutilize the knowledge in the same community of rock when he used the knowledge he had acquired to teach his guitar teacher. This illustrates the recycling effect developed by complex systems: the re-usage of resources in order to guarantee their survival in the environment (Holland, 1995).

From the interactions established with his friends, with the instruments, with the songs, with the linguistic and non-linguistic resources shared by the group, he was able to multiply his knowledge. Another characteristic of complex systems can be observed here – the multiplicative effect: the increased effect of initial resources due to the flows established among aggregates.

These two effects combined led to more motivation. He mentions that since then he has not stopped learning. As established by Ehrman (1996), the sense of self-efficacy leads to motivation and, ultimately, to autonomous learning. In this narrative, however, we also observed that the autonomous learning led to more motivation and to a sense of self-efficacy.

Finally, we should reflect on the constant interaction among the narrator's identity fractals that led to a sense of 'wholeness': *Let's say as a vocalist/guitarist I was/I am a good English teacher*. It is possible to notice here the way in which the narrator's identity fractals of teacher, vocalist, guitarist and speaker of English (implicit in the identity fractal of English teacher) are entangled. Moreover, they are amalgamated and integrated in order to create a sense of wholeness. One just exists in face of the others. The articulation of this multiplicity of 'selves' contributes to the formation of a sense of uniqueness.

Wenger (2000: 241–242) summarizes the complexity of this argument by stating that 'identity [...] is neither unitary nor fragmented. It is an experience of multimembership, an intersection of many relationships that you hold into the experience of being a person, at once one and multiple'. It was this complex process of being one and multiple at the same time, and the process of belonging to these different practices associated with his identity fractals that triggered the narrator's motivation to learn.

Conclusion

This study showed that the motivation to learn a second language, among other aspects, can be associated with engagement in valued enterprises. The desire to belong to multiple communities of practice contributes to the development of a new kind of motivation, which I call 'motivation as belonging'. In this sense, motivation is understood as woven together with processes of social belonging in which identity as a complex system plays an important role. To view identity as a complex system demands an understanding of the way the social identities fuse and merge alongside processes of discursive affiliation.

This view, brought by complexity theory, has striking implications for classroom practice. The multiplicity of social identities that arises through multimembership enables knowledge exchange and, therefore, maximizes learning. So, as Murray (2008: 139) points out, fostering a sense of community in class, exploring the possibilities presented by imagined communities, and bringing, for example, more pop culture to the class, would be good ways to trigger motivation and learning. In the same direction, I would also suggest that language educators bring the students' communities of practice – such as those formed around sports, leisure activities, ethnicity or other things that students value – into the classroom and prepare language tasks that could help increase the students' motivation to learn by attributing value to their social and cultural identities.

Another implication is the recycling effect, that is, the observation that learners use resources and artifacts from other communities of practice in order to maximize learning in an autonomous way. Through this observation, we have to acknowledge that although learning can take place in the classroom, it is not in any way limited to it. I would dare to say that learning takes place much more outside the classroom walls than inside them. As pointed out by Wenger (1998), all lived experiences are sources of learning.

This narrative also showed us that the butterfly effect, which states that the effects cannot be directly associated to simple causes, was observed in the learning process of this narrator. His motivation to learn arose out of unpredictable circumstances, and learning took place due to the interaction of the narrator with the cultural context, artifacts and discourses available to him. An understanding of this unpredictability and non-linearity can contribute to a rupture of crystallized classroom practices, based on unquestioned theories. In this sense, I hope this view can inspire social actions that favor those learners who, many times, are victims of the school system and are excluded from it due to linear and prejudiced views. The perspective of complexity theory helps reveal the complex nature of human beings and why, due to this nature, it is impossible to fit them in pre-fabricated, homogenous and essentialist models, be they theoretical or methodological.

Above all, the lens of complexity theory demands a new view of the language classroom; one that is able to see it not just as the context where the action of learning is enacted, but also as part of the action itself. Within this perspective, the classroom should be seen as a dynamic and emergent phenomenon that is created and re-created everyday as a result of the interactions developed in, with and through it. Teachers and learners should not be seen merely as participants in a specific social practice, but mainly and foremost as complex, adaptive, autonomous and diverse human beings, who are able to design new discursive attractors out of the possibilities presented in the social contexts.

Finally, it is important to observe that since participation in social practices and reconstruction of social identities is something that is constant as long as the person is alive, so are the opportunities to learn and the motivation to commit to valued enterprises. Regarding this point, an insightful observation was stated by the narrator whose voice was heard throughout this chapter: *By the way I haven't learnt how to be a good singer, but I still do it and I still study English doing that, I mean the learning process never ends for real. There's always something new as language is an unfinished process.* This in essence shows that participation in communities of practice creates conditions for learners to experience the complexity and ambiguity of learning in the real world and take advantage of autonomous learning. Therefore, the view presented here not only shows identity, motivation and autonomy as entangled in an ever-evolving process of social belonging, but helps to understand the never-ending nature of learning.

Notes

1. For a review of those theories, see Dörnyei (2001) and Sade (2003).
2. Bakhtin (2003: 268–269) defines discursive genres as 'utterances and their types' that act as 'a transmission chain between the history of society and the history of language'.
3. This process has been treated in the literature of the field as 'identity fragmentation'. However, for reasons I will make clear later, I suggest using the term 'identity fractalization' instead.
4. AMFALE stands for 'Aprendendo com Memórias de Falantes e Aprendizes de Língua Estrangeira' (Learning with Memories of Speakers and Learners of a Foreign Language). The full project, which is coordinated by Dr Vera Lúcia Menezes de O. e Paiva, and the narratives can be found at: http://www.veramenezes.com/amfale.htm.
5. We can infer he was in Junior School because he mentions he was 13 years old. At this age, regular Brazilian students attend Junior High School.
6. In the period mentioned by the narrator, soccer practice was much associated with the masculine gender. Nowadays, this practice has become common for girls as well.

References

Bakhtin, M.M. (1981) *The Dialogic Imagination – Four Essays*. Austin, TX: University of Texas Press.

Bakhtin, M.M. (2003) *Estética da Criação Verbal* (4th edn). São Paulo: Martins Fontes.

Deci, E.L. and Ryan, R.M. (1985) *Intrinsic Motivation and Self-Determination in Human Behavior*. New York: Plenum.

Dörnyei, Z. (2001) *Teaching and Researching Motivation*. Harlow: Pearson Education.

Ehrman, M.E. (1996) *Understanding Second Language Learning Difficulties.* London: Sage.

Gardner, R.C. and Lambert, W. (1972) *Attitudes and Motivation in Second Language Learning.* Rowley, MA: Newbury House.

Giddens, A. (1999) Modernity and self-identity: Tribulations of the self. In A. Jaworski and N. Coupland (eds) *The Discourse Reader* (pp. 415–427). London: Routledge.

Giddens, A. (2002) *Modernidade e Identidade.* Rio de Janeiro: Jorge Zahar Ed.

Holland, J.H. (1995) *Ordem Oculta – Como a Adaptação Origina a Complexidade.* Lisboa: Wesley Publishing.

Kramsch, C. (ed.) (2002) *Language Acquisition and Language Socialization – Ecological Perspectives.* London, New York: Continuum.

Larsen-Feeman, D. and Cameron, L. (2008) *Complex Systems and Applied Linguistics.* Oxford: Oxford University Press.

Lieblich, A., Tuval-Mashiach, R. and Zilber, T. (1998) *Narrative Research: Reading, Analysis, and Interpretation.* London: Sage.

Morin, E. (2008) *A Cabeça Bem-feita: Repensar a Reforma, Reformar o Pensamento* (15th edn). Rio de Janeiro: Bertrand Brasil.

Murray, G. (2008) Communities of practice: Stories of Japanese EFL learners. In P. Kalaja, V. Menezes and A.M.F. Barcelos (eds) *Narratives of Learning and Teaching EFL* (pp. 128–140). London: Palgrave Macmillan.

Paiva, V.L.M. de O. e and Nascimento, M. do (eds) (2009) *Sistemas Adaptativos Complexos – Linguagem e Aprendizagem.* Belo Horizonte: Faculdade de Letras da UFMG.

Sade, L.A. (2003) Querer é poder, querer e poder, querer sem poder: A motivação para o aprendizado de inglês na escola pública sob uma perspectiva semiótica social. MA dissertation, Universidade Federal de Minas Gerais.

Sade, L.A. (2009a) Fractals and fragmented identities. In G.R. Gonçalves *et al.* (eds) *New Challenges in Language and Literature* (pp. 109–127). Belo Horizonte: Editora da UFMG.

Sade, L.A. (2009b) Identidade e aprendizagem de inglês sob a ótica do Caos e dos Sistemas Complexos. PhD thesis, Universidade Federal de Minas Gerais.

Stewart, I. (1991) *Será que Deus Joga Dados? – a Nova Matemática do Caos.* Rio de Janeiro: Jorge Zahar Ed.

Ushioda, E. (2007) Travels of the intrepid motivation worm. On WWW at http://www.learnerautonomy.org/Ushioda2007.pdf. Accessed 15.2.10.

Wenger, E. (1998) *Communities of Practice: Learning, Meaning and Identity.* Cambridge: Cambridge University Press.

Wenger, E. (2000) Communities of practice and social learning systems. *Organization* 2 (7), 225–246.

Chapter 5

Identity, Motivation and Autonomy in Second Language Acquisition from the Perspective of Complex Adaptive Systems

VERA LÚCIA MENEZES DE OLIVEIRA E PAIVA

> *In this world, nothing is permanent except change.*
> American Proverb

Introduction

In this chapter, I discuss some characteristics of complex adaptive systems as a framework for the understanding of language and second language acquisition (SLA). In order to investigate what motivates the SLA system dynamicity, and how identity construction and autonomy influence its trajectories and changes, I will examine some empirical evidence drawn from a *corpus* of English language learning histories (ELLHs) written by Japanese and Brazilian English learners. It is my intention to demonstrate that small changes in identity, motivation and autonomy, among other factors, may trigger important developments in SLA.

It is not my intention in this chapter to present a documentary history of the origins of complexity theory, but I must draw attention to the fact that what we call complexity theory today encompasses findings from a number of fields. In mathematics, Poincaré (1921) demonstrated that even systems whose behaviors are well known, display indeterminate behaviors, and Mandelbrot (1982) worked on fractal geometry. In meteorology, Lorenz (2001) developed research on weather prediction and created the butterfly effect metaphor to represent the notion of sensitive dependence on initial conditions in chaos theory, i.e. the idea that small inputs can trigger enormous consequences. In chemistry,

Prigogine (1984) demonstrated the role of dissipative structures in thermodynamic systems and offered us the concept of self-organization. In biology, Maturana and Varela (1987) developed the concept of an autopoietic system, understood as a system that exhibits a self-structuring characteristic and that produces organizations continuously. Each of these researchers has contributed to the conceptual framework of what we now refer to as complexity theory.

Complexity is a new metaphor pervading different fields of knowledge and, as Waldrop observed:

> Instead of relying on the Newtonian metaphor of clockwork predictability, complexity seems to be based on metaphors more closely akin to the growth of a plant from a tiny seed, or the unfolding of a computer program from a few lines of code, or perhaps even the organic, self-organized flocking of simpleminded birds. (Waldrop, 1992: 329)

However, complexity has become more than a metaphor; it is now a new paradigm in science, which offers concepts to help us understand different phenomena in different fields of knowledge, including applied linguistics. Larsen-Freeman (1997: 141), in her inaugural work in this new perspective, sees 'many striking similarities between the science of chaos/complexity and language and SLA'. She presents several arguments for the understanding of language and SLA as a complex, non-linear, dynamic phenomenon. Later on, Larsen-Freeman and Cameron (2008) demonstrated the applicability and usefulness of complexity concepts in applied linguistics research, and offered us some methodological principles and practical implications for the empirical investigation of language development.

In the next section, I will discuss some characteristics of complex adaptive systems with the help of Lewin (1992), Holland (1995, 1998), Cilliers (1998), Williams (1997), Lorenz (2001) and Larsen-Freeman and Cameron (2008).

Complex Adaptive Systems

According to Holland (1995: 6), complex systems are 'made up of large numbers of active elements'. These interacting elements adapt themselves and change their behaviors because of the interactions; in other words 'any element in the system influences, and is influenced by, quite a few other ones' (Cilliers, 1998: 3). Those systems are non-linear because their changing behaviors are not proportional to their causes. They are also open systems, as energy or information flows into and out of the system due to its interacting process. As Larsen-Freeman and Cameron (2008: 29) point out 'The complexity of a complex system arises from components and subsystems being interdependent and interacting with each other in a variety of different ways'. The overall system behavior emerges from those interactions, but cannot be described as just a matter of the sum of each agent's behavior. A good example can be the emergence of a family due to the union of a couple or the emergence of a pidgin due to the interaction of groups of people speaking different languages. A pidgin is not the sum of two languages, but a new language that emerges from the interaction of members of two different linguistic communities, which expand and become more complex.

These systems are also dynamical systems. According to Lorenz (2001: 8), there are two kinds of systems: those that 'vary deterministically as time progresses' and those that 'vary with an inconsequential amount of randomness'. The latter seems to be the case of language and of language acquisition. Williams (1997: 11) points out that 'The word *dynamics* implies force, energy, motion, or change' and that 'A *dynamical system* is anything that moves, changes, or evolves in time'. During this dynamical process, agents learn from each other, they get feedback, they gain experience and change. These systems are also referred to as chaotic systems because, as explained by Holland (1998: 45), 'small changes in local conditions can cause major changes in global, long-term behavior'. This characteristic of chaotic systems is known as sensitive dependence on initial conditions. However 'initial' does not necessarily mean the time a system was created, but can refer to 'any stretch of time that interests an investigator, so that one person's initial conditions may be another's midstream or final conditions' (Lorenz, 2001: 9).

Lewin (1992: 20) argues that 'Most complex systems exhibit what mathematicians call attractors, states into which the system eventually settles, depending on the properties of the system'. Larsen-Freeman and Cameron (2008: 49) define attractors as 'states, or particular modes of behaviors, that the system "prefers"'. As Sade (2008) highlights, the concept of 'attractor' does not refer to something that attracts, but to long-term behavior or temporary stability.

When the systems exhibit properties that are found in different scales or stages, we say that they display fractal dimensions. The word fractal is used to name patterns with similar shapes whatever scale we view them in, due to its self-similarity property. One fractal example is the coast line. It exhibits similar shapes independent of the scale we observe it. Another example is a set of Russian dolls. The largest doll nestles a smaller one that nestles an even smaller doll, and so on. Their size varies, but the shape is similar. As Gleick (1988: 98) beautifully claims 'IN THE MIND'S EYE, a fractal is a way of seeing infinity'. When we think of fractals, we also think of recursive operations such as those we find in the language system. Language organizes itself from phonemes to words, from words to sentences, from sentences to utterance units, from utterance units to discourse, which itself triggers other discourses in an endless flow.

Most systems are made up of nested systems and to study a human complex system is a matter of seeing it as a nested living system. For example, SLA can be viewed as a nested system that, in turn, is an essential component in language itself, which can also be understood as a complex system, as we will see in the next section.

Language and Language Acquisition as Complex Adaptive Systems

I understand language as a non-linear dynamic and adaptive system, made up of interrelated bio-cognitive, socio-cultural, historical and political elements, which enables us to think and act in society. The Five Graces Group, a workgroup made up of 10 scholars sponsored by the Santa Fe Institute, offers us the following description of language as a complex adaptive system:

> The system consists of multiple agents (the speakers in the speech community) interacting with one another. The system is adaptive, that is, speakers' behavior is based on their past interactions, and current and past interactions together feed forward into future behavior. A speaker's behavior is the consequence of competing factors ranging from perceptual constraints to social motivations. The structures of language emerge from interrelated patterns of experience, social interaction, and cognitive mechanisms. (Five Graces Group, 2008: 1)

As language is in evolution, so too is SLA and any change in a subsystem can affect other elements in the network. It develops through dynamic and constant interaction among the subsystems, alternating moments of stability with moments of turbulence. As complex systems are in constant movement, after chaos – understood here as the optimal moment for learning – a new order arises, not as a final static product, but as a process, i.e. something in constant evolution.

Complex systems are also adaptive and, as such, SLA exhibits an inherent ability to adapt to different conditions present in both internal and external environments. As pointed out by van Lier (1996: 170), 'we can neither claim that learning is caused by environmental stimuli (the behaviorist position) nor that it is genetically determined (the innatist position). Rather, learning is the result of complex (and contingent) interactions between individual and environment'. By saying that, van Lier admits that SLA acquisition is much more complex than what several SLA theories have been trying to explain.

With this in mind, I assume that a complex view of SLA can simultaneously admit the existence of *innate mental structures*, as proposed by generativists, and at the same time sustain the notion that part of the language is acquired by means of repetition and the creation of *automatic linguistic habits*, as explained by the structuralists. In such a model, *input*, *interaction* and *output* are also considered of paramount importance for language acquisition as they trigger both *neural* and *sociocultural connections*.

It is my contention that *identity, motivation* and *autonomy* are key elements for successful sociocultural connections and SLA system evolution. Those interconnected elements work as a potent fuel to put the system into movement, contributing to its development and change. It is also my contention that minimal differences in identity, motivation and autonomy, among other factors, can cause very different results in the acquisition outcomes. In this chapter, I will focus on identity, motivation and autonomy and show their paramount importance for SLA as a complex system.

Identity

Learning a language is also a process of identity construction. Norton (2000: 5) defines identity as, 'how a person understands his or her relationship to the world, how that relationship is constructed across time and space, and how the person understands possibilities for the future'. As explained by Wenger:

> An identity is not an abstract idea or a label, such as a title, an ethnic category, or a personality trait. It is a lived experience of belonging (or not belonging). A strong identity involves deep connections with others through shared histories and experiences, reciprocity, affection, and mutual commitments. (Wenger, 2000: 239)

However, identity is not a unified experience of belonging, but an array of multiple memberships in a fractal dimension. Sade (2008: 15) explains that in a fractal 'no matter the number of internal fragmentations, the parts are interconnected into a whole which is self-similar to the parts'. Identity is a complex system that displays a fractalized process of expansion as it is open to new experiences. In SLA, this expansion occurs through one's engagement in diverse linguistic social practices, with which one identifies.

Motivation

Motivation has been traditionally understood as either an integrative or instrumental orientation, as proposed by Gardner and Lambert (1972). They define integrative motivation as 'a willingness to become a member of another ethnolinguistic group as an integrative motive' (Gardner & Lambert, 1972: 12), while the instrumental orientation is 'characterized by a desire to gain social recognition or economic advantage through knowledge of a foreign language' (Gardner & Lambert, 1972: 14). Later on, Deci and Ryan (1985) developed 'the self-determination theory' and added to the field two other notions of motivation '*intrinsic motivation*, which refers to doing something because it is inherently interesting or enjoyable, and *extrinsic motivation*, which refers to doing something because it leads to a separable outcome' (Ryan & Deci, 2000: 55). By separable outcome, they refer to the instrumental characteristic of extrinsic motivation and exemplify with a hypothetical student who does his work just to avoid parental sanctions and another who studies because she believes it is important for her future career.

All these theories contributed to our understanding of the construct of motivation. I must agree with Dörnyei (2003) when he says that 'theories do not necessarily exclude one another but may simply be related to different phases of the motivated behavioral process' and with Dörnyei and Csizér, who state that:

> Human motivation to learn is a complex phenomenon involving a number of diverse sources and conditions. Some of the motivational sources are situation-specific, that is, they are rooted in the student's immediate learning environment, whereas others appear to be more stable and generalized, stemming from a succession of the student's past experiences in the social world. (Dörnyei & Csizér, 2002: 424)

I see motivation as an important complex subsystem nested in SLA systems, which works as a moving force in any learning process. This seems to be consistent with Ryan and Deci's (2000: 54) position that motivation 'is hardly a unitary phenomenon' and with Dörnyei (1994, 2001), who sees it as a complex, multi-dimensional construct. I consider that motivation is not just a matter of being integrated into a speaking community or using the language for an instrumental reason as posited in the earlier work of Gardner and Lambert (1972), or of displaying intrinsic or extrinsic motivation orientation (Ryan & Deci, 2000). I view motivation as a dynamic force involving social, affective and cognitive factors manifested in desire, attitudes, expectations, interests, needs, values, pleasure and efforts. It is not something fixed, and as Winke (2005: 1) claims, it 'varies widely, ebbs and flows over the course of the year (or even during a classroom activity) and stems from various sources, internal to the learner, external, or both'. I would add that motivation varies over a period of time or over stages along the acquisition process, which is not restricted to the educational context, and that it is a necessary condition for autonomy.

Autonomy

In Paiva (2006), I argue that autonomy is a socio-cognitive system nested in the SLA system. It involves not only the individual's mental states and processes, but also political, social and economic dimensions. It is not a state, but a non-linear process, which undergoes periods of instability, variability and adaptability. It is an essential element in SLA because it triggers the learning process through learners' agency and leads the system beyond the classroom. Autonomous learners take advantage of the linguistic affordances in their environment and act by engaging themselves in second language social practices. They also reflect about their learning and use effective learning strategies.

Autonomy changes for reasons that are, usually, entirely internal to itself, such as a willingness to learn in a more independent way. In Paiva and Braga (2008: 463–464), we argue that 'autonomy, in the perspective of complexity, encompasses properties and conditions for complex emergence, and is inextricably linked to its environment'. Likewise, its dynamic structure governs the nature of its interactions with the environment in which it is nested. In this sense, the language learner agent influences, and is influenced by, his/her social practices in a constant movement of organization and reorganization, a process that, paradoxically, possesses a certain degree of freedom and dependency.

As human beings are different, so are their contexts and so are their SLA processes, which are mediated by different human agents and cultural artifacts. As a consequence, unequal learning experiences may occur in very similar situations. When we turn our observation to language teaching practices, we see that no matter how much teachers plan and develop their classes, students will react in different ways and unforeseen events will inevitably be part of their learning experiences. The seemingly orderly world of acquisition is, in fact, chaotic and chaos seems to be fundamental in such a process.

SLA consists of a dynamic interaction among different individual and social factors put into movement by inner and social processes. The random interaction among all the elements of the acquisition system yields the changes responsible for acquisition. The rate of change is not predictable and varies according to the nature of the interactions among all the elements of the system. A live acquisition system is always in movement and never reaches equilibrium, although it undergoes periods of more or less stability.

The Study

In order to investigate the complexity of SLA systems in what concerns three of its interacting elements – motivation, identity and autonomy – I 'listened' to the voices of Japanese and Brazilian English language learners by reading and analyzing a *corpus* of 20 ELLHs. As highlighted by Davis and Sumara (2006), 'personal memories might be characterized in terms of fractal structure in which virtually any recollection, when closely inspected, can explode into a vast web of associations'. I consider that each history will provide a clue to make us understand the intricacies of the complexity of SLA.

The 10 Japanese histories were selected from a *corpus* of 24 ELLHs collected in 2007 and published by Murray (2009) and the 10 Brazilian histories were chosen from a *corpus* of 19 ELLHSs written by my undergraduate students in 2007 and published on the homepage of my research project on language learning memories, which can be accessed at http://www.veramenezes.com/narmulti.htm. The criterion for the selection of the texts was the order of appearance in both ELLHs *corpora*.

After reading the 20 ELLHs, I selected some excerpts and summarized the data in two charts, one for each group. The charts were divided into five columns, the first for students, the second for initial conditions, the third for identity data, the fourth for motivational clues and the fifth for autonomy examples. The chart made it easier for me to compare the data and the excerpts taken from both *corpora*. The texts were not edited, as

I considered it important to keep the form of each ELLH. Subsequently, I analyzed each column in both charts in order to get a general portrait of those groups of English learners.

I will compare their language learning 'initial conditions' to see what motivates the SLA systems set-up processes and compare the two groups of learners in what concerns (1) their 'learning initial conditions'; (2) the connections among the systems' components – mainly identity, motivation and autonomy – which are supposed to underpin change and dynamics in the acquisition system; and (3) points of change or transition and self-organization.

Learning initial conditions

There seems to be at least two distinct phases common to all the students in the ELLHs, the first one is the first contact with English in junior high school and high school, and the second is represented by diverse experiences outside school. Some students in both groups tell us they were curious about English when they were children. They also say that they had early contact with the language, scaffolded by their relatives: a Japanese student imitated a cousin who used pictures to teach her some words; another learned the alphabet with his brother; and a Brazilian girl started learning English with her grandmother.

All of them register somehow their experience in junior high school or high school and most of them do not have good memories of that period. A Japanese student claims that she 'preferred going out with friends, listening to songs, reading books, watching movies, etc., to studying'. A Brazilian girl said that the only thing she had learned in junior high school was to hate the language and another said that the classes were boring. Only one Japanese woman presents explicit positive references to high school. She says:

> It has been said that Japanese high school English education is not effective for the students. Many people think that they are just like prep schools for the university; however, I can't agree with this idea. In my case without English education in high school I couldn't keep learning and speak English as I do now, I'm sure. I can say that the English education in my high school was well organized. Luckily we had good English teachers. I learned many things from their classes. Let me introduce how and what I did in school.

The other ELLHs emphasize experiences out of school. One important thing we learn when reading both Japanese and Brazilian ELLHs is that language social practices outside school are important agents to make the SLA system work. They are the initial conditions for a new phase in an SLA process. Some of these practices emerged in experiences such as: working in places where English was spoken; living abroad; studying abroad; traveling to the USA; traveling to Europe and using English as a tool for communication even in countries where other languages were spoken; having fun and pleasant moments with cultural artifacts; interacting with English speakers; and enrolling in private language courses. Those new initial conditions change the route of the systems as they offer opportunities for interactions in authentic linguistic social practices. Being hired by a hotel, for example, can highly increase learners' motivation and autonomy and establish a new phase in one's SLA system.

It is worth mentioning that, although those students seldom mention good experiences at school, they seem to realize the importance of formal studies for SLA. All the Japanese narrators, for instance, were enrolled at Akita International University's Center for Independent Language Learning and the Brazilians were enrolled in an undergraduate English Language and Literature Program in Brazil.

In the next section, I present some discussion on the interrelation between identity, motivation and autonomy and SLA.

The connections among identity, motivation and autonomy

For the sake of textual organization, identity, motivation and autonomy will be discussed in separate subsections, but I am aware that they represent interconnected elements in the SLA complex system.

Identity

Learning a language involves coping with fractal dimensions of the identity complex system. Besides being a learner, one has other identities, such as gender and social class identities, and additional ones can arise along the SLA process. For example, it is the identity of Michael Jackson's fan that urges a Brazilian learner to learn English. Listen to her: 'I've started to study English by myself, when I was about 15, because of Michael Jackson. He's been my idol since 1991, and I really wanted to understand him and his music since I was a child'. Another one took advantage of her identity of waitress to improve her English. All of them demonstrated in their ELLHs that they were highly motivated autonomous learners.

A good example of gender identity is found in the Japanese *corpus*. Being a female implies certain constraints in Japanese society. One narrator remarks that she worked in a trade company that used to send employees to study abroad, but females were not included in that policy. Others were housewives and mothers and those identities demanded, for instance, taking care of children, which interfered with their studies or even interrupted the flow of their SLA processes. Nevertheless, as chaotic systems exhibit unpredictable and irregular dynamics, it is the very identity of a Japanese housewife that moved one learner's SLA system. According to that narrator, she hated English in school and almost died of boredom, but something unexpected happened and she felt motivated and restarted learning English. She explains:

> It was spring at my age of twenty-eight. As my youngest child went up to kindergarten, I began thinking about my own life which had had no free time. I desired strongly that I could have something special providing me a sense of fulfillment. Whatever it was, I would be ok if it gave me satisfaction at that time. One day in those days, my husband once said to me: "I will take you to Hawaii some day." As I heard from him, I thought that's it. It was what I wanted to do. The idea of going shopping with fluent English in Hawaii suddenly popped in my mind. But at the same time I thought the English I would take must be practical, not useless. Now I come to think of my choice then, it was too childish, wasn't it?

That choice worked as a butterfly effect. The metaphor 'the flapping of a butterfly's wing in Brazil can cause a tornado in Japan' can explain what happened to that student's SLA system. The promise 'I will take you to Hawaii some day', in her own words 'was a direct trigger to make me her restart it'. The SLA system, which was temporarily at rest, was moved by sudden motivation and consequent autonomy as the learner took control of her SLA process.

She started following a radio language program, on NHK (Nippon Hoso Kyokai), the Japan Broadcasting Corporation, which broadcasts various language lessons on its international shortwave Radio Japan service. But again, her identity of mother was responsible for experiences of engagement in two different communities of practice. Let us listen to her again:

> One and half years later after I chose it, a new cute girl from America enrolled in the kindergarten where my youngest child had been. The America girl and my daughter became good friends and both families became very close. Thanks to this relationship, my poor

English was getting better little by little. I was lucky I could have the opportunity to use English. Necessity helped motivate me to brush up my skill. They returned to the US after their five-year stay in Japan. During their stay, I got a job introduced by her father and worked for a while using English.

We can see that new identities emerged: friend of an American family and worker. Not only had her SLA system changed, but also her identity system, which increased its complexity with the addition of new identities: autonomous language learner, friend and worker. She realized that she had changed: 'I know myself that relearning English made me change. I have come to care about my own life. I have become a little bit more outgoing than I used to be'. This remark is a good example of how interrelated complex systems are. Acquiring a language is interrelated with the complexity of identity construction, social life and family complex systems.

Motivation

The ELLHs reveal that motivation is not a linear phenomenon and small changes in the student's experiences can yield an enormous change in motivation, as we saw in the case of the Japanese housewife. On the other hand, motivation may disappear in the face of monotonous activities in the classroom, but can revive if the learner meets a new teacher, a new school or interesting experiences outside school. An example is the Brazilian student who said that 'the only thing she learned was to hate the language' in junior high school. She lost her motivation in high school, but it came back with a rewarding experience when she attended private lessons. She says: 'the teacher taught me not only there was not to be scared of, but also to love the language'. Then she started her major in English and motivation vanished, she hated the course and dropped out. Later on she traveled to Canada, lived there for six months, and when she returned to Brazil, she went to another university to get her degree as an English teacher.

English culture, especially music and literature, seems to be a source of extrinsic motivation. In both *corpora*, some learners register in their histories that they wanted to learn the language to understand the lyrics. The Brazilians say: 'I always liked foreign songs'; 'The music was my motivation to study English'; 'I was a big fan of a rock 'n' roll band called Guns 'n' Roses (certainly you know about them) and I really wanted to understand what those guys were saying in their songs'; 'I've started to study English by myself, when I was about 15, because of Michael Jackson. He's been my idol since 1991, and I really wanted to understand him and his music since I was a child'. The Japanese also talk about their affiliation to Western culture: 'I love Western music'; 'I was a lover of English poetry, especially Shakespeare, Wordsworth, Milton and so on'.

Motivation is also a changing phenomenon, it can grow or decrease and it can differ depending on the school or social experiences. One Brazilian girl mentioned she hated repeating dialogues, but loved listening to music. Several narrators confessed their fear of speaking in public, but said they wanted to interact with foreigners. A Japanese learner claimed she was always willing to participate in class, but others did not feel motivated in high school. A Japanese narrator confessed that, when she was in high school, she was shy and did not want to learn more than she already knew, but that changed and her fear of speaking disappeared during a two-month home stay in the USA. It is interesting to see that motivation varies from student to student and so does the degree of motivation in similar situations.

Autonomy

Identity, motivation and autonomy are interconnected elements in an SLA complex system as we can see if we go back to the Brazilian girl who was a fan of Michael Jackson. Her fan identity motivated her to learn English in order to understand her idol's discourse and she demonstrates she was a very autonomous learner in order to achieve her goals. Let us listen to her:

> I used to use a Dictionary in order to find the meaning of each word in songs or in texts written by him. (...) One thing that I can say is that I started learning English through comparing patterns and observing the language structure, comparing it to Portuguese and trying to memorize rules, and I used to make lists of words in order to memorize them and their meanings. Another thing that helped me a lot was the fact that I would spend hours studying and memorizing every rule I could notice, the uses, tenses, etc. of the words. After having a good vocabulary, I started working on pronunciation, which was the hardest part of the process for me, because the only source I had was music, although I used a Pronunciation Dictionary, too.

This student is the only one who talks about comparing structures and using a dictionary and translating. The other students in the Brazilian group mentioned practicing the language alone and monitoring pronunciation; listening to music and radio; repeating song lines; reading books; watching TV; looking for opportunities to communicate; and volunteering in a school. The Japanese learners also talked about similar strategies, which prove that learners autonomously create opportunities to use the language.

No matter how different student's routes are, the fact is that identity, motivation and autonomy have an enormous influence on the SLA system changes and self-organization. I would like to conclude this text by talking about points of change and self-organization in the SLA complex systems represented in both *corpora* of ELLHs.

Points of Change and Self-Organization

As we have seen in our *corpus*, each learner's SLA system displays a different dynamicity and their SLA systems follow different routes at different paces. The learners' experiences lend support to Larsen-Freeman and Cameron (2008: 158) when they say that 'language learning is not about learning and manipulating abstract symbols, but it is enacted in real-life experiences, such as when two or more interlocutors co-adapt during an interaction'. Our *corpus* of Brazilian and Japanese ELLHs demonstrate that the SLA system is always open to change: learning contexts are always changing and so are identities, motivation and autonomy. They change and adapt themselves with the emergence of a more complex order, a new linguistic behavior much more complex than the previous ones. As Larsen-Freeman and Cameron (2008: 44) point out, 'complex systems can change smoothly and continuously for periods of time but may then go through more dramatic types of change when they alter their nature radically, sometimes entering a period of turbulence, or "chaos", where the system keeps on changing dramatically'. Our narratives demonstrate that SLA systems undergo phase shifts and self-organize from second language school experience to linguistic social practices with the emergence of new identities, motivation and new autonomous learning strategies.

The main points of change identified in our *corpus* are: (1) from pleasant, early contact in a family environment initial condition, the system self-organizes and shifts from having fun to formal learning in junior or higher school. Some felt like crying, other felt bored, others were scared, but there is at least one who recognizes that she learned a lot in this phase. No matter what they feel, this is a phase common to all the students, although the rate of acquisition, autonomy and motivation are not similar. (2) A second point of change has to do with autonomous movements when highly motivated learners experience linguistic social practices by means of cultural artifacts (music, TV, reading, etc.). (3) New changes and new identity constructions (marriage, traveling, new neighbors, friendship, new jobs, etc.) occur and the system adapts and moves to another phase or attractor when it settles down until a new change happens. It is important to notice that some changes decrease the dynamicity of the process or even put the system at rest for a period of time. That is the case of the Japanese housewives who interrupted their studies when they got married. We heard the voices of successful ones, but, probably, others could have told us that their SLA systems had simply died.

As put by Larsen-Freeman and Cameron (2008: 60) and confirmed by our *corpus*, SLA is a matter of 'a succession of cycles of emergence'. The LLHs in our *corpus* provided enough evidence for us to state that acquisition results from what emerges from the interaction among different elements in an SLA system and that identity construction, motivation and autonomy are three of the most important elements that contribute to the emergence of points of change, self-organization and, consequently, for SLA.

References

Cilliers, P. (1998) *Complexity and Postmodernism: Understanding Complex Systems.* London and New York: Routledge.

Davis, B. and Sumara, D. (2006) *Complexity and Education: Inquiries into Learning, Teaching and Research.* Mahwah, NJ: Lawrence Erlbaum Associates.

Deci, E.L. and Ryan, R.M. (1985) *Intrinsic Motivation and Self-Determination in Human Behavior.* New York: Plenum.

Dörnyei, Z. (1994) Motivation and motivating in the foreign language classroom. *Modern Language Journal* 78 (3), 272–284.

Dörnyei, Z. (2001) *Motivational Strategies in Language Classroom.* Cambridge: Cambridge University Press.

Dörnyei, Z. (2003) Attitudes, orientations, and motivation in language learning: Advances in theory, research, and applications. *Language Learning* 53 (1), 3–32.

Dörnyei, Z. and Csizér, K. (2002) Some dynamics of language attitudes and motivation: Results of a longitudinal nationwide survey. *Applied Linguistics* 23 (4), 421–462.

Gardner, R.C. and Lambert, W.E. (1972) *Attitudes and Motivation in Second Language Learning.* Rowley, MA: Newbury House.

Gleick, J. (1988) *Chaos: Making a New Science.* New York: Penguin Books.

Holland, J.H. (1995) *Hidden Order: How Adaptation Builds Complexity.* Reading, MA: Addison-Wesley.

Holland, J.H. (1998) *Emergence: From Chaos to Order.* New York: Basic Books.

Larsen-Freeman, D. (1997) Chaos/complexity science and second language acquisition. *Applied Linguistics* 18 (2), 141–165.

Larsen-Freeman, D. and Cameron, L. (2008) *Complex Systems and Applied Linguistics.* Oxford: Oxford University Press.

Lewin, R. (1992) *Complexity: Life at the Edge of Chaos.* New York: Macmillan.

Lorenz, E.N. (2001) *The Essence of Chaos*. Seattle, WA: The University of Washington Press.

Mandelbrot, B.B. (1982) *The Fractal Geometry of Nature*. New York: W.H. Freeman and Company.

Maturana, H.R. and Varela, F.J. (1987) *The Tree of Knowledge: The Biological Roots of Human Understanding*. Boston, MA: Shambhala.

Murray, G.L. (ed.) (2009) *Restrospective: Learning English in Japan*. Akita: Center for Independent Language Learning, Akita International University.

Norton, B. (2000) *Identity and Language Learning: Gender, Ethnicity and Educational Change*. London: Longman/Pearson Education.

Paiva, V.L.M.O. (2006) Autonomia e complexidade. *Linguagem e Ensino 9* (1), 77–127.

Paiva, V.L.M. de O. and Braga J.C.F. (2008) The complex nature of autonomy. *Revista D.E.L.T.A.* 24 (especial), 441–468.

Poincaré, H. (1921) *The Foundation of Science: Science and Method*. New York: The Science Press.

Prigogine, I. and Stengers, I. (1984) *Order Out of Chaos: Man's New Dialogue with Nature*. London: Heinemann.

Ryan, R. and Deci, E.L. (2000) Intrinsic and extrinsic motivations: Classic definitions and new directions. *Contemporary Educational Psychology 25* (1), 54–67.

Sade, L.A. (2008) Complexity and identity reconstruction in second language acquisition. Symposium paper presented at AILA 2008 – 15th World Congress of Applied Linguistics, Essen, Germany.

The Five Graces Group (2008) Language is a complex adaptive system. On WWW at http://www.santafe.edu/research/publicat...papers/08-12-047.pdf.

Van Lier, L. (1996) *Interaction in the Language Curriculum: Awareness, Autonomy, and Authenticity*. London: Longman.

Waldrop, M.M. (1992) *Complexity: The Emerging Science at the Edge of Order and Chaos*. New York: Touchstone.

Wenger, E. (2000) Communities of practice and social learning systems. *Organization 7* (2), 225–246.

Williams, G.P. (1997) *Chaos Theory Tamed*. Washington, DC: Joseph Henry Press.

Winke, P.M. (2005) Promoting motivation in the foreign language classroom. *Clear News 9* (2), 1–6. On WWW at http://clear.msu.edu/clear/newsletter/files/fall2005.pdf.

Part 2

Independent Learning Settings

Chapter 6

Imagination, Metacognition and the L2 Self in a Self-Access Learning Environment

GAROLD MURRAY

Introduction

The exploration of contemporary notions of self and identity in the field of language education has opened up an intriguing area of study – the role of imagination in second (L2) and foreign language (FL) learning. In one line of inquiry, Norton (2001) has employed Anderson's (1991) construct of *imagined communities* in order to explore how learners' sense of belonging to target language communities that are not immediately accessible can impact on their identity construction and language learning. More recently, Dörnyei (2005, 2009), informed by Markus and Nurius's (1986) theory of possible selves – our images of what we can or might become – has proposed the L2 Motivational Self System model. While these two lines of inquiry have enhanced our understanding of the roles of self and identity in language learning and the ways in which learners' visions of themselves in the future influence what they do in the present, little, if any, research has focused closely on the role of imagination in specific L2 and FL learning contexts. A greater understanding of the functioning of imagination in relation to the learning process will benefit educators as they undertake the challenge of identifying the kinds of pedagogical interventions that might support the development of positive as well as potentially attainable L2 selves and enhance learners' sense of belonging to imagined target language communities.

This chapter explores the part played by imagination in the English language learning of a group of Japanese first-year university students. It reports on a research project investigating their experiences in a self-directed learning course, which blended self-access language learning with classroom-based instruction. Employing the combined theoretical perspectives of possible selves and imagined communities, the chapter illustrates how imagination mediated the role of these constructs in the daily learning experiences of the participants. The ensuing discussion examines the implications of the findings for language learners and educators, and considers the potential of this particular mode of learning as a pedagogical intervention capable of enhancing learners' visions of their L2 selves and enabling learners to work toward their realization.

Imagined Selves and Communities

The theoretical notion of possible selves, 'individuals' ideas of what they might become, what they would like to become and what they are afraid of becoming, was introduced to the field of psychology by Markus and Nurius (1986: 954). Applying this construct to the field of L2 learning and drawing on Higgins's (1987; Higgins *et al.*, 1985) notions of the 'ideal self' and the 'ought-to self', Dörnyei (2005, 2009) elaborated his theory of the L2 Motivational Self System, which consists of three components: the *ideal L2 self*, the *ought-to L2 self* and the *L2 learning experience*. Dörnyei (2009: 29) explains that, 'if the person we would like to become speaks an L2, the *"ideal L2 self"* is a powerful motivator to learn the L2 because of the desire to reduce the discrepancy between our actual and ideal selves'. The ought-to L2 self relates to 'the attributes that one believes one *ought to* possess in order to meet expectations and *avoid* possible negative outcomes' (Dörnyei, 2009: 29), while the L2 learning experience concerns motives related to the immediate learning environment and experience.

Imagination comes into play in Dörnyei's motivational model primarily in two ways. First, a possible self or one's ideal self is manifested as a mental image or composite of mental images. As Boyatzis and Akrivou (2006: 632) explain, 'the dream or image of a desired future is the content of the ideal self'. Secondly, learners who envision an ideal L2 self will most likely imagine themselves using the language in some social context or target language community (Yashima, 2009). Wenger (1998), who has explored how we develop our identities through participation in various communities of practice (Lave & Wenger, 1991), provides a conceptual framework for situating possible selves within an imagined social context.

Wenger (1998: 176) defines imagination as 'a process of expanding our self by transcending our time and space and creating new images of the world and ourselves'. He contends that while engagement in social groups in our immediate environment provides opportunities for identity construction, our imagination enables us to have a sense of belonging to communities that are not immediately accessible or are diffuse or distributed over a widespread geographical area (Wenger, 1998; Wenger *et al.*, 2002), i.e. imagined communities. Since Norton (2001) first introduced the concept into the field of language education, research has primarily explored how visions of future participation in imagined communities can influence individuals' language learning trajectories (Kanno, 2003; Kanno & Norton, 2003; Lamb, this volume; Murray, 2008a) and the (re)construction of learners' identities (Kinginger, 2004; Murphey *et al.*, 2004; Norton, 2001).

Much of the research to date exploring possible selves in the area of L2 and FL learning has been of a quantitative nature with the general aim of providing empirical support for Dörnyei's L2 Motivational Self System (Csizér & Kormos, 2009; Taguchi *et al.*, 2009; Ryan, 2009). One notable exception to this trend employed the dual perspectives of possible selves and imagined communities to investigate the experiences of Japanese English as a foreign language (EFL) students as they participated in a model United Nations (UN) project (Yashima, 2009; Yashima & Zenuk-Nishide, 2008). These researchers concluded that learning activities enabling students to participate in imagined international communities could be instrumental in the development of the future L2 self. The study reported on in this chapter builds on these previous inquiries in three ways: it demonstrates how another type of L2 learning experience might foster a learner's vision of an L2 self and facilitate its realization; it examines the role that imagination plays in this process; and, in doing so, it illustrates the link between imagination and metacognition.

The Learning Context

The study was carried out at a small Japanese university, which offered a liberal arts curriculum consisting of two majors, Global Studies and Global Business. English was the medium of instruction. Students were required to spend a year studying abroad at one of the university's partner institutions located in English-speaking countries as well as various parts of Europe and Asia. Before students could start taking courses toward their degree, they first had to successfully complete an English for Academic Purposes (EAP) program.

As a part of their EAP program, the students who participated in the study took a course called self-directed language learning, which was offered in the university's self-access center. The course had two main objectives: (1) to help students improve their language proficiency; and

(2) to help students develop their metacognitive knowledge and skills. Here, metacognitive knowledge is understood to be the knowledge that students have about themselves as learners and how they learn (Flavell, 1976), while metacognitive skills refer to the skills required to plan, monitor and evaluate their learning (Wenden, 1998). As a means of achieving these objectives, students developed and carried out their own personal learning plans. In keeping with Holec's (1981) model of learner autonomy, they determined their goals, chose appropriate materials, decided how they were going to use these materials, monitored their progress and assessed the outcomes. There were no teacher-based language lessons; however, instruction modeling learning strategies and activities were provided in mini-lessons delivered at the beginning of a class. Portfolios played a key role in the management and assessment of students' learning. In their portfolios, students collected evidence of learning, including the long-term learning plans that they developed, documents resulting from assessment strategies (e.g. graphs recording reading speed, tables indicating test of English as a foreign language (TOEFL) practice test results, etc.) and regular learning log entries documenting what they had done each day, a brief reflection on their experiences and their plans for the next class. Final grades were determined through a process of collaborative evaluation (Dickinson, 1987) in which both the student and the instructor reviewed the portfolio and allocated a grade according to a rubric of performance criteria. (For a more detailed account of the course, see Murray, 2009.)

The Study

A three-year study investigated the experiences of the students enrolled in the self-directed language learning course. Of the approximate 400 students who took the course during this period, 269 agreed to participate in the study. On entering the university, these students had a TOEFL score in the 400–500 range. Given that the students had to pass rigorous entrance examinations and chose to attend this university knowing their coursework would be in English, it is highly likely that they were motivated to become proficient in the language.

The design of the study drew on both quantitative and qualitative research methods with data from a variety of sources. A language beliefs questionnaire was administered in a pre-/post-test manner at the beginning and end of the course. As a class activity, the students compared their responses and briefly wrote about their reactions and insights. During the first two weeks, the students wrote a language learning history and, at the end of the semester, they wrote a reflection on this history in view of their experiences in the course. In addition, the learners' portfolios, containing their long-term learning plans, daily learning log entries and documentation resulting from self-assessment strategies, served as a rich, additional source of data. At the end of the course, the students completed a course evaluation questionnaire consisting of 20 Likert scale items and six open-ended questions. In addition to the data resulting from the course materials, two students in each class who were engaged with the coursework and who did not stand out from the others were asked to participate in interviews. A total of 27 individual interviews and two focus group discussions were recorded and transcribed.

Findings

A previous analysis focusing on the quantitative data indicated that the self-directed learning course was successful in meeting its stated aim of promoting the learners' metacognitive development (Cotterall & Murray, 2009). Furthermore, a thematic analysis of the qualitative data, in addition to supporting this finding, hinted at the role imagination played in the students' learning by offering evidence that they envisioned future English-speaking selves engaging in imagined target language communities. Informed by the literature on possible selves and imagined communities, the following thematic content analysis of the qualitative data – the interviews, language learning histories, open-ended questions on the course evaluation and the portfolios – examines the part imagination played at the various stages of the learning process from goal setting to assessment. Because of the large number of participants and the vast amount of data generated, the chapter will focus primarily, but not exclusively, on the experiences of three learners, who will be called Hiro, Rina and Mari. These learners were chosen partly because, as their teacher, I was able to gain a deeper insight into their learning approaches and beliefs, given the opportunities this provided to interact with them and observe their performance on a regular basis. An additional consideration in their selection was the range of different perspectives and approaches each of them brought to the learning situation, while sharing similar goals.

Imagination and goal setting

Imagination mediated the process of goal setting in two ways. First, it enabled the learners to have a vision of a possible self they could work toward. Secondly, picturing this self operating in an imagined target language environment helped them identify intermediate goals, or the steps they needed to take in order to make their future self a reality, which in turn led to the emergence of a learning plan (Taylor *et al.*, 1998). While future possible selves might be viewed as long-term developmental goals comprised of interim goals, they are more than a set of goals (Pizzolato, 2006); rather, they are '"self states" that people experience as reality' (Dörnyei, 2009: 16). The data in this study suggest that the learners had images of an ideal self – although not always clearly articulated – and in the self-directed learning course they set goals designed to help them move from their present toward their imagined future self state.

Hiro, for example, had a vision of an ideal self that was distinct from the goals he set in order to realize that self. Explaining in an interview why he was learning English, Hiro said, 'I want to become an International person and I want to work in a foreign country using English'. His vision of an international person was inspired by a dynamic Japanese EFL teacher who had lived abroad and whose lessons actively engaged his students. Recounting this experience in his language learning history, Hiro concluded, 'I thought that I wanted to learn English at university and become an international person like him'.

A number of the participants recounted similar stories in their language learning histories and echoed Hiro's desire to become an international person. Their comments indicated that their understanding of the term was akin to the concept of *international posture*, which Yashima (2002, 2009) has identified in her research designed to explain how students in an FL setting, like Japan, might relate to the target language community. She describes international posture as an 'interest in foreign or international affairs, willingness to go overseas to stay or work, readiness to interact with intercultural partners, and, one hopes, openness or a non-ethnocentric attitude toward different cultures' (Yashima, 2002: 57). While the term posture suggests possessing a set of attitudes, for the learners in this study, the attributes Yashima outlines serve more as a description of the self they hoped to become – a self, embracing a global identity (Arnett, 2002) of which an English-speaking future self was one aspect.

Not only did the learners' visions of their ideal selves appear to extend beyond images of themselves as English language speakers, but a number of the participants viewed becoming an English speaker as an interim goal on the road to making this self a reality. When the participants were asked, on the course evaluation questionnaire, how they thought they would use English in the future, a number of the responses indicated that they saw English as a tool to help them realize their ideal self. For example, one anonymous learner wrote, 'My dream is to be a flexible global thinker. I want to make efforts to study English as a first step for my dream'. In the self-directed learning course, the learners set intermediate goals designed to guide their efforts to make this first step a reality.

The intermediate goals that Hiro, Rina and Mari set for themselves in the self-directed learning course appeared to be strongly influenced by their visions of a future self participating in imagined communities – more specifically, they wanted to improve their ability to participate in everyday conversations. Hiro, for example, said, 'Now I visit there [the Centre] and watch movies... when I go abroad I have to talk with them [English speakers]. So I want to watch a drama with daily conversations'. Rina, whose future self appeared to have a more career-oriented focus reflecting an ought-to L2 self, said, 'In the future I want to be a tour guide so I have to study English and history'. Mari, on the other hand, did not explicitly articulate her vision of a future or ideal self; nonetheless, as the discussion of her choice of course content in the following section makes apparent, her goals were also influenced by her vision of a possible self engaging in imagined target language communities.

Imagination and content

Seeing themselves engaging in imagined communities with people of their own age influenced the students' choice of content in the self-directed learning course. Many of the students chose to work with DVDs of movies and television programs so they could learn slang and idiomatic expressions that they could use in conversations with their future English-speaking peers. Speaking of her choice of content, Mari had this to say:

> I watched the DVD, *How to Lose a Guy in 10 Days*. I chose this movie because it was my favourite.... I thought it would be useful for me to learn because the DVD has a lot of slang, and the American way of speaking in English, and phrases I would use in daily life.

Mari's comments not only point to her emerging metacognitive awareness of the need to be knowledgeable about the pragmatic and sociocultural aspects of language use – or, as she put it, 'the American way of speaking' – but also illustrate the connection between metacognition and imagination (Oyserman *et al.*, 2006). Her experience suggests that having images of themselves using the language in target language communities helps learners know which aspects of the language they need to learn and, subsequently, which materials would be appropriate.

In addition to drawing attention to the relationship between meta-cognition and imagination, Mari makes another point meriting closer attention – she chose this movie because it was her favorite. Many of the students had favorite movies or television programs that they worked with – in some cases – the whole semester. Elsewhere, I have argued that DVDs present imagined communities that can provide learners with a form of peripheral engagement through the power of the imagination (Murray, 2008b). Writing on this topic, Wenger (1998: 203) says, 'Stories can transport our experience into the situations they relate and involve us in producing the meanings of those events as though we were participants'. Mari's comments suggest that she was having this kind of experience and finding it beneficial for her language learning. When asked in an interview if she thought her work in the course helped her meet her goal of participating in everyday conversations, she replied, 'I think so because DVDs have daily conversation with daily phrases and if you listen carefully to the conversations maybe you can see it in yourself'. Mari's comment suggests that the DVDs provided potential models of English-speaking selves. Furthermore, her peculiar turn of phrase, 'see it in yourself', gives us a clue to the role of imagination in the construction of her future English-speaking self. She suggests that she was relating these expressions to who she was as a person – trying them on to see if they fit her emerging L2 self. It would seem that Mari's imagination enabled her to picture herself using these expressions in similar situations to see if they would work for her.

Like Mari, Hiro, in his efforts to realize his future self, also used DVDs to reach his goal of being able to participate in everyday conversations. In addition to this, he worked with a monthly news magazine produced for Japanese EFL learners. Hiro said, '_CNN English Express_ was very helpful for me because this book writes about current events in the world and I can gain a broad vision and I could gain a lot of information in the world'. Many students in the self-directed learning course used this material to increase their vocabulary; however, Hiro suggests that he found an additional purpose – it provided him with information that was helping him visualize the communities he might participate in one day. The experiences of these learners suggest that they chose content that supported the work of their imagination by providing material that helped them develop clearer images of imagined communities, por-trayed models of potential L2 selves and aided them in building a linguistic repertoire appropriate for the L2 self that they envisaged.

Imagination and learning strategies

Imagination was not only instrumental in learners' choice of content, but there is evidence that it was also an integral aspect of how they worked with the content, i.e. their learning strategies and activities. In the following quote, Rina explains the role that imagination played in strategies she employed to improve her speaking proficiency:

> I prefer to read to watch DVD's. When I watch DVD's, it has already shown me the situation and characters, but when I read the book I can imagine the character, or setting, or situation....Creating the image helps me when I encounter the same situation in daily life.... I always try to image and relate to the situation... and so I try to memorize the whole situation, including speaking and facial expression, or gesture and I try to use this expression in daily life.

Throughout the course, Rina combined reading and listening strategies – in other words, she listened to an unabridged audio recording as she read the book – which enabled her to memorize 'the speaking expression'. Rina found that using her imagination to visualize the language being used in the imagined community was effective in helping her to remember the expressions and to identify when and how to use them in daily life.

Other students also found DVDs helpful in this regard. Comments similar to the following appeared in many daily learning logs and learning plan assessments: 'I have learned that watching DVD is best for me because I can visualize when and how to use the conversation'. However, Mari, who experienced working with both DVDs and books accompanied by audio recordings, concurs with Rina. When asked in an interview what was the most useful thing she did in the course to learn English, Mari replied, 'Reading books... because, if I watch DVDs, I don't need to imagine the situation because the picture is already there. But, if I read a book, I have to use my imagination to go over the story so my brain works more'. While the learners' comments were constrained by their emerging metacognition and meta-language, they nonetheless demonstrated an awareness of the importance of employing learning strategies and activities, which required active use of their imagination.

Imagination, monitoring and assessment

The learners' remarks also indicate the extent to which imagination is an important aspect of the strategies required to monitor and self-assess the learning process and outcomes. Wenger (1998: 217) notes that, 'the combination of engagement and imagination results in a *reflective* practice'. Conversely, the opportunity to reflect on engagement in learning practices can invoke the processes of the imagination. Elsewhere, Wenger (1998: 185) writes, 'Imagination requires the ability to disengage—to move back and look at our engagement through the eyes of an outsider'. When we ask students to reflect on their engagement in order to monitor or assess their learning, we are asking them to do just this.

Many comments suggesting that imagination figured prominently in the monitoring and assessment of learning appeared on the course evaluation questionnaire in response to the questions, 'Has your perception about how you best learn a language changed as a result of having taken this course? If so, how?' and 'How did your attempts to measure your learning progress in this course affect your language learning?' For example, one student responded, 'I think this course gave us the opportunity to look at ourselves objectively and think deeply how we can improve our English skills'. Another student wrote, 'I liked this course because there are discoveries of myself, the style of learning as a language learner'. The opportunities that the course provided for reflection encouraged the students to step back and visualize themselves as learners, which led to insights into their identities as language learners. One student even made a distinction between the type of learning that went on in other courses in the EAP program and the self-directed learning course, writing, '*Academic Writing* is for writing. *Focused Listening* is for listening. But, *Self-Directed Learning* is for everything. Students have a chance to see themselves and find their weakness in learning English and they can improve and develop these things'. Taking these metacognitive insights into account, learners were then able to revise and refine their goals, which in most cases necessitated modifying their learning plan.

Discussion

The data collected in this study illustrate the concomitant operation of the processes of imagination and metacognition in the students' learning experiences. Wenger (1998: 185) contends that, 'in terms of participation, imagination needs an opening. It needs the willingness, freedom, energy, and time to expose ourselves to the exotic, move around, try new identities, and explore new relations'. The course in self-directed learning provided students with autonomy, time and space for their imagination to do its work. Furthermore, the course supported students' exploration of learning opportunities by offering instruction in strategies and activities, and encouraging them to experiment. In short, the course offered students opportunities to personalize their learning, to engage directly in the learning process, to experiment, to reflect on their experiences and to seek the support they required. This combination of affordances not only facilitated the work of imagination, but at the same time enabled the students to develop their metacognitive knowledge and skills (Cotterall & Murray, 2009). For the learners in this study, the role of imagination was particularly evident in the metacognitive skills areas of planning and assessment.

As for planning the learning, Wenger (1998: 185) writes that imagination helps us in 'defining a trajectory that connects what we are doing to an extended identity, seeing ourselves in new ways'. This echoes Markus and Nurius's (1986: 961) comment that possible selves 'can be viewed as cognitive bridges between the present and future, specifying how individuals may change from how they are now to what they will become'. When the students in the self-directed learning course identified weaknesses in their language proficiency and planned ways to improve, they were defining trajectories leading from who they were at that time as English language learners to their extended identities as English speakers. Projecting into the future and visualizing their possible selves participating in imagined English language communities provided learners with a model of a future English-speaking self to which they could aspire.

This notion that determining language learning goals entails having a vision of a possible self as an FL speaker makes goal setting a much more complex process than it appears to be on the surface. The challenge for educators is to ascertain how they might encourage or facilitate the emergence of learners' L2 selves. In the self-directed learning course, activities such as completing a learner profile, requiring students to identify things they would need or like to be able to do in English in the future, and writing a language learning history, which they concluded by considering how they would continue to develop their language skills, helped the students to focus on who they were as L2 learners, consider their trajectories and determine their learning goals.

Once learners have set their goals, they need to be able to choose materials and activities that fuel their imagination by presenting them with potential imagined communities and possible models for their L2 selves. For this reason, language educators should consider incorporating pop culture artifacts into the curriculum (Chik & Breidbach, this volume; Murray, 2008b). In this study, DVDs of movies and television programs, young adult fiction and magazines were very popular with the learners and appeared to enhance their visions of target language communities that they might participate in one day. The data also suggest that these media helped students envisage their L2 selves participating in conversations in these imagined communities.

In addition to materials, the data revealed another source of ideal L2 selves – language teachers. In their language learning histories, a number of learners indicated that their desire to learn English was inspired by a teacher whom they respected and who made language learning 'fun'. In some cases, they mentioned admiring these teachers and wanting to become like them because in their eyes they represented an 'international person'. Yashima (2009: 153) recalls a college student telling her that, 'a native speaker is too remote a goal. I can never identify with them. But Japanese teachers are more accessible goals'. According to Bandura's (1986, 1997) social cognitive theory, seeing people, i.e. models, similar to oneself succeed, is one way of creating and strengthening self-efficacy beliefs, thereby enhancing motivation. The experiences of the learners in this study suggest that bilingual teachers who share the learners' first language and culture can positively influence learners' self-efficacy as well as inspire the development of ideal L2 selves by serving as models. This calls into question current thinking and practice in Japan and other parts of the world, which place a high value on English classes being taught by so-called 'native' English speakers.

The second area of the learners' experience in which imagination figured most prominently was assessment. Wenger's (1998: 185) contention that '[imagination] requires the ability to proceed without being too quick with the constraints of a specific form of accountability', suggests that as language educators we may need to rethink assessment and evaluation practices. Current practices seem to focus on the ought-to L2 self based on educators' projections of learning outcomes. The experiences of the students in the self-directed learning course point to the need for open-ended assessment procedures and collaborative evaluation methods that encourage learners to document what they recognize they are learning in relation to the goals they set for themselves. In some cases, what they note may lie outside the bounds of anticipated outcomes. As teachers, we need to acknowledge and value these unforeseen aspects of our students' learning.

We also need to be aware of the potential role of the ideal L2 self in self-assessment practices. Markus and Nurius (1986: 956) contend, 'possible selves furnish criteria against which outcomes are evaluated'. Evidence provided by the study, combined with my observations over a four-year period as I worked with the learners in the self-directed learning course, has led me to conclude that the learners assessed their learning by comparing their present L2 self with their ideal L2 self. A danger lies in the learners' tendency to focus on the large, more salient gaps that exist between the two visions in various skill areas. This situation can blind learners to the more subtle incremental changes that characterize gains in L2 proficiency. In the self-directed learning course, learners were encouraged to look for small signs of progress and to document these on graphs or tables so that they could see their language-related development over time.

While notions of progress and development tend to be future oriented, Wenger reminds readers that the past, mediated by the imagination, has a role to play in the present and future. He writes, 'It is through imagination that we see our own practices as continuing histories that reach far into the past.... By taking us into the past and carrying us into the future, it can recast the present and show it as holding unsuspected possibilities' (Wenger, 1998: 178). Learners in the self-directed learning course wrote language learning histories at the beginning of the course and reflections on their histories at the end. The purpose was to cue their metacognitive development by having them focus on who they were as language learners and document changes in their thinking during the course. They were encouraged to consider why they wanted to learn English and to conclude both their history and reflection by outlining how they intended to proceed with their language learning. This activity could be extended by having the learners write *anticipated life histories* (Segal, 2006) in which they would focus more specifically on their future English-speaking self. As it was, the histories and reflections enabled the participants in this study to trace their identity as language learners and the trajectory of their English learning from their junior high school days to the present, and into the future through their visions of the communities they could see themselves participating in someday. It is my contention that this exercise helped them to see more clearly the possibilities the course in the self-directed learning offered in the present.

Conclusion

The underlying purpose of this chapter has been to support the work of language educators as they seek to foster learners' motivation by designing L2 learning experiences that facilitate the development and realization of learners' visions of their L2 selves and enhance their sense of belonging to imagined target language communities. To this end, the chapter examined the role that imagination played in a learning context, which combined self-access learning with classroom-based instruction. The data illustrated how the processes of imagination and metacognition were interconnected in the daily learning experiences of the students. While imagination mediated the learners' visions of an L2 self, it was their metacognitive knowledge and skills that mediated the steps they took toward its realization. The findings of this study lend support to Dörnyei's (2009: 37) contention that, 'the ideal self needs to come as part of a "package" consisting of an imagery component and a repertoire of appropriate plans, scripts and self-regulatory strategies'. The high degree of learner autonomy that this particular learning context provided was a key factor in facilitating the work of imagination and metacognition. For the learners in this study, the L2 learning experiences afforded by a combination of self-access language learning and classroom-based instruction contributed to the development of their current L2 selves and enabled them to plan and implement action aimed at making their visions of future selves participating in imagined target language communities a reality.

One of the limitations of the research in relation to the discussion presented in this chapter was that the study was not specifically designed to investigate the L2 self system or the role of imagination in this particular learning context; rather the serendipitous emergence of imagination as an aspect of the participants' experience led to the current exploration of the data in this respect. This unexpected outcome points to the value of taking a person-in-context approach (Ushioda, 2009) in future inquiries and employing research methods that make it possible to focus on the L2 selves of individuals in specific learning contexts (Lamb, 2009). Taking such an approach enabled this inquiry to explore the role of imagination in one learning context, to illustrate the relationship between imagination and metacognition, thereby demonstrating the motivational potential of a mode of learning integrating self-access learning and classroom-based instruction.

References

Anderson, B. (1991) *Imagined Communities: Reflections on the Origin and Spread of Nationalism* (rev. edn). London: Verso.

Arnett, J.J. (2002) The psychology of globalization. *American Psychologist* 57 (10), 774–783.

Bandura, A. (1986) *Social Foundations of Thought and Action: A Social Cognitive Theory.* Englewood Cliffs, NJ: Prentice Hall.

Bandura, A. (1997) *Self-Efficacy: The Exercise of Control.* New York: Freeman.

Boyatzis, R.E. and Akrivou, K. (2006) The ideal self as the driver of intentional change. *Journal of Management Development* 25, 624–642.

Cotterall, S. and Murray, G. (2009) Enhancing metacognitive knowledge: Structure, affordances and self. *System* 37, 34–45.

Csizér, K. and Kormos, J. (2009) Learning experiences, selves and motivated learning behaviour: A comparative analysis of structural models for Hungarian secondary and university learners of English. In Z. Dörnyei and E. Ushioda (eds) *Motivation, Language Identity and the L2 Self* (pp. 98–119). Bristol: Multilingual Matters.

Dickinson, L. (1987) *Self-Instruction in Language Learning*. Cambridge: Cambridge University Press.

Dörnyei, Z. (2005) *The Psychology of the Language Learner.* Mahwah, NJ: Lawrence Erlbaum.

Dörnyei, Z. (2009) The L2 Motivational Self System. In Z. Dörnyei and E. Ushioda (eds) *Motivation, Language Identity and the L2 Self* (pp. 9–42). Bristol: Multilingual Matters.

Dörnyei, Z. and Ushioda, E. (eds) (2009) *Motivation, Language Identity and the L2 Self.* Bristol: Multilingual Matters.

Flavell, J.H. (1976) Metacognitive aspects of problem solving. In B. Resnick (ed.) *The Nature of Intelligence* (pp. 231–235). Hillsdale, NJ: Lawrence Erlbaum.

Higgins, E.T. (1987) Self-discrepancy: A theory relating self and affect. *Psychological Review* 94, 319–340.

Higgins, E.T., Klein, R. and Strauman, T. (1985) Self-concept discrepancy theory: A psychological model for distinguishing among different aspects of depression and anxiety. *Social Cognition* 3, 51–76.

Holec, H. (1981) *Autonomy and Foreign Language Learning.* Oxford: Pergamon Press.

Kanno, Y. (2003) Imagined communities, school visions, and the education of bilingual students in Japan. *Journal of Language, Identity, and Education* 2, 285–300.

Kanno, Y. and Norton, B. (2003) Imagined communities and educational possibilities: Introduction. *Journal of Language, Identity, and Education* 2 (4), 241–249.

Kinginger, C. (2004) Alice doesn't live here anymore: Foreign language learning and identity reconstruction. In A. Pavlenko and A. Blackledge (eds) *Negotiation of Identities in Multilingual Contexts* (pp. 219–242). Clevedon: Multilingual Matters.

Lamb, M. (2009) Situating the L2 self: Two Indonesian school learners of English. In Z. Dörnyei and E. Ushioda (eds) *Motivation, Language Identity and the L2 Self* (pp. 229–247). Bristol: Multilingual Matters.

Lave, J. and Wenger, E. (1991) *Situated Learning: Legitimate Peripheral Participation.* Cambridge: Cambridge University Press.

Markus, H. and Nurius, P. (1986) Possible selves. *American Psychologist* 41, 954–969.

Murphey, T., Chen, J. and Chen, L-C. (2004) Learners' constructions of identities and imagined communities. In P. Benson and D. Nunan (eds) *Learners' Stories: Difference and Diversity in Language Learning* (pp. 83–100). Cambridge: Cambridge University Press.

Murray, G. (2008a) Communities of practice: Stories of Japanese EFL learners. In P. Kalaja, V. Menezes and A.M. Barcleos (eds) *Narratives of Learning and Teaching EFL* (pp. 128–140). Basingstoke: Palgrave Macmillan.

Murray, G. (2008b) Pop culture and language learning: Learners' stories informing EFL. *Innovation in Language Learning and Teaching* 2, 1–16.

Murray, G. (2009) A self-directed learning course. In A. Smith and G. Strong (eds) *Adult Learners: Content, Context, and Innovation* (pp. 61–70). Alexandria, VA: TESOL.

Norton, B. (2001) Non-participation, imagined communities and the language classroom. In M. Breen (ed.) *Learner Contributions to Language Learning: New Directions in Research* (pp. 159–171). Harlow: Pearson Education.

Oyserman, D., Bybee, D. and Terry, K. (2006) Possible selves and academic outcomes: How and when possible selves impel action. *Journal of Personality and Social Psychology* 91, 188–204.

Pizzolato, J.E. (2006) Achieving college student possible selves: Navigating the space between commitment and achievement of long-term identity goals. *Cultural Diversity and Ethnic Minority Psychology* 12, 57–69.

Ryan, S. (2009) Self and identity in L2 motivation in Japan: The ideal L2 self and Japanese learners of English. In Z. Dörnyei and E. Ushioda (eds) *Motivation, Language Identity and the L2 Self* (pp. 120–143). Bristol: Multilingual Matters.

Segal, H.G. (2006) Possible selves, fantasy distortion, and the anticipated life history: Exploring the role of imagination in social cognition. In C. Dunkel and J. Kerpelman (eds) *Possible Selves: Theory, Research and Reflections* (pp. 79–96). New York: Nova Science.

Taguchi, T., Magid, M. and Papi, M. (2009) The L2 motivational system among Japanese, Chinese, and Iranian learners of English: A comparative study. In Z. Dörnyei and E. Ushioda (eds) *Motivation, Language Identity and the L2 Self* (pp. 66–97). Bristol: Multilingual Matters.

Taylor, S.E., Pham, L.B., Rivkin, I.D. and Armor, D.A. (1998) Harnessing the imagination: Mental simulation, self-regulation, and coping. *American Psychologist* 53, 429–439.

Ushioda, E. (2009) A person-in-context relational view of emergent motivation, self, and identity. In Z. Dörnyei and E. Ushioda (eds) *Motivation, Language Identity and the L2 Self* (pp. 215–228). Bristol: Multilingual Matters.

Wenden, A. (1998) Metacognitive knowledge and language learning. *Applied Linguistics* 19, 515–537.

Wenger, E. (1998) *Communities of Practice: Learning, Meaning, and Identity.* Cambridge: Cambridge University Press.

Wenger, E., McDermott, R. and Snyder, W.M. (2002) *Cultivating Communities of Practice: A Guide to Managing Knowledge.* Boston, MA: Harvard Business School Press.

Yashima, T. (2002) Willingness to communicate in a second language: The Japanese EFL context. *The Modern Language Journal* 86, 54–65.

Yashima, T. (2009) International posture and the ideal L2 self in the Japanese EFL context. In Z. Dörnyei and E. Ushioda (eds) *Motivation, Language Identity and the L2 Self* (pp. 144–163). Bristol: Multilingual Matters.

Yashima, T. and Zenuk-Nishide, L. (2008) The impact of learning contexts on proficiency, attitudes, and L2 communication: Creating an imagined international community. *System* 36, 566–585.

Chapter 7

Identity, Motivation and Plurilingualism in Self-Access Centers

E. DESIRÉE CASTILLO ZARAGOZA

Introduction

In the literature on self-access centers (SACs), learners are implicitly considered to be learning only one language, and thus one aspect of learners can be analyzed. But in reality, SACs are generally multilingual and learners may engage in learning more than one language at a time, allowing other facets of the learner to emerge. Although learners are using multilingual SACs to engage in plurilingual learning projects, this has so far received no attention in the literature. This chapter addresses this gap in the literature by reporting on an exploratory research project, which examines the identity, motivation and autonomy of learners who are working to improve their proficiency in more than one language in two SACs in Mexico.

Throughout this chapter, in accordance with the Council of Europe's usage of the terms, I employ the words multilingual and plurilingual to refer, respectively, to the learning context and the act of learning or using more than one language. In this sense, multilingual describes an environment or milieu in which two or more languages are spoken or expressed, e.g. a society that uses different languages, learning material presented in different languages, language centers that offer access to more than two languages, etc. Plurilingual describes a person who is capable of using several languages (cf. Riley, 2003), as well as the activity of learning two or more languages at the same time, e.g. a plurilingual learning project.

By learning several languages in a SAC, which means that learners are working by themselves in a more autonomous way, it may be assumed that learners have a particular and strong motivation toward languages. As they invest in the languages, they are investing in their

91

own identities (Norton, 2000). Based on the notions of the second language (L2) Motivational Self System (Dörnyei, 2009), in this chapter we will see how Mexican learners are engaging in a bi- or plurilingual learning project, learning more than one foreign language in order to build a plurilingual identity, and this despite the fact that there is no explicit language policy of multilingualism in Mexico. We will also see how learners can have different attitudes toward the languages being learned, thus revealing different facets of their identities. Moreover, by working, in part, by themselves in a more autonomous way, learners can see and reveal other aspects of their person, which are less likely to be seen when learners are analyzed through the single lens of only one language they are learning, as is usually the case in classrooms.

In order to illustrate these points, the chapter begins by briefly reviewing concepts of motivation and identity and their link with plurilingualism. It then establishes the context by discussing the linguistic and SAC situation in Mexico. This is followed by a description of the methodology and the results of the study.

Motivation, Identity and Plurilingualism

The notions of integrative/instrumental motivation (Gardner, 1985), as well as those of extrinsic/intrinsic motivation (Deci & Ryan, 1985) have, for some time, informed our understanding of why people learn languages. However, increasing interest in notions of the self and identity have led to a shift in language learning motivation from the area of social psychology. As Dörnyei and Ushioda (2009) explain, motivation is in the process of being reconceptualized and retheorized in relation to self and identity. In fact, they point out that the well-known concept of integrative orientation, introduced by Gardner and Lambert (1972), is under debate, because, among other issues, researchers question how to apply the integrative orientation 'when there is no specific target reference group of speakers' (Dörnyei & Ushioda, 2009: 2), as can be the case with English.

In this reconceptualization of motivation, Dörnyei (2009) presents the L2 Motivational Self System, which is constituted by what one wants to become (ideal L2 self), by the attributes one thinks one has to possess in order to meet expectations and to avoid possible negative outcomes (ought-to L2 self) and by the situated motives related to the immediate learning environment and experience (L2 learning experience). Dörnyei contends that these elements will have an influence on learners: learners will do what they think has to be done in order to reduce the discrepancy between the actual and the ideal self, or to avoid negative outcomes.

With regard to plurilingualism, as Dörnyei and Clement (2001) and Csizér and Dörnyei (2005) point out, there have been few studies that focus on the motivational disposition related to learning several target languages within the same community. However, studies that have explored this topic (for examples, see Csizér & Dörnyei, 2005; Dörnyei & Clement, 2001; Humphreys & Spratt, 2008; Schmidt & Watanabe, 2001) demonstrate that learning several languages at one time is possible and that learners' attitudes toward the languages being learned can be different at any given moment. However, it is also important to note that all these studies were conducted in a classroom setting, were quantitative in design, and focused on the stable and generalized motives of the learners to learn languages.

In contrast to this approach, Ushioda (2009, this volume) states that it is also important to be interested in a 'person-in-context relational view of motivation'. She invites the researcher to look at the learner as a whole person within a particular context, their current situation, as well as their past and future. It will be more in keeping with this approach that the study reported on here will examine the work learners do out-of-class in a SAC and not just in a classroom. Thus, I will look at learners from the same language background, who are learning two or more languages as the participants in what I will call a bi- or plurilingual learning project, not from the perspective of the generalized and stable motives that learners have to learn languages, but more from their own particular perspective and situation.

Self-Access Centers, Autonomy and Plurilingualism

SACs, which have been developed since the 1970s for a number of reasons – as a response to linguistic theories, social movements and improvement in technology, for example (e.g. Benson, 2001; Gremmo & Riley, 1995) – have now spread to many parts of the world. SACs offer the possibility for learners to actively engage in the learning of languages. Such centers are also usually related to the idea of autonomy (e.g. Esch, 1996; Holec, 1995), as well as to the vision of learners as users of the language and not just learners of the language (e.g. Esch, 1996; Littlewood, 1997). To those ends, they offer different kinds of services.

Regarding plurilingualism, even if SACs can be considered multilingual by virtue of the languages they offer, the link between plurilingualism and autonomy in self-access language learning has only just been formalized with regard to the role of the advisor (e.g. Castillo & Gremmo, 2003; Gremmo & Castillo, 2006). Although centers are usually multilingual and advisors can advise in and for several languages, to my knowledge there is no evidence of research on the relationship between plurilingualism and learners working in SACs. While learners may have access to a variety of resources, the research literature on SACs usually takes a monolingual posture. Therefore, it appears to be taken for granted that learners in SACs are learning just one language.

It is interesting to note that an increasing number of Mexican learners realize that it is important to learn other languages besides English, despite the fact that there are some circumstances that might hinder their awareness of this issue. For example, Mexico is a *de facto* monolingual country with Spanish as the official language (Terborg *et al.*, 2006). Also, its citizens have been encouraged to learn English, thus creating a population of Spanish/English learners. The country does not have an explicit multilingual educational policy on teaching foreign languages, and geographically, Mexico is surrounded by English- and Spanish-speaking countries (USA, Belize and Guatemala). Thus, despite these circumstances, learners are using classroom and/or SAC environments in order to learn other languages and achieve the construction of a plurilingual identity.

Regarding SACs, contrary to the usual way of establishing them, which is from the bottom-up (Holec, 1996), i.e. that an educational institution sees the importance of establishing one, in Mexico, SACs started from the top-down. Indeed, they started in 1993, when the Mexican Ministry of Education decided to put a center in each state university, leading to a total of 31 SACs. This decision was taken in response to the lack of language teachers in Mexico (especially English teachers) and to the increase in demand for language learning generated by the North American Free Trade Agreement (NAFTA), initiated in 1994. Today, there are more than 200 centers throughout the country. Although, initially, SACs were intended to offer just English (Castillo Zaragoza, 2006), now they are multilingual, offering the possibility to learn several foreign languages and, in some SACs, native languages such as Maya (Chávez Sánchez, 1999).

Regarding this situation, it is important to state two things. First, we are principally talking about learning foreign languages, which is why the role of the center is important; oftentimes, it may be the only source of contact with the language (e.g. Gardner & Miller, 1999; Little, 1997). Second, we are referring to state universities, where the student population and their socioeconomic status can vary, but where the lower- and middle-class population also has access. This allows learners to use resources they would normally not have access to because of their cost or scarcity.

The Study

Objectives

This research is exploratory and its purpose is to better know a public that has not received any attention until now: learners working with more than one language while using classrooms and/or SACs, in general, and in particular in Mexico. The current study explores who these learners are (identity), what languages they learn (identity related), why they are learning them (motivation) and how they can manage learning several languages at the same time (autonomy).

Participants and data collection

In order to answer the above-mentioned questions, 33 semi-structured interviews were carried out at SACs in two different universities (SAC1 and SAC2), obtaining a corpus of 24 hours of recording. One university is located in the north and the other in the center of Mexico. The principal purpose of the interview was to understand a learner's work in a SAC from a plurilingual perspective (e.g. Castillo Zaragoza, 2006; Cenoz *et al.*, 2001; Sciriha, 2001).

Participants had to be learning two or more languages and working in the SAC of their own volition. The centers did not have official information regarding the fact that learners were learning more than one language. Therefore, receptionists at the centers helped identify learners with those characteristics. Of the different learners who were approached during their visit to the center and were invited to take part in an interview, 33 agreed to be interviewed. I cannot say that I interviewed the totality of the population with those characteristics, as there were no records of this trait; however, I did contact all the learners identified by the receptionists at the time of my visit.

Regarding the interview population, it is essentially young. Of the 33 learners interviewed, 23 (70%) are between 18 and 25 years old, 6 (18%) between 26 and 35 years old, and 4 (12%) between 36 and 50 years old. It is important to highlight that SAC1 is open to all kinds of users, namely, students, university employees, as well as people from the community. On the other hand, SAC2 just accepts students, ex-students and employees. This explains, in part, the young interview population, as most of the interviews were done at SAC2.

Regarding the number of languages being learned, it was found that, out of 33 learners interviewed, 3 were learning 5 languages simultaneously (9%), 1 was learning 4 (3%), 6 were learning 3 (18%) and 23 were learning 2 (70%). As can be observed, most were learning two languages.

Results

Portrait of learners regarding the use of classrooms and self-access centers

Learners can vary their use of the classroom and the SAC. This is possible because learners have different interests, objectives, obligations, hopes or desires regarding the languages chosen, as will be shown later. However, because they can work in two environments, learners can use the classroom and the SAC differently. In fact, it was observed that, out of the 33 learners, 8 were using both the classroom and the SAC together to learn each one of the languages chosen. The rest varied their use, going just to the SAC to learn one or more languages while using the SAC and the classroom together for one or more of the remaining languages.

To exemplify this, I refer to the case of a learner from SAC1 who is working with four languages: French, German, Japanese and Italian (she had previously studied English). At the time of the interview, she was taking classes for two languages (German and Japanese) and working in the SAC with three (French, Japanese and Italian). Concerning the languages she is learning, she has decided not to work with German in the SAC, because, as she said, she is just studying it to have some basic notions of the language and she is not as interested in this language as she is in the others. This can be related to the study by Csizér and Dörnyei (2005), who claim that the fact of learning a language can have an attitudinal interference with other languages, and, that there can be a 'competition' among languages for limited language learning capacity. As we will see later, learners have to manage different languages, and this forces them to make decisions in their own plurilingual learning scheme. For instance, they create hierarchies among the languages being learned. Thus, for the learner in this example, the work in the SAC is more related to the languages she is most interested in.

One point needs to be emphasized. Learners give great importance to SACs and to the process of learning by themselves. Indeed, they do not just go to classes, but they also go to the center, underlining the importance they give to learning languages and their motivation to learn them.

Reasons to learn different languages

Next, I will discuss what these Mexican learners consider as the main reasons to engage in a bi- or plurilingual learning project. First, languages are seen as important for increasing knowledge, as this learner points out:

> The more languages you know, the more (...) knowledge you can develop from the world. Because (...) if you only know Spanish you'll only learn from the areas written in Spanish (...) new things that come out of what documents or from Internet pages in English and in other languages (...) if you know English, you can read them.

This learner talks about how learning a new language helps him with reading, one of the most important activities he is required to do at the university, but also how he has a vision of his future self as a foreign language reader.

Other learners can imagine themselves going to another country, on a mid-term project, to continue their academic studies. It is in anticipation of the projects they want to carry out in the future, the L2 self they want to become, that they have particular learning behaviors. For example, consider a learner who is studying for a BA in economics and learning English and French simultaneously. She attends classes and goes to the SAC for both languages:

> **R:** Is it important to be trilingual?
> **L:** Yes, one because for my field of study. I don't just want a BA, I want to pursue Doctorate studies. Then I need more than three languages. Then, if I finish with the university first, I also want to acquire the three languages that I don't have. Two and a half years to finish the BA meeting all the requirements, then study a Master's in Canada, and because over there they speak French and English, well I expect to have full command of both.

This learner has a clear vision of a future self, and she is making decisions regarding the languages she thinks she will need, and thus she is reducing the discrepancy between the current self and her possible future self (e.g. Dörnyei, 2009; Ushioda, this volume).

Continuing with the academic environment, due to globalization and study exchange programs, Mexican universities now offer new opportunities to study in universities in other countries. This enables students to have other visions of future L2 selves, as well as actual models, such as friends who have done this:

> I'm studying Industrial Engineering then a lot of my peers have gone on exchange programs to France, and I've noticed that French is required, English is a basic requirement, I've noticed that it is with a second language and French that my peers leave for France and well I also don't want to go without knowing something.

An added reason is that learning languages can help students to be different from others. Some students mentioned that they want to learn other languages besides English, because 'English is a common language being learned', and if they want to be different from the others, if they want to have a different and significant capital in the academic and labor markets, they need to invest in other languages (Norton, 2000). That is the case of this student who is learning five languages at the same time (English, French, Chinese, Italian and Portuguese). She is using the SAC for the five languages and also attending classes for the last four. In her program of study, she was acknowledged as an advanced student of French by one of her teachers and was asked to do a special task, as can be seen in the following excerpt:

> **R:** And in engineering do you use it? Is it useful?
> **L:** Yes, because in fact last semester I used French a lot because the teacher knew that I was doing French, and he told me that I should look for some laws about (...) annual operations plan, something like that (...) which is related to industry and processes. (...) And that law, when I looked, it wasn't in any other language except French. So I started to translate everything it said there (...), so now I was able to present it to the class in Spanish.

This recognition of being different from others may encourage and reinforce learners in pursuing their plurilingual identity and learning project. This is also reflected in Ushioda (this volume), for whom motivation and identity are 'co-constructed processes'. The experiences of these learners also support her claim that, 'Motivation is not located solely within the individual but is socially distributed, created within cultural systems of activities involving the mediation of others' (Ushioda, 2006: 154).

Further to the idea of how the environment can contribute to motivation and identity, learners' professional identity encourages them to learn languages. But also, their own experience has shown them that what they consider as an asset becomes a necessity, and they are therefore encouraged to learn more languages, to different degrees:

> **R:** Is it important to be polyglot?
> **L:** For my field of studies, totally and absolutely, because I've worked for Disney's Cruises and because in those places there are many visitors from other places that don't speak English and (...) I was required for everything because they knew that I also spoke to some degree several languages....That's when I realized that knowing other languages is not just to show off, I really need it....

So, after realizing that knowing several languages can be more than a utilitarian tool or of cultural value, learners become engaged in learning languages they like. Furthermore, it may be supposed that because they have had a direct and positive experience using a foreign language, they develop a more realistic goal, instead of relying on abstract situations where they imagine they might use the language.

As mentioned before, motivation and identity are co-constructed processes, and the learners interviewed are building a plurilingual identity. Languages have a strong influence on who they are and who they want to become. Learners can have different motives for learning them, but it is a fact that they are investing in them and that they do not limit themselves to the classroom, but also work out-of-class and thus exercise their autonomy.

Attitudes toward the languages

It has been observed that learners have different motives to learn languages, so it is not surprising that they have different attitudes toward the languages being learned (Humphreys & Spratt, 2008). For example, a 25-year-old learner who is in her eighth semester of Industrial Engineering is learning five languages simultaneously. She has different attitudes toward the languages she is learning, which reflect the different reasons she has for learning each one of them:

> **R:** And why those languages?
> **L:** Well, English is basic (...) and French was more because I liked the way it sounds (...) and later Italian (...) also because it caught my attention. And Chinese it was more thought out, perhaps about the future of my career because you see that China now is growing a lot,

it is helping itself to a good part of the market. So I said, well I am going to study Chinese too. And Portuguese that one was more as a hobby. I said something (. . .) that it will not be so difficult. I said Portuguese because it is similar to Spanish.

For her, romance languages are for pleasure, and the other two (English and Chinese) are for career objectives. She loves languages, and she says she grew up with English, and later started with French.

On the other hand, it has been observed that when students, from a self-perspective, have principally an instrumental image of English, with a prevention focus – i.e. regulating the presence or absence of negative outcomes (Dörnyei, 2009, 2010), which is more related to the ought-to L2 self – they are less interested in investing time and effort in learning it. However, if they see something else besides the utilitarian aspect, thus having a promotion focus – i.e. hopes, aspirations and accomplishments (Dörnyei, 2009, 2010), which is more related to the ideal L2 self – the interest in learning English grows, such as in the case of the following learner:

> **R:** And why English?
> **L:** Well, I'm interested(. . .)before you study it, like, because studying a foreign language is mandatory, and now it's because you like to study it, isn't it? And now because you like it, the route that takes you to study it is different.

Because she is no longer obliged to learn English, the learner now likes it. Her motivation has changed, as have her language-oriented activities. For instance, she attends conferences where native speakers talk. She participates in workshops to find out what other materials the center offers for listening and reading. She takes risks with her learning, e.g. using Skype to chat with strangers in the two languages she is learning (English and Portuguese). By doing this, her motivation has changed, and it seems that this has contributed to a change in the way she is working to learn the languages on her own.

Meanwhile, considering that learners are studying two or more languages, for those who just see the utilitarian part of learning English, with a prevention focus, their greater investment may be in the other languages they are learning, if these were chosen for other motives besides obligation. This notion is supported by Humphreys and Spratt (2008), who found that the compulsory language can have a more instrumental value, and the chosen language can be seen as more affective. An example of this is provided by a learner, who is studying

English and Japanese during the last semester of her program in International Relations:

> I wanted to start with Chinese, but I began to listen to it and I said, "Ay, it sounds horrible, I don't want it", even though for my career, yes, it would be really good, no? But I said no, something that I like and that interests me, so that I can truly dedicate myself to it, no? So Japanese was the option and, well, I'm much more interested in studying Japanese than English, which is like required. Japanese, yes, I'm convinced that this is the language that I like and it is the language that I will study.

Regarding differing attitudes toward languages being learned, let us look at one last example of a student who is in the last semester of Law School. She does not like English, but she loves German, which she sees as her passion:

> **R:** You told me that German started through a reading, didn't it? An opera from Wagner, and English why are you studying it?
> **L:** Oh, English, more than anything because lately I've discovered that it's very important (...) I'm studying Law and it's really necessary and (...) I feel that I don't have a good command of English (...)
> **R:** And why do you think that you see that difference?
> **L:** Between English and German?
> **R:** Yes, one is easier than the other?
> **L:** Well, I like German writing and I like the authors and the writers very much. On the other hand, I don't like the English ones. It's like having mixed feelings between liking or not liking the United States. It is a great country, however, there is a great deal of inequality and many times a lot of racism, then it's like English is a language that I don't identify very much with. With German is different, I like to read German authors, I don't know, I like the language and its culture, that's why I find German easier to learn.

This learner has a preference for German, and she prefers to continue working on her German at the SAC despite the fact that in the classroom she has better grades than in English. Regarding grades, this is related to Schmidt and Watanabe's (2001) finding that when learning a language is primarily for grades or fulfillment of requirements, learners are more likely to measure the difficulty of the task to see if they can perform it well enough. On the other hand, the fact of having a positive perception of a community and its culture (in this case German) makes this learner have a positive attitude toward the language and invest in that language. By contrast, her sense of obligation toward English, plus her negative image of the community she associates with English, results in her having a different behavior toward it and preferring to work by herself in the language she likes the most.

In summary, when students are learning different languages at the same time, they can have different attitudes and motivations regarding each language. Indeed, when learners are working with two or more languages simultaneously, they make different decisions regarding their learning, e.g. creating hierarchies among the languages learned. It was also observed that learners will not work in the same way and with the same material with each one of the languages (Castillo Zaragoza, 2006). Because of space limitations, it is not be possible to expand on this topic, but in essence, this is due to different reasons such as the importance learners give to each language, how they perceive each one of them, the reasons they are learning each one of them, the kind of materials they can find, as well as the fact that they do not have the same level of proficiency in each language, among others.

Discussion

This study is interested in learners who are working on a bi- or plurilingual learning project and have the possibility to use two contexts, classroom and/or SAC. It focused on their work done in SACs, because it is an environment where they can work by themselves; also, because they are in a setting where they are not necessarily told what to do, they must rely on their own resources, e.g. beliefs and knowledge of what a language is and how to learn it. As such, they can be more themselves: they can act in relation to who they are, and also they have the possibility to explore.

As Ushioda (2006: 155) states, there is interdependence between the 'individual and social forces that coalesce in the individual learner's motivation. This dynamic interdependence may be largely positive in a supportive social or pedagogical setting, leading to the healthy growth and co-construction of individual motivation'. As the learners in this study have come to see the importance of plurilingualism and a plurilingual identity, and as they are looking for the resources to create this identity, they recognize that SACs offer a possibility in this construction.

While their reasons for engaging in a bi- or plurilingual learning project vary, it was found that the motives given by the interviewees to learn several languages are related to their current identity, as well as the possible selves they imagine, e.g. their future selves as students or workers. It was also seen that when students are learning different languages simultaneously, they can have different attitudes/motivations regarding each language, a finding supported by the work of Csizér and Dörnyei (2005) and Humphreys and Spratt (2008). In fact, the latter study found that the compulsory language can have a more instrumental value, and the chosen language a more affective one – a finding corroborated by this study. When learners have chosen for themselves a language or languages in addition to the compulsory one, and when they work by themselves (e.g. in SACs), they can give preference to their second and other languages. Furthermore, it is with the added languages that they can express themselves, and do what they like, what interests them.

It has also been observed that when a SAC allows learners to work in the way they like and need, learners can appropriate that space (Castillo Zaragoza, 2006). Thus, if SACs afford the opportunity to learners to work more in relation to who they are, as well as to experiment, learners can adapt the center in order to meet their needs and reflect their identities. In this study, this was evident in how learners made use of SACs for their bi- or plurilingual projects. In fact, because learners go to SACs on their own, the work in the center can be more closely related to their objectives, their needs, their desires, their pace, their schedules and their projects, i.e. it can correspond to their current and possible future selves (Dörnyei, 2009).

When learners are sorted and observed for just one language as is usually the case in a classroom, only one part of their persona can be observed or explored. When working by themselves, learners have the possibility to show in general who they are (plurilingual learners); that is why by observing them working with several languages in a SAC, we can better see the complexity of the person and, in particular, the learner, in whom identity, motivation and autonomy are interlinked.

One final point needs to be emphasized. While it has been shown that learners work with different languages, it is important to say that they do not necessarily know how to work with them in an efficient manner. For example, they do not always seem to be able to transfer learning strategies that they have used with one language to the study of another language (Debaisieux & Valli, 2003), thereby extracting the maximum advantage from that knowledge. They need to know how to apply learning strategies to all languages. They also need to under-stand how to take advantage of all the resources available, external

(SACs and classroom) as well as internal (the knowledge and experience they already have). Offering workshops in SACs, which focus on learning how to learn languages in general (and not a specific language), could be of great benefit to them. This is just one example of the implications of this kind of research.

Conclusion

Mexican learners have seen the importance of plurilingualism, and in order to achieve it, they use the resources in their environment, such as classrooms and SACs. Learners use SACs in order to work in a bi- or plurilingual program, which is not explicitly encouraged by the centers. In a SAC, their identity regarding plurilingualism can be better observed, as it is there that they can work toward the realization of their desires and projects, by themselves, at their own pace and with the resources they have personally selected.

This investigation reinforces what has been found previously, namely, that what learners are, and also what they want to become (ideal L2 self), or think they have to become (ought-to L2 self), has a strong influence on the decisions they make toward their language learning. But this work also illustrates that learners may have different attitudes/motivations with each language, and the relationship that they have with each language uncovers new facets of themselves. By working in SACs, learners are able to develop themselves more fully, discovering links between who they are, who they want to become, and why and how they learn. This study reveals the intertwining of identity, motivation, autonomy and plurilingualism.

References

Benson, P. (2001) *Teaching and Researching Autonomy in Language Learning.* Harlow: Pearson Education Limited.

Benson, P. (2007) Autonomy in language teaching and learning. *Language Teaching* 40, 21–40.

Castillo, D. and Gremmo, M-J. (2003) Autodirection, plurilinguisme, interdisciplinarité: Conseiller dans un centre de ressources multilingue. *Le Français dans le Monde: Vers une Compétence Plurilingue: Recherches et Applications,* Juillet, 178–192.

Castillo Zaragoza, E.D. (2006) Centres de ressources pour l'apprentissage des langues au Mexique: Représentations et pratiques déclarées de conseillers et d'apprenants. PhD thesis, Université Nancy 2.

Cenoz, J., Hufeisen, B. and Jessner, U. (2001) Towards trilingual education. *International Journal of Bilingual Education and Bilingualism* 4 (1), 1–10.

Chávez Sánchez, M. (coord) (1999) *Directorio Descriptivo.* Mexico: UNAM.

Csizér, K. and Dörnyei, Z. (2005) Language learners' motivational profiles and their motivated learning behavior. *Language Learning* 55 (4), 613–659.

Debaisieux, J.M. and Valli, A. (2003) Lectures en langues romanes. *Le Français dans le Monde: Vers une compétence plurilingue: Recherches et Applications*, Juillet, 143–154.

Deci, E.L. and Ryan, R.M. (1985) *Intrinsic Motivation and Human Behavior*. New York: Plenum.

Dörnyei, Z. (2009) The L2 motivational self system. In Z. Dörnyei and E. Ushioda (eds) *Motivation, Language Identity and the L2 Self* (pp. 9–42). Bristol: Multilingual Matters.

Dörnyei, Z. and Clément, R. (2001) Motivational characteristics of learning different target languages: Results of a nationwide survey. In Z. Dörnyei and R. Schmidt (eds) *Motivation and Second Language Acquisition* (pp. 399–432). Honolulu, HI: University of Hawai'i. Second Language Teaching and Curriculum Centre.

Esch, E. (1996) Concepts of autonomy in language learning. In R. Pemberton, F. Li, W. Or and H. Pierson (eds) *Taking Control. Autonomy in Language Learning* (pp. 35–48). Hong Kong: Hong Kong University Press.

Gardner, R.C. (1985) *Social Psychology and Second Language Learning: The Role of Attitudes and Motivation*. London: Edward Arnold.

Gardner, D. and Miller, L. (1999) *Establishing Self-Access: From Theory to Practice*. Cambridge: Cambridge University Press.

Gremmo, M.J. and Castillo, D. (2006) Advising in a multilingual setting: New perspectives for the role of the advisor. In T. Lamb and H. Reinders (eds) *Supporting Independent Language Learning: Issues and Options* (pp. 21–35). Frankfurt am Main: Peter Lang.

Gremmo, M.J. and Riley, P. (1995) Autonomy, self-direction and self access in language-teaching and learning: The history of an idea. *System* 23 (2), 151–164.

Holec, H. (1995) Avant-propos. *Mélanges Pédagogiques* 22, 3–4.

Holec, H. (1996) De l'apprentissage autodirigé comme une innovation. *Mélanges Pédagogiques* 24, 91–110.

Humphreys, G. and Spratt, M. (2008) Many languages, many motivations: A study of Hong Kong students' motivation to learn different target languages. *System* 36 (2), 313–335.

Little, D. (1997) Responding authentically to authentic texts: A problem for self-access language learning. In P. Benson and P. Voller (eds) *Autonomy and Independence in Language Learning* (pp. 225–236). London: Longman.

Littlewood, W. (1997) Self-access: Why do we want it and what can it do? In P. Benson and P. Voller (eds) *Autonomy and Independence in Language Learning* (pp. 79–92). London: Longman.

Norton, B. (2000) Fact and fiction in language learning. In B. Norton (ed.) *Identity in Language Learning* (pp. 1–19). London: Pearson.

Riley, P. (2003) Le 'linguisme' – multi, poly, pluri? Points de repère terminologiques et sociolinguistiques. *Le Français dans le monde: Recherches et Applications*, Juillet, 8–17.

Schmidt, R. and Watanabe, Y. (2001) Motivation, strategy use, and pedagogical preferences in foreign language learning. In Z. Dörnyei and R. Schmidt (eds) *Motivation and Second Language Acquisition* (pp. 313–359). Honolulu, HI: University of Hawai'i, Second Language Teaching and Curriculum Centre.

Sciriha, L. (2001) Trilingualism in Malta: Social and educational perspectives. *International Journal of Bilingual Education and Bilingualism* 4 (1), 23–37.

Terborg, R., García Landa, L. and Moore, P. (2006) The language situation in Mexico. *Current Issues in Language Planning* 7 (4), 415–518.

Ushioda, E. (2006) Language motivation in a reconfigured Europe: Access, identity, autonomy. *Journal of Multilingual and Multicultural Development* 27 (2), 148–161.

Ushioda, E. and Dörnyei, Z. (2009) Motivation, language identities and the L2 self: A theoretical overview. In Z. Dörnyei and E. Ushioda (eds) *Motivation, Language Identity and the L2 Self* (pp. 1–8). Bristol: Multilingual Matters.

Chapter 8

'Why am I Doing This?' Maintaining Motivation in Distance Language Learning

LINDA MURPHY

Introduction

Developments in technology are encouraging the growth in distance language learning and teacher education, often as part of a 'blend' of face-to-face and technology-mediated learning, although the exact combination and amount of each may vary widely (Hall & Knox, 2009). Learners in such programmes are generally responsible for scheduling their study time and are expected to set personal goals, select their route through the material, monitor their own learning progress and maintain their motivation within the framework of a language learning pro-gramme, which may offer more or less guidance and structure. In other words, they may enjoy an increasing degree of autonomy in their study. Autonomous learners are, by definition, motivated learners, but even autonomous learners experience setbacks or changing circumstances. Self-motivation is crucial in distance learning, but, as Oxford and Lee (2008) ask, how do learners keep going when the going gets tough? This chapter explores self-motivation from the perspective of distance language learners. It begins with a brief overview of the relationship between distance language learning, autonomy, motivation and learner identity with reference to self-determination theory (SDT; Ryan & Deci, 2000) and Dörnyei's second language (L2) Motivational Self System (2005, 2009). These theoretical frameworks are then used to analyse the experience of distance language learners of French, German and Spanish at the Open University (UK). The findings provide some insight into ways in which distance language programme designers and learners may enhance self-motivation.

Theoretical Background

Distance learning is not necessarily synonymous with autonomous learning and in the past has been seen as 'learning by yourself', following the prescriptions of course writers, rather than a way of taking more control over one's language learning (Benson, online). White (2007: 100) has shown how distance learning has developed and changed 'from a concern with the production and distribution of learning materials to a concern with communication and learning as a social process supported largely by ICT', where learners are encouraged to decide the content and goals of their learning. Even where reliance on printed materials remains, programme designers are increasing the degree of learner choice and decision-making to enhance learners' capacity for autonomy (Murphy, 2008).

Despite the fact that technology has potentially removed some of the most problematic aspects of distance language learning, i.e. the physical separation of learners and teachers and the lack of opportunity to develop interactive competence in the target language, distance learners still have to schedule and pace their own learning. Many have a range of other commitments and responsibilities besides language learning, which may reduce time and energy for interaction with other learners. On the other hand, their past language learning experience may mean that they enjoy learning in the company of others and find it hard to monitor and evaluate their own progress when they cannot compare themselves with fellow learners. They can experience distance learning as both an isolated and an isolating activity. A situated view of learning highlights the significance of social identity and the learner's context in relation to motivation and self-motivation. This is particularly significant in the case of adult distance language learners, who have to find a way of reconciling a distance learning environment, their own life contexts and their personal attributes and aspirations (White, 2005).

A number of researchers have described phases in the motivational process (e.g. Dörneyi & Ottó, 1998; Williams & Burden, 1997), which Hiromori (2009) divides into pre- and post-decisional phases, the latter covering implementation and sustaining motivation. For the reasons noted above, the initial enthusiasm and motivation for learning a language through a distance education programme may be hard to sustain, depending on the unique combination of personal circumstances, experience, expectations and individual attributes. The aim of the study reported here was to explore how learners sustain motivation and overcome demotivation in distance language learning, an area that has not been investigated to any great extent to date, but is increasingly important as more and more people engage in forms of distance language learning.

Benson (2007) explains the way in which autonomy has been linked to the study of language learning motivation through Ryan and Deci's (2000) SDT. This emphasises the significance of intrinsic motivation, interest in the subject and learning process itself. Ryan and Deci identify three innate psychological needs related to intrinsically motivated processes: competence, relatedness and autonomy. They describe intrinsic motivation as being shaped by working towards what are termed 'optimal challenges', gradually extending the individual's capabilities and promoting feelings of achievement. This is supported by feedback or interaction prompting positive self-evaluation and enhanced feelings of competence. The study described below examines distance language learners' experiences in maintaining their motivation and looks for evidence of the motivational impact of competence (feelings of achievement and skill development), relatedness (positive interaction with others and feedback on performance) and autonomy (making decisions about their learning). For reasons already discussed, each of these may be problematic in a distance learning setting, depending on the nature of the programme and the circumstances or experience of individual learners.

Intrinsic motivation is an important factor in maintaining motivation to study at a distance as in other settings, but much research has also focused on the personal goal orientation of language learners, their individual reasons for studying a language and how these reasons and the context for learning may sustain study. For many years, the social-psychological approach of Gardner and his associates in Canada and the notion of 'integrativeness' dominated this research, but a number of issues have gained prominence recently, as summarised by Ushioda and Dörnyei (2009), who propose re-theorising language learning motivation in relation to 'self' and 'identity'. Dörnyei (2005, 2009) sets out a model of motivation, termed the L2 Motivational Self System, rooted in earlier psychological theories of self, which comprises three components: (1) ideal L2 self (the L2 specific version of one's ideal self – what we would like to become as a speaker of the target language); (2) ought-to L2 self (the attributes one believes one ought to possess in order to meet expectations and avoid possible negative outcomes); and (3) L2 learning experience (concerns motivation related to the immediate learning experience, e.g. impact of teacher, peer group and success) (Dörnyei, 2009: 29). He emphasises the significance of the imagery involved in picturing the ideal L2 self. 'Language learning is a sustained and often tedious business, and I felt that the secret of successful learners was their possession of a superordinate vision that kept them on track' (Dörnyei, 2009: 25). In the same volume, Ushioda (2009: 220) argues for 'a more contextually embedded, relational view of motivation and identity'. She emphasises the need to focus on people rather than on learners and to remember that 'language learner' is just one aspect of a person's identity (Ushioda, 2009: 216). She makes a powerful case for encouraging students to express their own identities through the target language by having more choice and control over their input (Ushioda, 2009: 223) in a more autonomous learning environment: arguments that she develops further in this volume.

The study of distance language learners reported here did not initially set out to explore the relevance of the L2 Motivational Self System or the notion of learner identities, but aimed to identify the self-motivational strategies that learners deployed and the importance of intrinsic motivation. However, the experiences of the distance learners themselves and the language in which they described them indicated the relevance of these concepts. Thus, the study now links distance language learning, autonomy, motivation and learner identity through reference to SDT and Dörnyei's L2 Motivational Self System.

The Research Study

Context

The study was carried out with a sample of part-time, adult distance language learners of French, German and Spanish, studying with The Open University (UK) during 2005–2006. The learners were studying at beginner level on 30 credit point courses requiring an average of six hours study per week. No previous knowledge of the language was expected. The university had only recently begun offering language courses at beginner level and courses had been extended over a full year to reduce the amount of study time per week and the pace of study in line with the results of market research. There were concerns about how students maintained their motivation over a part-time course of this length and the relatively high level of drop-out experienced in beginner language courses in all settings.

Students were provided with print and audio materials and their study was supported by a personal tutor, who also facilitated regular, optional tutorials that were held either face-to-face at a local venue or online via a synchronous audio conferencing system, depending on the version of the course that students registered for. Asynchronous and synchronous conferencing systems could be used by students to communicate with each other at any time. Students' performance was accredited via the completion of six tutor-marked assignments, which included speaking, reading, writing and listening tasks and an end of course assessment (ECA) of writing and speaking skills.

Aims of the study

In light of the concerns about learner motivation over a lengthy distance language course and the theoretical issues outlined above, the study aimed to investigate the experiences of individual learners in order to understand how motivation is maintained and how it might be supported. The specific research questions were as follows:

(1) What do adult beginner distance language learners report as negative influences on their motivation?
(2) What helps students to maintain motivation? What role does intrinsic motivation, including feelings of competence, relatedness and autonomy play?
(3) Do learner experiences reflect elements of the L2 Motivational Self System and the importance of learner identities?
(4) How might the findings be used to enhance distance language programme design and support for learners?

Method of investigation

The study can be described as exploratory-interpretative (Grotjahn, 1987) in that it was non-experimental, produced qualitative data and used interpretative analysis. Data collection was through verbal reports from learners (Cohen, 1987). Cohen (1987: 32) identifies three types of verbal report data that give researchers access to learners' conscious strategies and thought processes: self-report, self-observation and self-revelation. The key distinction is whether the reports are retrospective or concurrent with the activity. In this study, retrospective reports were felt to be more appropriate and feasible. Possible methods for gathering retrospective verbal reports include learner diaries, logs or journals, questionnaires and interviews (McDonough, 1995).

As this research involved a dispersed group of part-time students and the aim was to explore motivation maintenance over the period of a course, it was decided to gather data via a monthly learner log. The log comprised a set of questions with space for open responses. Students were asked to identify the highs and lows of study that month, how they overcame difficulties, what kept them going and support they received from other people.[1] This 'questionnaire' style of log was designed to be easy to use with minimal briefing and aimed to keep additional work to a minimum. Logs were sent to the student sample from February to September with a reply-paid address label. Courses start in November, but a February starting point was chosen to allow students time to settle into their course. A postal return, rather than an electronic log, was chosen to avoid technical problems. Students were assured that replies would be anonymised and that individuals would not be identifiable in any reports. They were free to withdraw from the project at any time.

Instructions and questions were piloted with a small sample in 2004. In 2005 and 2006, log sheets were sent to a random sample of 191 beginner language students of French, German and Spanish (91 in 2005 and 100 in 2006), who had responded to a large-scale survey on their language learning experience and expectations and had indicated willingness to participate in keeping a log. The sample included students from both versions of courses, i.e. the version with face-to-face tuition and the version with tuition via online synchronous conferencing. It had been anticipated that the self-motivation strategies that students used might depend on the version of tuition they chose, but the pilot study in 2004 did not bear this out and also indicated that motivational differences were not related to the language studied. Therefore, these two variables were not considered further.

Of the 191 students who agreed to keep a log, 53 participated during 2005 and 48 during 2006. Their ages ranged from 22 to 75. Just over half of the participants were female with almost two-thirds in the 40–60 age range, a common profile for Open University (UK) language courses (Coleman & Furnborough, 2010). Responses were collated and comments were typed up month by month. Each student was referred to by a number and year. For example, responses from student number 5 in 2006 are referred to as 5/06. As might be anticipated in a longer-term voluntary activity, the number of participants dwindled after the first month, but 17 continued to complete logs regularly in 2005 and 15 in 2006. Qualitative analysis of comments was carried out using NVivo 8 (2008). Negative influences on motivation were extracted and grouped into broader categories by constant comparison. The responses to setbacks and difficulties were examined for evidence of self-motivation and intrinsic motivation, including feelings of autonomy, competence and relatedness. They were then re-examined in relation to learner identities and the L2 Motivational Self System.

Findings and Discussion

The findings from the investigation are presented and discussed in relation to each of the four research questions.

Negative influences on motivation

Table 8.1 summarises the external and internal factors that students reported as negatively affecting their motivation.

In studies involving full-time higher education students (e.g. Ushioda, 2001) the factors that students perceive as negatively influencing their motivation tend to be almost entirely related to the institutional language learning experience. Table 8.1 shows similar experiences

Table 8.1 Negative influences on motivation

Institutional	*Other*
External factors negatively affecting motivation	
Unhappiness with aspect of course content	Lack of time/other commitments causing worry re falling behind
Unhappiness with tutor/tutorials	Bereavement/illness
Isolation (studying through distance institution)	
Workload	
Technical problems	
Difficulties with understanding audio material	
Other difficulties with course, particularly grammar	
Internal factors negatively affecting motivation	
Concerns about speaking and being understood	Concerns re memory
Low scores/lack of progress	Loss of motivation
Difficulties with understanding audio material	Other difficulties with course, particularly grammar

related to the institutional context negatively affecting motivation among these part-time distance learners. Lack of contact with other students was seen as a particular drawback, despite the opportunities for online conferencing. Individuals might not be able to make the tutorial date and time due to other commitments, or be unable to get to the venue for face-to-face tutorials. The following comments illustrate these concerns:

> Tutorials difficult to get to because of distance from home town (22/05).
> The lack of contact with other students is a problem (12/05).

Negative factors were also related to the course materials. For example, as in the following log entry, some students were demotivated by the speed of the audio material and their inability to understand without reading a transcript:

> I have to listen over and over again to the audio, often stopping the CD after each sentence (29/06).

Others were not always sure what to do, reflecting findings by White (1999), who identified ambiguity as a particular problem for some distance learners. They reflected their concern or frustration in their log in comments such as:

> Sometimes I need to look at the answer to see what is required. A bit ambiguous (8/05).

For some students, lack of interest in the topics used as vehicles for language instruction reduced motivation. This student of German sums up the impact on study when learner interest is not engaged:

> I found Thema 7 quite boring and as a result struggled to complete it (30/06).

Others were demotivated because they found the pace of instruction moved too fast for them and they would have liked more practice. The following comment was echoed by other participants:

> The text gets harder very quickly and there is very little re-inforcement of each section as it is completed (33/05).

However, as might be expected, there were other external influences stemming from the part-time students' social context, the personal and professional roles that they fulfil and demands on their time that compete with their studies. The following comments illustrate some of these roles and demands:

My mother needs a lot of time at her age (30/05).
Death of father – last few months caring duties increased (37/06).
The hardest part of "Portales" is now we are in the holiday zone of August, long holidays, and family obligations etc (35/06).

At the same time, students identified influences that could be said to stem from internal attributions. In some cases, individuals linked their difficulties around grammar or audio material with what they perceived as personal deficiencies or circumstances, e.g.:

I found it difficult to understand the grammar, particularly verb conjugation. It is over 50 years since I had anything to do with English grammar!! (26/05).

Lack of confidence in their ability to speak the language in front of others and be understood was seriously demotivating for some. Others expressed concerns about memory, as illustrated in these log entries:

Starting to get shellshock! I can't remember things I did on the course even 1 unit back even when I look at the book! (9/05).
Difficulty in recalling words and phrases to use spontaneously (25/06).

On occasions, this was bound up with perceived lack of consolidation in the course materials, i.e. more related to the institutional learning experience. Similarly, difficulties with grammar were sometimes attributed to personal shortcomings, whereas other students attributed them to poor explanations and lack of practice activities.

Lack of confidence in speaking skills and memory was sometimes combined with the impact of low assignment scores and a perceived lack of progress, which combined to seriously undermine motivation, as shown in comments such as:

I feel I am not progressing well. Retaining vocabulary and grammatical structure is hard (29/05).
Because I don't understand some of the basic fundamental aspects I am struggling to keep going (28/06).
Most of the class are faster learners than me and it daunts me. I feel as if I'm miles behind them (8/06).

Some students simply talked about having lost motivation or enthusiasm. This was evident in comments from the later months in the course, particularly during the summer. Some typical comments at this point in the course included:

> I found it a struggle to maintain my study schedule after returning from my holiday (30/06).
> End of course boredom – anxious to move on (37/06).

Thus, there was a range of external and internal factors that negatively affected students' motivation. Factors related to the language learning experience illustrate how students feel when they find the challenges of a course less than 'optimal' and do not experience a sense of progress or the kind of positive self-evaluation that enhances their intrinsic motivation, as argued by Ryan and Deci (2000). These feelings of competence and the other components of intrinsic motivation are the focus of the next section, which explores what helps in maintaining motivation.

Sources of support for positive motivation

As well as indicating the impact of perceived lack of progress on motivation, students provided plenty of support for the view that intrinsic motivation is enhanced through engagement in tasks that provide the 'right' degree of challenge and result in increasing feelings of competence. These might be course tasks or activities related to personal goals and interests. A sense of progress and achievement was frequently reported as boosting motivation and keeping students going. The following log entries illustrate this clearly:

> I have had a real sense of satisfaction studying German. I have made more progress than I anticipated I would and can read a German magazine now with a great deal of understanding (16/06).
> I am inspired when I recognise that my comprehension is getting better (16/05).
> Feel pleased to have actually written and spoken at a little more length in French – even if that is only 80 words and 1 minute (27/05).

These achievements fed into students' enjoyment of the language and language learning, as expressed by one participant:

> I'm interested in the subject. I just love every aspect of learning (35/05).

Rather than relying on assignment scores to indicate progress, students were looking for ways of measuring how far they had come in relation to their personal goals and interests. But there were also explicit comments about the impact of positive assignment scores on motivation, e.g.:

Very pleasing [....] score boosted my confidence and continued enthusiasm (30/06).

The significance of relatedness, positive interaction with others and feedback on performance, which also prompted positive self-evaluation and enhanced learners' feelings of competence and skill development, was clear from a variety of log entries. This interaction took place with the tutor and fellow students or with other speakers of the target language. Logs indicated how students looked for opportunities to speak their target language as much for the motivational benefits as for language practice. As well as the confidence and motivation gained from sustaining successful communication with native speakers of the language, partici-pants recorded similar gains from speaking the target language with fellow students. The following comments exemplify their experience:

Having a short conversation on the phone with a Spanish speaker and being understood and able to keep the conversation going (12/05).
I managed to speak to a German visitor at work and she remarked how well I spoke. That boosts confidence (31/06).
Sometimes I talk to German and Austrian people via the internet. They give me confidence in speaking the language in real time (30/06).
Confidence in talking French to other students (28/5).

Just as isolation was noted as a factor negatively affecting motivation, logs provided evidence of the motivational gains from interaction with others, not necessarily in the target language or directly concerned with it. This came about through talking to fellow students in tutorials, in self-help groups or via online conferences. Writing about their interaction in these settings, participants commented on what they felt they gained:

Maintains my motivation and we learn a lot of words (32/06).
Talking through problems – sharing ideas (8/06).
The contact with other students is helpful. Hearing about other students' experiences with the course is useful (12/05).
Camaraderie (46/06).

For some, attending tutorials helped them feel that they were part of a wider community of learners as reflected in this log entry about what was gained from this experience:

Sense of being part of a group (45/05).

Talking to friends, family or colleagues was similarly important to some students. The role that 'significant others' can play in sustaining motivation is summed up in this log entry:

Provided support when I felt disheartened (33/05).

These examples and the earlier comments about the negative effect of lack of contact illustrate the importance of relatedness for motivation. It is surprising, therefore, that although students reported interaction with a range of people, including the tutor, fellow students, family, work colleagues, friends and others, overall the volume of contact was limited. At most, 50% of respondents attended a tutorial each month, and on average around 10% contacted their tutor. Very few reported contact with other students via online conferences. On average, 23% of respondents mentioned contact with other speakers of the language each month. It seems that more effort may be needed to involve students in contact with others to enable them to experience the motivational benefits.

All distance students receive feedback from their tutor on their performance in assignments. It is essential that this feedback leads learners to reflect on and evaluate their own achievements and recognise their responsibility for them, so that they can take pride in their progress and see how they might take it further. Such feedback fosters learners' beliefs in their own potential and capacity for language learning (Ushioda, 1996: 57), which in turn feeds into their capacity to take more responsibility for their learning and deal with factors negatively affecting their motivation.

Examples of students seeking opportunities outside the course to use the language provide some evidence of control and decision making. They were also free to schedule their study time and pace their studies, although they were provided with a recommended calendar. They could exercise a degree of choice over the activities and course content and were encouraged to reflect on their progress and focus on the activities that were most relevant to their personal goals and needs (Murphy, 2008). Logs provided many examples of the ways in which students used the materials to overcome specific language difficulties or adjusted their study schedules to cope with other commitments. For example, students reported finding additional practice materials; repeated listening with and without transcripts; oral repetition, recording themselves and comparing with other models; reviewing previous work and comparing with present performance; using other reference materials such as grammars and dictionaries; using the internet and radio. They coped with lack of study time or disruptions by prioritising; adapting their study plan; reviewing study methods and creating more opportunities for study as reflected in the following responses:

Selected key course elements to focus on (34/05).
Rearranging other commitments to keep up (19/06).

Nevertheless, many comments about the volume of course work and lack of time for study due to other commitments also indicated that intrinsic motivation was seriously diminished by a feeling of being 'out of control', well illustrated here:

Feel like I'm studying in a rush and not remembering everything I should (18/05).
I'm studying at 11 at night and am shattered at work most of the time (8/06).

These findings confirm the importance of experiencing feelings of competence and a sense of relatedness for the maintenance of motivation, as argued by Ryan and Deci (2000). Similarly, they highlight the way that many students took their own decisions about what to study and how to develop their skills, and demonstrate the importance of a sense of autonomy. Although students recognised that a degree of pressure might be necessary to keep them going, the sense of being 'swept along' because of time pressures and volume of course work was clearly detrimental to motivation.

The L2 Motivational Self System and learner identity

Of the three elements of the L2 Motivational Self System, the influence on motivation and the maintenance of motivation of the L2 learning experience are apparent in the discussion above. However, in a distance learning context, this L2 learning experience also necessarily includes the other aspects of the learner's life context, which may have a very significant impact on motivation. Relatively few log entries appeared related to the ought-to L2 self. Possible negative outcomes did not seem to spur learners on and help to maintain motivation as they had done in Ushioda's (2001) study of full-time learners. Perhaps this is due to the greater commitment needed and risks inherent in full-time study, or to the fact that, for many part-time learners, language study is but one challenge among many and their personal/professional status often does not depend on the outcomes. However, there were some occasional references to possible negative outcomes as a spur to maintaining study effort. For example:

> Determination not to waste my OU fee (35/06).
> I didn't want to fail! (42/05).

There were far more references to persistence being part of their make up as learners/distance learners, which seemed to reflect an ideal learner self: one who does not give up but completes what they have set out to do, not just in language learning. A selection of log entries illustrate this point:

> I sometimes wonder "why am I doing this" – but I am determined to keep going (28/06).
> I won't give up the course. I will finish it!! (33/06).
> I don't quit! (37/06).
> Not being "put off" (29/05).
> Sheer bloody mindedness! (26/05).

This 'persevering learner' identity was obviously important in enabling some students to maintain their motivation through serious difficulties.

Dörnyei emphasises the motivational power of the vision of the ideal L2 self. The desire to reduce the gap between actual and ideal selves pulls the learner towards their ultimate goal. Logs provided many expressions of visions of the ideal L2 self, often as someone who could live and communicate successfully in a country where the language is spoken. For example:

> I spend a lot of time in France, and I want to be able to communicate effectively with people (20/05).
> Just my own desire to be able to communicate in Spanish (21/06).
> My reason for doing French – to live there and run a B and B in France by 2008 (9/05).
> When my German is adequate, I would like to study in Germany for an academic year (13/06).
> My sister-in-law lives in France and I'm determined to be able to follow at least some of the conversations with neighbours etc when I stay with them (12/05).
> I wish to be able to speak fluent German as my mother is German and I have a lot of family still in Germany (26/06).

For some, the ideal self was more a matter of academic success as shown in reasons for keeping going, such as:

Wanting to get a distinction at the end of the course (15/05).
Wanting to achieve a degree in modern languages (51/05).

As noted by Ushioda (2009), individuals are not just 'language learners', but have multiple identities. Respondents often referred to other roles and identities, such as mother, child of aged parents, worker, perseverer, conscientious learner or member of a specific interest group. Comments showed how these other roles or identities could conflict with study, or had to take priority, but also how they might help motivation, as in the following log entry:

> I belong to a local needlework group [in France]. Wanting to understand the techniques is a motivating influence (29/05).

The experiences reported by students in this study certainly reflected the way that having a vision of their ideal L2 self sustained motivation. However, they also were in accord with Ushioda's view (2009; this volume), indicating the way in which this ideal self may coexist or come into conflict with other ideal selves in the learner's identity framed by life contexts, in which language learning is but one element.

Future distance language programme design and learner support

A number of issues have been highlighted by this study, which could be addressed in programme design or which need further research. The concerns about workload, isolation and lack of choice are institutional demotivators that can be addressed. The need for and benefits from interaction signal that this as an area that needs to be developed, both to enhance feelings of relatedness and reduce isolation, as well as to increase opportunities for positive feedback and a sense of growing competence. Open University students are encouraged to attend tutorials, to join self-help groups and to look out for opportunities to use their developing language skills. However, many respondents indicated that they were under extreme time pressure from other commitments. Therefore, ways are needed to integrate interaction into the course content and assessment rather than allowing it to be an 'optional extra' over and above course work. Perhaps also, more explanation should be given and more emphasis placed on the self-motivational aspects rather than the linguistic benefits to be gained from interaction, and these could also be emphasised through more explicit teaching on self-evaluation.

The motivational impact of successful interaction reinforces the need for meaningful, communicative interaction in tutorials, whether online or face-to-face, through activities that provide 'optimal challenges' as far as possible: differentiated tasks that enable students to gain confidence in using the language they have been studying while giving them opportunities for choice and control over what they are doing. In view of the range of possible negative influences on motivation experienced by distance learners, course materials could acknowledge more explicitly the probability that motivation may dip, and create opportunities for learners to share the strategies they have and talk though how to handle difficulties, e.g. via an online forum. Opportunities to talk about issues affecting motivation, and strategies and techniques to overcome them could also be included in tutorials.

As noted above, feedback on assignments needs to foster self-evaluation and reflection on achievement or progress made so that learners believe in their capacity to learn and see how to build on that achievement. Courses need to include more explicit support for the development of self-evaluation, which may lead learners to 'notice' progress towards key learning points or personal goals. Tutor development should support dialogue between learners and tutors, which avoids a judgemental approach. Further research is needed to establish the development needs of tutors in this respect.

Finally, the variety of identities expressed by students emphasises the need for programme designers to be more aware of the range of interests and calls on learners' time. This suggests that efforts to increase choice and flexibility in study patterns should be re-doubled.

Conclusion

The data examined in this study give a clear picture of negative motivational factors influencing part-time distance language learners studying at beginner level. The study also illustrates the importance of feelings of competence or engagement in optimal challenges, feedback gained through interaction and a sense of 'control'. It provides some evidence of the power of the ideal L2 self in maintaining motivation, but also of the significance of other competing or complementary learner identities. Although further research with learners at higher levels is needed to see if their experience is different from those at beginner level, the findings from this study highlight the interrelationship between identity, motivation and autonomy. The participants' vision of themselves was a significant factor in sustaining motivation, whether or not this vision had a language learning focus. At the same time, the individual's multiple identities, the circumstances of the study environment and learning experience influenced the extent to which learners felt able to control their learning. Those who exercised their capacity for autonomy, making conscious decisions and choices about their learning, enhanced their motivation to achieve goals in keeping with their vision rather than feeling overwhelmed and frustrated.

From the point of view of course designers and teachers, findings from the study point to the need to monitor learner workload more closely and enhance learners' control of the study process by increasing opportunities for choice and decision-making. This is vital if learners are to be able to engage their multiple identities, roles and interests to the benefit of their language learning. Feedback practices need to be reviewed to ensure that they foster self-evaluation and recognition of achievement and to identify staff development needs. The findings also suggest a need to integrate interaction with other speakers of the language into the courses and probably into assessment as well, since this is most likely to influence learner attitudes and encourage them to allocate time for this purpose. Course materials and tutors could also raise awareness and facilitate exchanges related to factors affecting motivation and self-motivational strategies, including visualisation of the ideal L2 self. The implementation of such measures would hopefully lead to a reduction in the occasions when learners wonder 'why am I doing this?'

Note

1. A copy of the questionnaire is available from the author on request.

References

Benson, P. *What is autonomy?* On WWW at http://ec.hku.hk/autonomy/what.html.
Benson, P. (2007) Autonomy in language teaching and learning: State-of-the-art article. *Language Teaching* 40, 21–40.
Cohen, A.D. (1987) Using verbal reports in research on language learning. In C. Faerch and G. Kaspar (eds) *Introspection in Second Language Research* (pp. 82–95). Clevedon: Multilingual Matters.
Coleman, J.A. and Furnborough, C. (2010) Learner characteristics and learning outcomes on a distance Spanish course for beginners. *System* 38, 14–29.
Dörnyei, Z. (2005) *The Psychology of the Language Learner: Individual Differences in Second Language Acquisition*. Mahwah, NJ: Lawrence Erlbaum Associates.
Dörnyei, Z. (2009) The L2 Motivational Self System. In Z. Dörnyei and E. Ushioda (eds) *Motivation, Language Identity and the L2 Self* (pp. 9–42). Bristol: Multilingual Matters.
Dörnyei, Z. and Ottó, I. (1998) Motivation in action: A process model of L2 motivation. *Working Papers in Applied Linguistics 4* (pp. 43–69). London: Thames Valley University.

Grotjahn, R. (1987) On the methodological basis of introspective methods. In C. Faerch and G. Kaspar (eds) *Introspection in Second Language Research* (pp. 54–81). Clevedon: Multilingual Matters.

Hall, D. and Knox, J. (2009) Issues in the education of TESOL teachers by distance education. *Distance Education* 30 (1), 63–85.

Hiromori, T. (2009) A process model of L2 learners' motivation: From the perspectives of general tendency and individual differences. *System* 37, 313–321.

McDonough, S. (1995) *Strategy and Skill in Learning a Foreign Language*. London: Arnold.

Murphy, L. (2008) Supporting learner autonomy: Developing practice through the production of courses for distance learners of French, German and Spanish. *Language Teaching Research* 12 (1), 83–102.

Oxford, R.L. and Lee, K.R. (2008) The learners' landscape and journey: A summary. In C. Griffiths (ed.) *Lessons from Good Language Learners* (pp. 306–317). Cambridge: Cambridge University Press.

QSR International Pty Ltd (2008) NVivo8, qualitative research software.

Ryan, R.M. and Deci, E.L. (2000) Intrinsic and extrinsic motivations: Classic definitions and new directions. *Contemporary Educational Psychology* 25 (1), 54–67.

Ushioda E. (1996) *The Role of Motivation. Learner Autonomy 5*. Dublin: Authentik.

Ushioda, E. (2001) Language learning at university: Exploring the role of motivational thinking. In Z. Dörnyei and R. Schmidt (eds) *Motivation and Second Language Acquisition* (pp. 93–125). Honolulu, HI: University of Hawai'i, Second Language Teaching and Curriculum Centre.

Ushioda, E. (2009) A person-in-context relational view of emergent motivation, self and identity. In Z. Dörnyei and E. Ushioda (eds) *Motivation, Language Identity and the L2 Self* (pp. 215–228). Bristol: Multilingual Matters.

Ushioda, E. and Dörnyei, Z. (2009) Motivation, language identities and the L2 self: A theoretical overview. In Z. Dörnyei and E. Ushioda (eds) *Motivation, Language Identity and the L2 Self* (pp. 1–8). Bristol: Multilingual Matters.

White, C.J. (1999) Expectations and emergent beliefs of self-instructed language learners. *System* 27 (4), 443–457.

White, C. (2005) Contribution of distance education to the development of individual learners. *Distance Education* 26 (2), 165–181.

White, C. (2007) Innovation and identity in distance language learning and teaching. *Innovation in Language Learning and Teaching* 1 (1), 97–110.

Williams, M. and Burden, R. (1997) *Psychology for Language Teachers*. Cambridge: Cambridge University Press.

Chapter 9

Beliefs, Identity and Motivation in Implementing Autonomy: The Teacher's Perspective

HAYO REINDERS and NOEMÍ LÁZARO

Introduction

Recent discussions of identity and motivation in language acquisition have increased our understanding of the highly personal, variable and contextually influenced learning processes our learners engage in (e.g. Breen, 2001; Ushioda, this volume; van Lier, 2007). But what about the teacher? What factors affect teacher motivation and identity? This study was motivated by an interest in understanding teachers' roles as agents in the learning process and, in particular, their roles as facilitators of autonomous learning in self-access centres (SACs).

This chapter reports on a large-scale investigation that took place over three years in which extensive interviews were held with teachers of 46 SACs in five countries. The purpose of this chapter is to (1) elicit teachers' beliefs about learner autonomy in self-access, (2) identify conflicts between teachers' beliefs about autonomy and students' (self-access) language learning behaviour, and (3) identify conflicts between teachers' beliefs and institutional constraints. The study is based on an ethnographic approach to develop an understanding of the participants' personal theories (Borg, 2003) of supporting autonomous language learning. It does this through a combination of open-ended interview questions and a SWOT analysis (strengths, weaknesses, opportunities and threats) (Thompson & Strickland III, 2001) of the language support offered in the centres. A categorical content analysis (L'Ecuyer, 1990) reveals a complex and sometimes conflicting interaction between the teachers' beliefs and their everyday roles, which suggests that the concept of agency cannot be separated from those of motivation and identity.

Understanding the Teacher's Role

With the so-called 'social turn' in education (Lea & Nicoll, 2002), there is currently a growing interest in understanding the role of the teacher in the wider sociocultural-educational context and, similarly, an interest in understanding the teacher as an active individual within that context, responsible for his/her own development. This requires an understanding of the teacher as a person; 'The aim of teacher education must be to understand experience' (Freeman, 2002: 11). Freeman (2002c: 1) provides a comprehensive review of both the conceptual and research literature on teacher knowledge and learning to teach. In his paper, he focuses on 'the hidden side of teaching', where the 'hidden side' refers to teachers' mental lives. Teachers' beliefs and their sense of identity are examples of these 'hidden' characteristics and have been shown to strongly affect teaching practice (Richards & Lochkart, 1991).

How teachers' beliefs emerge and CHANGE over time, and how teachers' sense of 'self' and identity develop, has been the focus of an increasing amount of research over the years. Borg (2003) proposed an influential model of 'teacher cognition', which encompasses all of a teacher's beliefs, knowledge, assumptions, perspectives, etc., that determine teaching practice, and that are, in turn, affected by the practice of teaching. For example, experiences gained in the classroom shape a teacher's views on pedagogy, as does taking a professional course or communicating with other teachers.

With Borg's model as the theoretical framework for this chapter, we are particularly interested in teacher cognition in relation to one particular type of teaching, namely, the 'facilitating' that occurs in a SAC. Teachers (also often referred to as 'facilitators') working in a SAC find themselves needing to use a different or additional set of skills than those they draw on in a classroom. There are a number of obvious differences between a self-access and a classroom environment that affect the day-to-day role of the teacher. Many tasks that in the classroom are commonly considered to belong to the teacher, in a SAC are carried out by the learner, with or without the help of a teacher. Examples include identifying learning needs, setting goals, selecting materials and monitoring progress. Facilitators thus provide individualised help at times when learners need it, which involves a great deal of flexibility. The range of learners' levels, interests and needs are what usually surprises new facilitators (Moore & Reinders, 2003). Another challenge for facilitators is the difficulty of focusing on *skills* as opposed to content;

in classes generally a certain amount of material needs to be covered (e.g. a course book or a number of topics), whereas in self-access, facilitating involves preparing learners and supporting learners in their self-directed learning. As a facilitator, it is impossible in most cases to know if a student will return or not, therefore the focus is always on helping learners discover ways of improving their language by themselves.

These differences between the language classroom and the SAC mean that for teachers, working in self-access can be challenging. Looking at Borg's model (see above), the prior language experience that teachers have is usually limited to classroom learning; most teachers have had little, if any, prior experience of developing autonomy as a learner, and most teacher education courses do not cover the topic in detail (Reinders & Balcikanli, 2010). From our personal experience, for many people, working in this type of environment is a conscious decision, based on convictions about optimal ways of learning and teaching, and a process that requires a great deal of self-discovery. However, little formal research has so far been done to investigate exactly what motivates facilitators and what challenges exist for them in implementing self-access in practice. In other words, there is little information about the 'hidden side' of facilitation as a professional practice, and the relationship between teachers' cognition on their teaching practice, and vice versa, the effect of teaching practice on teachers' cognition. The main purpose of this study was thus to fill this gap in the literature and, in particular, to explore the relationship between teachers' identities in terms of their beliefs and perceptions of self; their motivation to promote learner autonomy; and their practice of fostering it in the context of a SAC.

Teacher Beliefs about Autonomy and Self-Access

Teachers' beliefs about autonomy

In order to explore teacher cognition, it is important to start from the individual. Kumaravadivelu (2001: 541) talks about teachers as 'autonomous individuals' who 'construct their own context-sensitive pedagogic knowledge'. Similarly, Borg (2003: 81) has described teachers as, 'active, thinking decision-makers who make instructional choices by drawing on complex, practically-oriented, personalised, and context-sensitive networks of knowledge, thoughts, and beliefs'. To better understand the roles of teachers in the self-access environment it is thus paramount to investigate their knowledge, thoughts and beliefs. In practice, this has not often been done. According to Vieira (2007), teachers are sometimes simply seen as tools to reach certain educational goals, rather than as an integral and active part of the educational process.

> If we see teachers as expert technicians, the notion of professional autonomy makes little sense, since expert technicians are not supposed to move beyond or subvert normative expectations. This view of teachers is not compatible with the idea of pedagogy for autonomy, unless we envisage pedagogy for autonomy as a specific kind of regime to be followed uncritically. The resistance of many teachers to educational and political discourses of autonomy is often a sign of rebellion against this instrumental view of their role as technicians who should conform to top-down policies and reforms, more than a sign of rejection of the idea of autonomy itself. (Vieira, 2007: 23)

Aoki (2008) too, emphasises the personal nature of implementing autonomy and argues that teacher education is about seeing teachers as individuals who develop their educational identities, as they attempt to develop their learners' identities as autonomous learners:

> If identity is the central concern of teachers, learning to support learner autonomy may not be about acquiring knowledge or even generating knowledge as assumed by advocates of reflective practice but about transforming identity. In other words, teacher educators should ask themselves "who do I want teachers to become?" rather than "what do I want teachers to know and to be capable of?" (Aoki, 2008: 15)

Perhaps surprisingly, considering the attention that learner autonomy has received over the years, not very much is known about the relationship between teachers' identity and beliefs about learning and teaching on the one hand, and how this affects their practice of fostering autonomy on the other. To understand teaching practice in a particular context, it is important to investigate teachers' beliefs about that context and we therefore now look at the case of self-access.

Teachers' beliefs about self-access

A number of previous studies have investigated teachers' beliefs about learner autonomy and their own roles in its development. One of these (Reinders *et al.*, 2011) is a diary study charting the experiences of two novice language advisors working in a university SAC. It was clear from the advisors' comments that the facilitation process requires good support and, ideally, good preparation and training. Other studies have come to similar conclusions. For example, de los Angeles Clemente (2001) found that in one university in Oaxaca, Mexico, teachers who were asked to work in the SAC without proper preparation and training, developed a dislike of the work, and a disbelief in the potential of independent learning. In addition, they felt anxious about their new roles. Clearly, the process of moving from classroom teaching to facilitating learning in SACs can be a daunting one.

Although studies such as the above help us to understand more about how teachers think about autonomous learning and their roles in supporting this process, much less is known about how the implementation of autonomy works in practice, especially at an institutional level. It is unclear, for example, to what extent teachers' beliefs about autonomy are matched by their students' beliefs, and to what extent teachers are supported within their teaching and institutional context in implementing a pedagogy for autonomy. Understanding how 'autonomy in practice' works and what impediments may exist, will help better prepare teachers for their roles as facilitators of autonomy and deal with the constraints that exist. Their ability to deal with these constraints, or indeed their willingness to do so, of course depends on their own beliefs about what learning and teaching should be like. It is clear that cognition and practice are closely, and mutually, related.

The Study

The data for this chapter come from a large-scale study conducted between 2003 and 2007 in which 46 SACs were visited in five countries and in-depth interviews were held with staff. The purposes of that study were to chart current thinking about theory and practice in self-access and to identify issues in its implementation in different countries. As part of the interviews, a SWOT analysis was carried out (see below). The interviews also included questions about teachers' beliefs about autonomy and self-access and their motivations for working in this type of environment; it is this subset of the data that we are exploring here. Below, we will describe the research questions, participants, procedures, instruments and the types of analyses conducted using this dataset.

Research questions

The research questions this study aimed to answer were:

(1) What are teachers' beliefs about autonomy in self-access?
(2) What conflicts exist between teachers' beliefs about autonomy and students' (self-access) language learning behaviour?
(3) What conflicts exist between teachers' beliefs and institutional constraints?

Through these questions, we aim to investigate how teacher identity and motivation develop and change in the context of developing autonomy in self-access.

Participants

Participants in this study were teachers in 46 centres in five countries, 35 were part of a tertiary institution and 11 were part of a language school. All were visited in person by one of the authors (see Table 9.1).

Instruments

The semi-structured interviews consisted of 35 questions (most of them open ended), divided into nine thematic blocks, adapted from Gardner and Miller (1999). Together they cover the main pedagogical and practical issues related to self-access as identified by Gardner and Miller and in the wider self-access literature. The nine themes included: learners' and teachers' attitudes towards autonomous learning in the

Table 9.1 Participants in the study

	Total no. centres	*Tertiary education centres*	*Languages schools*
Germany	10	10	
Hong Kong	6	6	
New Zealand	13	8	5
Spain	15	9	6
Switzerland	2	2	
Total	46	35	11

SACs, the counselling service, learner training, learner profiles, materials, activities, assessment and evaluation. The questions about the themes were structured through a SWOT analysis. This is a tool originally used for management purposes, which looks at strengths, weaknesses, opportunities and threats of organisations (Thompson & Strickland III, 2001). More recently, it has been adapted for use in educational research as it encourages an investigation of a learning or teaching context from multiple angles, unaffected by prior expectations. Strengths in this context are the capabilities and resources that are advantages for the operation of the centre. Weaknesses are the aspects that limit or reduce the potential of the SACs. Opportunities are the external factors that ensure the optimal functioning or future of the centre and threats are the external elements that could negatively impact on the centre and even affect its existence.

Analysis

The interviews were transcribed for content and this was analysed by using the categorical analysis model (Bardin, 2003) within an open categorisation framework (L'Ecuyer, 1990), which has no predetermined set of categories, in order to ensure that the resulting categorisation corresponded to the reality as felt and expressed by the participants and not to the prior conceptions of the researchers. The transcripts of the interviews were analysed by both researchers, coded and then transcribed (for more information, see Lázaro, 2009).

Results

The results discussed below focus on teachers' beliefs about autonomy, mismatches between teachers' and learners' beliefs and, finally, the relationship between individual and institutional views on autonomy. Together, these affect teachers' identity and motivation in the context of enabling learners' ability to control their own learning. The three sections will show the way that teachers' cognitions are constructed based on these three key points.

Teachers' beliefs about learner autonomy in self-access

Several questions in the interviews asked participants to reflect on the implementation of autonomy in self-access and their roles in this process. We have grouped comments related to similar issues together and report these here with representative quotations taken from the interviews.

The development of autonomy is, to many of the teachers we interviewed, primarily about treating learners as equals. In the words of one of the centre managers when talking about the teachers in the centre:

> Advisors in the centre, they treat them [the students] as equals. They try to show them that they respect them, they expect respect in return. They have very high standards, they expect very high standards from the students. They try to provide students with some sort of scaffolding or a framework by which the students would do better than what they would on their own. (New Zealand)

Perhaps related to this is the notion that teachers need to be able to offer alternatives to existing power relations:

> The advisors really try to break down some of the power relationships that are traditionally present between teacher and student. The adviser tries to ensure that the student realizes that he or she is responsible for their own learning. (Hong Kong)

Some teachers also indicated that they felt they had a responsibility to actively shape a context that allows for the development of autonomy(cf. Winch, 2007). Autonomy, in their view, is thus something that needs to be 'taught' or the development of which needs to be 'guided'.

> Understanding why they need learner training is a process. Students don't understand why they have to learn this. They need guidance and support. Without this, learner training does not work. (Spain)

This implies an increasing (support for) individualisation of the learning process:

> One of the strengths of the advising sessions is the capacity to adapt to the student's needs and his or her situation. I think this is the most powerful aspect of self-access. (Switzerland)

Self-access and autonomy are about the development of lifelong learning skills:

> It actually enables the learner to continue learning when they leave the school. That's the biggest single thing, I think. (New Zealand)

The view of learner autonomy as an individualised process towards lifelong learning, to many teachers implied a degree of conflict between recognising the individual's role while still providing the necessary guidance. For several teachers, this form of guidance towards autonomy was seen as a form of negotiation:

> The idea for us is to offer them an advising service at the beginning, so that learners can feel comfortable and can start taking their own decisions. After that you can leave more space and let the learner make their own choices more. We wouldn't want to give learners a set "autonomy curriculum" but it is necessary to start with a certain number of limited options and to offer guidance in the beginning. (Spain)

Conflicts between teachers' beliefs about autonomy and students' (self-access) language learning behaviour

Looking back at Borg's model, it is clear that classroom practice plays an important part in the development of teachers' cognition. Our beliefs affect our teaching practice, BUT similarly, our teaching experiences affect our beliefs. A mismatch in teachers' and learners' beliefs is thus likely to have an impact on teachers' views on autonomy. Below, we report incidences in the interviews where teachers reported a potential mismatch or conflict between their own view on autonomy in self-access and their students' (self-access) language learning behaviour. As in the section on beliefs, we have grouped comments related to similar issues together and report these here with representative quotations taken from the interviews.

One recurring issue is that many teachers feel their students are too dependent on them and do not take responsibility for their learning.

> In general I would say that students are not used to autonomous learning. That means that they expect that an advisor will be always guiding their learning process. Obviously one of the goals of the centre and its staff is to get the students to be more and more autonomous, so that they learn to analyse their learning process and so that they can use the learning materials in a more considered way. (Spain)

Students' dependence is probably closely related to another issue that was mentioned by many teachers, namely, students' lack of interest in developing learner autonomy. Many reasons were cited for this, but the most common was that students simply do not think it is important. In the words of a teacher in New Zealand:

> For a numbers of years students have said: "Really, I want a teacher to teach me. I don't want to learn on my own" And I think half of that is financial: "I pay money, so I expect to be taught". They see it as a

complete waste of time. Part of it, it's educational background about what is expected. "If I go to school I have a teacher teaching me".

Some students feel that their money and time are better spent in class. There is also a common perception that, for students, independent learning is hard, or like 'asking them to run before they can walk' (New Zealand), often the result of not having been exposed to it in their formative school years. As a result, some students may even fear it, as this teacher from Spain says:

> The learner has a very paradoxal attitude towards autonomy. On the one hand, the freedom and flexibility sound very attractive, as does the "anything you want, whenever you want" idea. It's easy to convince them like this. But after a while students realise that it's not so easy, and especially if they pay for their education, they start to develop doubts. It's like looking at a blank page and asking yourself: where should I start?

For some teachers, this lack of interest in autonomy is difficult to understand:

> The program has good staff who believe in the idea of independent learning. The problem is that they can't understand that not everyone wants to be independent in their learning process. (New Zealand)

Not only are students sometimes less than enthusiastic about the idea of directing their own learning, they also often do not see the importance of tools such as learning plans, records and portfolios. Many students see it as an extra job and may consider it not a good use of their time. Teachers think they often also don't know how to use these kinds of tools properly:

> In most cases the reflection done by students it is not deep enough. They don't understand the process of the portfolio. They see it as a product/assignment. (Germany)

Many teachers thought that their students had the wrong view of what self-access is and how it contributes to student learning. Many felt that students used self-access as a 'quick fix' to deal with last-minute problems. This also applies to their views on language counselling sessions.

> You get also a lot of students that do like the service, but they basically want you to correct all their mistakes. And that's not what we do. [...] Some students really like it, some others get really annoyed as they just want a grammar check. (New Zealand)

Learners also feel that because self-access learning is often not credited and progress is not measured through formal tests, that it is not helpful.

> Test are potentially useful, as most of the students do not consider their peers as a source of information, a source of feedback. People think that they themselves are not really good judges of their own progress when it comes to language, and we try to show them that yes it is a valuable source of information. (New Zealand)

Some teachers report developing tests to make self-access more acceptable to students:

> As the students are very exam oriented, it is difficult for them to assess without pre- and posttest and to see progress. They feel they can't measure it. (Hong Kong)

It is clear from the comments reported above that considerable mismatches exist between teachers' and learners' beliefs about autonomy. Teachers display different ways of responding to these, in some cases accommodating them (such as in the last example), but in all cases reflecting on them. Since reflection is the starting point for all professional development (Freeman & Richards, 1996), these mismatches are likely to have an impact on the ways in which teachers see themselves within the contexts they work in.

Potential conflict between teachers' beliefs and motivations and institutional constraints

The way in which teachers are perceived is likely to have an effect on how they think of themselves. If teachers are not valued or if the goals they are working to achieve are not shared by their colleagues or the wider institution, then this may have a detrimental effect on teachers' identity and motivation.

In all the centres we visited, there were issues with regard to the integration of self-access and autonomy in the wider educational context. Often, there was a lack of coordination between students' self-access learning and their classroom work. In the words of one German teacher, 'the activities in the SAC are simply not coordinated with those in the courses'. And according to this New Zealand teacher:

> I think that the weakness is that you need a lot of classroom and staff to help students become independent and sometimes I think that we lack that. So like teachers teaching students how to be independent

so that when they come to the self-access they are doing the things that would help them to move in independent learning.

Frequently, this lack of integration is due to curriculum constraints where the role of foreign languages and of autonomous language learning in particular, is not given much room in terms of budget or timetabling considerations. Often, self-access learning is not compulsory and therefore only very motivated students, or those with severe learning difficulties, make use of the available support.

Actually the curriculum at the university has no language component. Students do not need to have language training, nor the university has the obligation of offering such training. This situation makes it very hard for the centre and the staff to get the necessary funding and recognition. (Germany)

Sometimes, this lack of integration is a result of working in a large institution where the position of the SAC is not clearly defined:

We haven't been able to engage all departments within the institute. We haven't been able to convince people that students should come. In a big institution you get lecturers who follow up the students and say them go to the support language centre and then they ring us and ask us: has this person been there? But many other don't. I guess, maybe we should have a stronger link with some departments. (New Zealand)

Implementing autonomy can also be a frustrating experience due to a lack of understanding from colleagues in other departments about what autonomy is.

It is very hard to change people's minds and their way of thinking. Convincing people takes time and it doesn't always work. In Hong Kong there are very few teachers concerned about the importance of learner autonomy. (Hong Kong)

This lack of understanding results in teachers in the SAC being perceived as somehow doing less valuable work and their professional contribution not always being recognised. In some cases, SAC counsellors are labelled 'administrators', which does not accurately reflect their roles. In some cases, their work is not adequately acknowledged.

According to the new guidelines, work in the SAC now gets less recognition and in practice this means that SALL involves more work for the teachers. This is dangerous, as these teachers may not be interested in working in the SAC anymore. (Hong Kong)

A perennial problem in self-access and one reflected in most of the interviews, is the lack of funding. In some cases, this is the result of a lack of institutional integration (no one takes financial responsibility for the centre), and sometimes it may be a result of the lower status of SACs and SAC teachers than other 'more academic' departments.

> The strength of the centre is the team behind it. Nevertheless there is a part of the team with bad working conditions, and this leads to the situation of people leaving the centre. So, once you have trained a person for the work in the centre he/she leaves and you have to start from the beginning. This is very frustrating for the staff responsible for the centre. (Spain)

This lack of funding particularly affects centres' ability to hire sufficient staff.

> We lack trained staff for working in the centre. We can't afford to hire professional staff, so we rely on students. As students come and go every semester or every year, there is no consistency. For us it would be much better if we could have permanent staff. (Switzerland)

In a number of centres, teachers in language departments are expected to carry out tasks in the SAC without proper training and without proper remuneration. SAC time is often paid at a lower rate than classroom time.

> We can't ask teachers to work in the centre, without having their time there recognised. If they don't get their effort acknowledged some-how, you can't ask them to invest their free time there. (Germany)

Several teachers point out that institutions may want to use SACs as a way to reduce teaching costs, and that they do not see the need to invest sufficiently in ensuring good quality self-access support. This also negatively impacts on the teachers' views of self-access:

> Teachers' attitudes has been a big thing. In the beginning it was really hard [on the teachers], because the school basically did it [establish the SAC] because they wanted to save some money. Management often views lab time, even self-access time as a sort of money saving and at the end it's not really. It's simply an alternative to classroom teaching. (New Zealand)

With or without the support of management and other colleagues, the work in the flexible environment that is a SAC can be frustrating. As there is often no timetable, no curriculum and no set materials or classes, the usual ways for teachers to obtain feedback about their own and their students' progress may not be easily available. This can affect teachers' motivation:

> In the beginning, working in the centre can be very exciting for the teachers, but then comes the time when they have to work alone without much support, and that's hard and sometimes a source of disillusionment. They do not have much experience and neither their colleagues. They ask themselves: "Am I doing it right? Does this really work?", and they feel really insecure and lonely. (Spain)

It is clear from the comments above that the institutional context has a significant impact on how the work in the centres is perceived. There is a lack of understanding or appreciation of the professional identity that facilitators bring to the institution, and this has an impact on teachers' self-perceptions and motivation.

Discussion

The results of this study show a complex interaction between teachers' beliefs, identity and motivation in implementing autonomy in the context of self-access. Previous research on classroom teaching has found similar interactions. For example, Borg's framework of teacher cognition (1997, cited in Borg, 2003: 82) gives prominence to contextual factors and classroom practice, including the learners' role therein.

In terms of teachers' beliefs about autonomy, the study found a great deal of overlap between the respondents. Autonomy is widely seen as involving (the development of) equality, and respect between teachers and learners. Other key concepts include empowerment, and related to this, the provision of guidance and the facilitation of learning (as distinct from teaching). The development of autonomy is also seen as a key aspect of successful teaching and a requisite for learner success. In practice, however, these ideas were not shared by many of the students. Teachers felt students did not recognise the importance of developing autonomy and lacked the necessary independent learning skills. It was generally felt that it was not so much cultural differences, but rather a lack of previous education that underlies this phenomenon. Students are simply not used to the idea of taking responsibility for their learning.

The interesting, and in our view crucial, question this raises, is how educators will respond to this challenge. Some facilitators adapt by making the self-access environment more like the classroom. An example of this is the implementation of tests to accommodate students' desire for a formalisation of their self-access learning. The majority of the facilitators, however, especially report an enormous need for learner training. Barcelos (2008) argues that a large part of the reluctance that students may have towards the idea of autonomy, may result from misunderstanding and miscommunication. Barcelos (2008: 194) calls for transparency and argues that 'teachers need to be more explicit to students about the roles they want to play, clearly explaining their purposes and rationale behind each activity [...]'.

This leads to the question of whether as educators we sometimes think we 'know better' and force our ideas of what constitutes good teaching and good learning onto our students, and whether there is an alternative. Barcelos (2008: 194) suggests occasional adaptation to students' beliefs. In this view, education, and in particular autonomy education, is a process of negotiation.

The main lesson from the results of this study is that these types of challenges are commonplace. Facilitators can expect to have to answer such questions for themselves in their own teaching context. This requires adequate personal/mental and professional preparation. In reality, however, many teachers lack this preparation. In terms of Borg's framework, teachers' extensive experience of classrooms, which defines early cognitions and shapes teachers' perceptions, is based predominantly on classroom teaching. Most facilitators do not have alternative models to guide them, and explicit training in self-access learning is not generally available.

The other point to note is that dealing with different beliefs and possible conflicts that result from this (think of a student refusing to do self-study as an alternative to classroom learning) is likely to challenge teachers' identity as someone who has the students' well-being at heart. That in itself may be a fairly healthy process, but not having the requisite preparation for that process may negatively impact teachers' motivation, and as we have shown, it can indeed do. In the words of this SAC manager commenting on her staff:

> In some cases teachers feel lost. The other day a teacher commented that she felt frustrated as she didn't know if her work at the centre had any impact or not, or what kind of impact. What happens is that there's a lack of feedback.

Without easily accessible professional development opportunities and academic support, individual facilitators may not have enough opportunities to reflect on and further develop their personal belief systems. If the development of learner autonomy depends on the presence of teacher autonomy (Smith & Erdoğan, 2008), then surely, the development of that autonomy has to be a priority.

Further challenges to implementing autonomy relate to Borg's 'contextual factors'; in the case of self-access, the challenges stem mainly from institutional constraints. Most of the respondents in the study reported similar problems with a lack of professional recognition. In many cases, this was thought to be a result of a lack of understanding on the part of colleagues of what autonomy is and what the role of a facilitator entails. This often resulted in a lack of integration of self-access learning into the wider (language) curriculum, an issue that has been widely reported in previous literature (e.g. Cotterall & Reinders, 2000; Gardner & Miller, 1999). This highlights the importance of awareness raising; an area where SACs have important work to do. Unfortunately, the lack of understanding of the work that facilitators do, in practice often translates into decreased status and pay. The lack of recognition for self-access also means that fewer (financial) resources are available for facilities and, importantly, staff academic development. This is reflected in the common labelling of SACs as a service department and of facilitators as 'administrators'. This has a clear effect on facilitators' sense of identity and motivation. They see themselves not simply as providing an administrative service, but as people who work at the heart of the teaching–learning interface and who build deep and powerful connections with their students.

Finally, teachers' sense of their personal development as professionals is informed by 'classroom practice' (as suggested by Borg's framework) and experiences. But, in self-access learning, the 'normal' means of making sense of these experiences, and of measuring success (through course completion, feedback from students, tests results, etc.) are almost absent. For many teachers, this means that working in self-access is often a form of isolation; both institutionally, as well as professionally.

Conclusion

This study has shown that facilitating self-access learning comes with both rewards and challenges. One of the rewards is the knowledge that one is actively acting on one's beliefs, by implementing autonomy in a flexible learning environment. This seems to be the motivation for most of the teachers in our study:

I would say that although human resources does not value our work so much, the teachers in the centre are all people who believe in learner autonomy and have always believed in it since the day the centre was opened. (Spain)

The many challenges, however, negatively impact on facilitators' identities and motivation. One of the implications of this study is that there needs to be far more accessible and far more specific preparation for teachers intending to work as facilitators, and far more ongoing support. Without such professional preparation, both students and facilitators are likely to be negatively affected. The study has also shown the value of teachers' voices as an important source of information in investigating the reality of implementing autonomy.

References

Aoki, N. (2008) Teacher stories to improve theories of learner/teacher autonomy. *Independence* 43, 15–17. On WWW at http://learnerautonomy.org/aoki2008.pdf.

Barcelos, A.M.F. (2008) Teachers' and students' beliefs within a deweyean framework: Conflict and influence. In P. Kalaja and S.M.F. Barcelos (eds) *Beliefs about SLA: New Research Approaches* (pp. 171–199). Deventer: Kluwer Academic.

Bardin, L. (2003) *L'analyse de Contenu des Documents et des Communications*. Paris: Presses Universitaires de France.

Breen, M.P. (2001) *Learner Contributions to Language Learning. New Directions in Research. Applied Linguistics and Language Study.* Harlow: Longman.

Borg, S. (2003) Teacher cognition in language teaching: A review of research on what language teachers think, know, believe and do. *Language Teaching* 36, 81–109.

Cotterall, S. and Reinders, H. (2000) Learner's perceptions and practice in self access language learning. *TESOLANZ* 8, 23–38.

de los Angeles Clemente, M. (2001) Teachers' attitudes within a self-directed language learning scheme. *System* 29, 45–67.

Freeman, D. (2002) The hidden side of the work: Teacher knowledge and learning to teach. A perspective from north American educational research on teacher education in English language teaching. *Language Teaching* 35, 1–13.

Freeman, D. and Richards, J. (1996) *Teacher Learning in Language Teaching.* New York: Cambridge University Press.

Gardner, D. and Miller, L. (1999) *Establishing Self-Access.* Cambridge: Cambridge University Press.

Kumaravadivelu, B. (2001) Towards a postmethod pedagogy. *TESOL Quarterly* 35 (4), 537–560.

L'Ecuyer, R. (1990) *Methodologie de L'analyse Developpementale de Contenu.* Québec: Presses de l'Université.

Lázaro, N. (2009) *Tendencias Pedagógicas en Centros de Autoaprendizaje de Alemania, Suiza, Hong Kong y España.* Madrid: UNED.

Lea, M.R. and Nicoll, K. (2002) (eds) *Distributed Learning: Social and Cultural Approaches to Practise.* London: Routledge.

Moore, N. and Reinders, H. (2003) Teaching for self-study. *Modern English Teacher* 12 (2), 48–51.

Reinders, H. and Balcikanli, C. (in press, 2011) Learning to foster autonomy: The role of teacher education materials. Novartis.

Reinders, H., Sakui, K. and Akakura, M. (forthcoming, 2011) Roles in language advising and fostering autonomy: A journal study. Hasald/HKUST.

Richards, J. and Lockhart, C. (1994) *Reflective Teaching in Second Language Classrooms.* Cambridge: Cambridge University Press.

Smith, R. and Erdoğan, S. (2008) Teacher-learner autonomy: Programme goals and student-teacher constructs. In T.E. Lamb and H. Reinders (eds) *Learner and Teacher Autonomy: Concepts, Realities and Responses* (pp. 83–102). Amsterdam: John Benjamins.

Thompson, A.A.J. and Strickland III, A.J. (2001) *Strategic Management: Concepts and Cases.* New York: McGraw-Hill.

Van Lier, L. (2007) Action-based teaching, autonomy and identity. *Innovation in Language Learning and Teaching* 1 (1), 46–65.

Vieira, F. (2007) Teacher autonomy: Why should we care? *Independence* 41, 20–29. On WWW at http://www.learnerautonomy.org/Vieira2007.pdf.

Winch, C. (2007) *Education Autonomy and Critical Thinking.* London: Routledge.

Part 3

Cultures and Contexts

Chapter 10

Identity, Motivation and Autonomy: A Tale of Two Cities

ALICE CHIK and STEPHAN BREIDBACH

Introduction

Students majoring in English or taking a degree course in foreign language education in English in most cases are successful language learners themselves. Students generally enter tertiary education with a sound knowledge of English. In general, a fairly high degree of language competence is required on entry to most European and Asian universities for studying English. However, looking at the issue from the point of language learning autonomy and language learning awareness, a number of questions can be raised: When the learners possess a high level of proficiency, is it related to their level of learner autonomy and awareness? Are the students more motivated to learn because they are more aware of their learning and more autonomous in making language learning decisions for themselves?

This chapter reports on a language learning histories (LLHs) exchange project between a group of Hong Kong undergraduates and German postgraduates in 2008. Both parties were learning English as a second language (L2), with the Hong Kong students majoring in English while their German counterparts were preparing for future careers as English teachers. These learners wrote and shared their multimodal LLHs through course wikis, and asynchronous responses were also posted. Drawing on the autobiographical narratives written by four learners, two from Hong Kong and two from Germany, we explore their lifelong development of language learning. In particular, we will discuss the ways that they capitalized on popular cultural resources to enhance and maintain motivation and also create personal spaces for English language identity construction outside the regular language classrooms. In light of the growing body of academic works on the L2 self, the narratives examined in this chapter illuminate how popular culture can serve as an overarching link in the cultivation of identity, motivation and autonomy.

Learning a second or foreign language does not follow a straightforward path, and classroom-based learning is certainly not the only path followed (Benson & Nunan, 2005). Students also seek alternative paths to improve proficiency, i.e. via English language popular culture (Lam, 2000; Murray, 2008, Norton & Vanderheyden, 2004). Out-of-class foreign language learning can be conceptualized along a continuum from 'self-instruction' to 'naturalistic' learning (Benson, 2001). Academics have long promoted the use of English language popular culture to motivate learners (see, e.g. Cheung, 2001; Duff, 2002, 2004; Marsh, 2005; Moffatt & Norton, 2005). In the context of schooling, Duff (2002) argues that, through participatory inclusion and exclusion, popular culture is an avenue for constructing identities. Examining internet participants' language use, Black (2008) and Lam (2004) both suggest that foreign language learners are given different language learning opportunities in the online communities. Throughout their studies, the learners crafted their personal spaces because they found learning in such contexts less hostile and they also received more opportunities to use English. Davis (2007) points out the incidental mini-English lessons available from digital photo sharing sites. However, these types of opportunities largely depend on the learners' initiative to join communities. The investigations also focused on learners, immersed in English-speaking environments, utilizing popular cultural practices as their sideways entrance into English-speaking communities, which they have greater difficulty accessing in reality.

While there is an emerging body of work on the phenomenon of learners engaging in new literacies or digital literacies, there is also a more traditional sense that language learners are consuming English language popular culture, not necessarily passively, as their way of supplementing traditional classroom teaching and learning. In an experimental setting, Koolstra and Beentjes (1999) show the effectiveness of using Dutch subtitles for English audio tracks in TV programs in order to help Dutch children learn vocabulary. Learners from non-English immersion environments are also using popular culture to aid their learning. Murray (2008) describes how Japanese English learners use radio and TV programs to reach out to imagined communities in order to learn English. His work has been particularly interesting in setting up the investigation of a sense of identity development in the learning of English. The intricate link between motivation, identity and language learning is an emerging field, in particular, the relevance of an L2 self. Dörnyei (2005, 2009) argues that the L2 Motivational Self System comprises three components: ideal L2 self, ought-to L2 self and L2 learning experience. Though the last component is still fairly much a theoretical concept, and it is beyond the scope of this chapter to investigate it, we are interested in using our narratives to illuminate the operation of the first two components. With the ideal L2 and ought-to L2 self, a learner has to imagine future possibilities and act on these learning possibilities to activate motivation. One area of particular interest for our exchange project is the different ways that learners from two cultural contexts view themselves as English learners and as users beyond their language classrooms.

Background to the Study

The aims of the personal LLHs exchange project were to help students realize the highly individual nature of language learning, to develop an awareness of the variety of possible ways language acquisition can take place, and to recognize how learning languages at school can be experienced in fundamentally different ways. We hoped that our students would be able to appreciate a variety of influencing factors that can foster learning autonomy and influence language learning identities. For the English students, we felt that they would learn to appreciate their individual autonomous efforts in shaping their English learning paths, rather than pointing to standardized ways of learning as can often be found in institutional contexts. For the pre-service teachers among our research partners, we felt it would be desirable for them to become more aware of the process of and the factors influencing the learning of an L2.

The Hong Kong participants started learning English from a young age, either in a kindergarten setting (from about age 4) or at home. They all had English as a core academic subject from primary one (age 6) onward, with weekly exposure of about 4–6 hours, which increased to about 7–9 hours in secondary education (Nunan, 2003). All Hong Kong students have to pass English examinations in the state public examination, held at the end of secondary education, as a pre-requisite for university admission. The German participants started learning English slightly later than their Hong Kong counterparts (primary three, age 8) and experienced less exposure (2 weekly hours throughout primary 3–4, 5 hours in secondary 1–2, 3–4 hours in secondary 3–6 and 5 hours in upper secondary 1–3). There is no general requirement for English language competence at a particular level for state university placement, except for the study of English itself and internationalized English-medium courses in some subjects (e.g. European Business Studies, International Law).

The 12 Hong Kong participants, who were Year 1 English majors, took a compulsory reading and writing core course in their first semester in 2008 with the first author, and later volunteered to participate in the exchange. The English LLHs course was one component of their reflective practices. Though students were provided with some guidelines, they were given a high degree of freedom in composing their LLHs. For the Hong Kong students, uploading their LLHs onto an online course site and providing peer feedback constituted an important assessment component. The LLHs were freely available online and exchanges between fellow students were vibrant. The two German participants took an optional MEd course on L2 acquisition with the second author. Due to differences in semester structure, the German students did not write their LLHs until mid-November and eventually uploaded their LLHs onto their online course site.

From the courses, we collected the participants' LLHs as well as the discussion threads produced during the exchange. Finally, both authors interviewed the participants to ascertain their views on the exchange. We adopted a narrative approach in analyzing the data obtained. First, we extracted themes from the LLHs by using content analysis (Lieblich *et al.*, 1998). In a second step, the discussion threads and interview data were woven into the narratives of the learners.

While it is possible to see a general pattern of overarching narratives in their LLHs, there is a stronger coherence to the chronological development aligned to the institutional path. Though many also touched on the importance of non-classroom-based activities, which ranged from watching English language TV programs to traveling overseas, some learners believed that their most important experience of learning English was related to institutional learning. For the more reflective writers, some focused a lot more on their English learning in their own personal spaces. The analysis of the LHHs revealed a distinct structure of the narratives. On the one hand, the narrative is structured around one or more of four distinct parameters: people, places, events and media.

On the other hand, these parameters function as the focal points of one or several critical incidents within nearly all of the LHHs analyzed. Within the dramaturgy of the narrative, such critical moments take the function of cathartic moments, turning points, that is to say, where the development of the L2 self takes a new direction or gathers fresh momentum. In some cases, these parameters appeared as isolated narrative elements of a language learning biography (Antje, Jessie and Mandy), whereas in others, two or more parameters seemed to be deeply entwined (Susanne). The deviating paths into the personal and out-of-class popular cultural activities will be the focus of this chapter. In the following section, we will focus on four particular learners who devoted most of their learning energy to consuming English language popular culture, thereby highlighting the parameter 'media' in particular. The use of 'media' was most unusual, in the sense that these learners were actively seeking individualized learning spaces through English language popular culture.

The Participants' Narratives

Jessie and Mandy, from Hong Kong, were English majors with English-medium secondary education backgrounds. They were both highly motivated and dedicated when providing feedback to fellow students. Susanne and Antje, from Germany, took a Master of Education course geared toward teaching in primary education. Both had gone through German mainstream education with English being taught as a foreign language but without English-medium instruction. Both were exceptionally keen and highly motivated students and displayed a fairly high level of proficiency in English.

Jessie's story

> The curriculum did actually help me in improving my English, although not in every aspect of it but I would say in many areas of it, such as writing and reading...TV does the rest. (LLH, September 2008)

Jessie is an outgoing, friendly and bright student. She started 'exchanging long e-mails in English' with an Israeli pen pal on a weekly basis in Secondary Two. At the time, she was not concerned about learning English; she was more interested in getting to know a friend from a foreign country. The e-mail exchanges became the foundation for her to see herself using English outside the language classroom. When it comes to English TV dramas and films, Jessie immediately transforms into a different person. She follows various TV dramas, like *Prison Break* and *Gossip Girl*, and is astonishingly knowledgeable about these programs. However, her passion for English language popular culture was a happy result of coincidence:

> I like grammar, I could not figure the order but my "unusual" passion for grammar led me on and my performance in grammar motivated to *go further* and *dig deeper*. It started with *pure boredom*

when I began to madly go after American dramas, movies and shows, but it ended up having a profound impact on me and my English; not to mention my long-time passion for foreign music. All these essentially contributed to my early exposure to this lingua franca. These are, in my opinion, some of the most interesting and effective ways to learn English. As a source of interest can always be an impetus for a learner. With constant contact with the English language, not only did it stir my interest in pursuing higher English fluency, but I had also acquired a large bank of commonly-used vocabulary, collocations, phrases and sentence structures which had benefited me enormously in every aspect of my English. Certainly, these hobbies had also done wonders to my spoken English which had always been my weaker part (LLH, October 2008, original emphasis)

Jessie's passion for English language popular culture enabled her to keep in touch with the 'real world'. The English learning part was purely incidental. For her, the learning was not the most important aspect of using the language; it was being able to 'see' the world in English. Jessie was fully immersed in English language TV programs and films because 'they allowed me to see the world differently, and so I am different from other people who are learning English in Hong Kong', the expansion of worldview is only coincidental to language learning.

Susanne's story

Without the technical possibilities provided by computers and the internet, my English would not be what it is today. (LLH, November 2008)

Susanne is a sharp-, yet open-minded person, with a taste for a good intellectual challenge. She describes herself as a language person who, initiated to languages by her multilingual father, has always considered learning languages as her own way of life. Just like Jessie, Susanne enjoys grammar, and language learning for her has been something profound and playful at the same time: 'I loved it and still do – translating Latin texts is like solving puzzles for me'.

With Latin being her first foreign language at school, she started formal English learning in grade 7 (at the age of 12). Still, her first encounter with English was at the age of 9, when she tried to guess the meaning of words from pictures in cartoon books. In later years, Susanne's passion for rock music paved the way for her to take control of her language learning in a pleasurable way, often to compensate for frustrating English classes at school.

> I think I was in the fifth class when I began listening to pop and rock music. I liked singing along a lot, although at first the only thing I could do was to imitate what I heard – and most times what left my mouth was probably anything but English. But when I started buying records, I often got the songtexts as well, and from that time on I started to read those texts, so that I'd be able to sing the correct words. Also, as I acquired knowledge of English at school, I gradually tried to understand what was sung. The connection to music made English the "absolute language of cool" for me. I remember studying the texts of my favourite bands over and over. What I nearly don't remember at all though are the English lessons at school. (LLII, November 2008)

After graduating from school, where she dropped English in the final year, she did not use her English for a number of years. This period came to an end with the purchase of her first computer, when she became intrigued by the possibilities offered by computer games:

> At that time, most of the interesting programmes were written in English. Therefore, my interest in English was revived by computer games such as *"Warlords"*, *"Diablo"*, and especially the computer version of *"Magic the Gathering"*. As this is originally a trading card game where you have to at least read, if not memorize all your available cards in order to be able to use them well, I did a lot of English reading during that time and again acquired a particular new vocabulary (one of my words definitely originating from that time was "opponent"). (LLH, November 2008)

Also, the internet opened up access to TV shows such as *Friends, Coupling* and *The Thin Blue Line*. The first on the list, however, was *Futurama*, which she says:

> I watched over and over again. The first time I watched an episode I was just able to follow the storyline, but the more often I watched it, the more jokes and allusions I understood. (LLH, November 2008)

Access to and the use of popular culture products was important for Susanne in order for her to take active control of her language learning. It helped to link her language learning affinities with existential experiences and emotions in her youth, and to catalyze her decision to embark on a career in English language teaching.

Mandy's story

> Don't you agree sitting in the classroom is too boring and dull? Learn beyond the classroom and practice in daily life just makes you love English! (LLH, September 2008)

Mandy was less vocal on the course, mostly because she felt that she was not an avid reader. However, she was a passionate writer and had no difficulty in expressing her love of video gaming. Her older cousin introduced her to video games as a child (between 5 and 6). Mandy recalled that in the early 1990s, video games on sale in Hong Kong were mostly imported directly from Japan and only came in Japanese. 'Hardcore' video gamers like her cousin were used to playing these Japanese games. English-language video games were rare and 'more expensive' (this is still true today). As a young child, she was attracted to all the games, but she did not understand much Japanese, other than the simple 'Yes' or 'No' on the screen. Her older cousin provided her with all the gaming instructions, but she realized that her ability to recognize words was minimal and the overall gaming experience unsatisfactory. This was even more obvious with role-play games (RPGs). Playing video games from a young age proved to have long-term effects, she was hungrily reading through walkthroughs and gaming instructions in Chinese.

Mandy's passion led her to discover English-language video games. With a better knowledge of English than Japanese, Mandy was quick to realize that the only way to gain more satisfaction from RPGs, which 'provide their consumers much space of imagination even after knowing the completed story lines of the games', was to play these games in English. For her, 'full understanding of the story line and other elements of a game is the basic and must achieved condition to fully enjoy playing it'. When the game *Dissidia: Final Fantasy* (Square Enix) was released in Japanese in December 2008, Mandy was both excited and tormented: she had been yearning for the game ever since she first heard of it, yet 'experiencing the Japanese version first might result in a miserable playing experience, and would certainly ruin the later playing experience of the English one' (interview, June 2009). Mandy waited until the release of the English version on 25 August 2009.

Mandy did not make a strong attempt to communicate with other video gamers on online forums 'because I really have no time', and she did not particularly like online gaming. Instead of simply pushing buttons like her cousin, she thought of herself as belonging to a wider community of video gamers who understand their games thoroughly because of a common language, English. 'It is through this incident I felt that I am an English video gamer. I know that I like video games, but it is English video games that I play. I cannot be a *Japanese* video gamer. It doesn't seem to make sense, because most of the games I play originated from Japan, but it is the language that matters'. While Mandy said that she did not like reading novels in English, she had no problem consuming the fantasy narratives in English-language video games. In fact, she loves those games for the narratives!

Antje's story

Eight years of language learning at school did not prepare me enough to have proper conversations with native speakers in English. (LLH, November 2008)

Antje started to learn English in grade 5. For her, it was a subject like any other, and she did not feel any special leaning toward the language. This changed when she was 15 and experienced what she calls the 'hardship of the inability to express myself' during a holiday language trip to England where she lived with a host family for three weeks. Learning English now made perfect sense to her:

Despite the fact that it was very hard to express myself clearly and to understand what people were saying at first, I began to enjoy speaking English. I finally had the opportunity to use it in a natural setting and I realized that learning a foreign language is indeed very useful. The vacation in England showed me how important it is to acquire another language and also how much fun it can be to be finally able to actually make use of it. Additionally I became more open towards and more interested in foreign cultures. (LLH, November 2008)

Later, Antje decided to work as an *au pair* in the USA for a year, but she experienced communicative handicaps as the variety of English she was exposed to in America had little in common with what she had learned at school.

The language difficulties I had at the beginning showed me that the kind of English I had learned at school differed vastly from the English, which is spoken in the USA. It only enabled me to understand the main details but in the beginning I had immense problems to follow the conversations around me. This changed after three to four months and the two years I spent living in North

Carolina helped me to become a fluent English speaker what would not have been possible with the little language input I received at school. (LLH, November 2008)

To this very day, Antje has kept in touch with both her former host-families, and she is in contact either via e-mail or the telephone with the family in the USA on an almost daily basis. In a comment in one of the course wikis, Antje discloses that the US series *The O.C.* had become her favorite, and even though she was generally reluctant to estimate to what extent such resources helped her to settle into American English, in the course discussions she repeatedly used the metaphor of 'feeling at home' whenever she watched these TV series again.

Antje conceptualizes language use and cultural knowledge as a way of participating in human relationships, which is expressed through a strong emphasis on the interpersonal and pragmatic dimension in foreign language learning in her learner's story. Against this background, popular culture and communication technologies play a vital, yet mediating role, as they serve as a means to an end rather than as a means of enjoyment in themselves.

Discussion

Few of our students decide to focus on English in their studies and future careers (as English teachers or professionals in English language) to make amends for what they perceive as an insufficient language learning outcome from their own days at school. Having normally not been asked to reflect on their strategies and general ways of language learning, most tend to consider their own success to be self-evident, or owing to benign circumstances and sometimes even to coincidence. The exchange project that we report on makes use of LLHs in order to initiate reflection about what prompts individuals to choose English as their course of study at university. Working with LLHs helps us, as teachers, to become aware of and understand our students' learning motivation and learning needs. Not only does it help our students on their way toward becoming a reflective practitioner (Schön, 1987), but also ourselves to the same degree.

Institutional foreign language teaching often centers on approximative and yet normative assumptions of why and how learners are motivated to learn a language. Learners are seldom given the opportunity to voice their subjective views on the issue. Qualitative research has reconstructed structures of subjective sense attributed to contexts of social action, such as instructed learning at school; such research has been able to show that normative expectations put forth by the institution may be blatantly at odds with the objective sense structures realized by the students (Meyer *et al.*, 2008). In the LLHs, one dimension that stood out was the way the participants found common ground in their language learning in different cultural contexts. And this common ground is English language popular culture. Hong Kong participants came to the realization that popular culture, mainly American, has become an important source of input for English learning. It is also quite noteworthy that many of the Hong Kong students felt they were perhaps watching the same Hollywood films or American TV programs as their German counterparts. One German participant noted the following observation on Jessie's LLH:

> I like the idea that as learners of English we keep changing our learning habits. You can start by cramming vocabulary and grammar into your head, but it surely takes some other measures to actually become fluent in English. Like you, I like to follow a variety of news programs as well as TV shows. (LLH, December 2008)

In response, Jessie thought 'it is funny that the whole world seems to be watching American TV in English' to learn English. In understanding how these four learners view themselves through an L2, it was necessary to consider the popular cultural practices that they engaged in. For Jessie, it was not simply the watching of American TV shows and films that mattered to her, it was the fact that she was *not* watching Chinese TV shows and films. Similar to Jessie, Mandy also said that she is an English video gamer. The language of the video games is more important than the habit of gaming. Susanne recognized that learning through video games might have been a shared habit, but the different types of games also enabled the foreign language gamers to build different vocabulary banks. The personal choices in English language popular culture enabled these learners to exercise their autonomy in textual consumption and language use. In turn, the ability to enjoy these popular cultural practices also motivated them to take their learning of English beyond the limitations of classroom practices. Another aspect that struck both researchers was the strong emotional involvement these learners displayed in discussing their out-of-class English use. Jessie was practically screaming when talking about her favorite TV programs and movies, and Mandy was thrilled and fairly vociferous when recommending the latest video games. The emotional responses were a good indication of the source of motivation for these two learners to use English.

LHHs can be seen as a way of giving the learners a voice when it comes to negotiating motivation and L2 identities; in teacher education, reflective work on LHHs has proven to be a means of professional development, as Antje aptly puts it:

> Before the correspondence with the students from Hong Kong I never imagined that exchanging learner biographies with others would reveal such essential aspects that would help me to further develop my personal teaching philosophy. Getting to know the different paths in the language learning processes, looking at diverse possibilities and resources for language learning that I was not aware of before and thereby realizing what a great influence a teacher actually has on the language learning progress of his or her students, helped me immensely to further develop my understanding of teaching. It became clear to me that there is not just the one and only way of learning a second language, but that instead there are several possibilities and resources that a language learner may make use of. (LLH, December 2008)

This reflection from Antje highlighted a shared motivating factor among the Hong Kong and German learners: the appropriation of English language popular culture for individualized learning. First, both Mandy and Jessie admitted that they did assume that if they themselves were watching American TV programs in Hong Kong, the rest of the world was probably doing the same thing. So they were not surprised, but bored to a certain extent, that 'the German students appeared to be doing very similar things as we do'. However, they were surprised to see that these German students were not only consuming English language popular culture passively, but they were also appropriating these texts as learning resources. Mandy agreed that it was beneficial to see that learners from Hong Kong had taken different steps and strategies to enrich their English learning outside the classrooms; this was more motivating than simply learning from their German counterparts about what was happening outside Hong Kong. Jessie had a more difficult time in believing that the German students also had to struggle with English, but she agreed that the learning mediated through English language popular culture 'was certainly more motivating than textbooks' (e-mail, March 2009).

Conclusion

Many of the Hong Kong participants focused on their own experience as collective memories. Though some came to see that educational experience of the same system gave way to individual differences, many responded less positively and thought that every Hong Kong student had the same experience. It took the reading of the German learning histories for the participants to realize that their own learning paths were unique. The German students also realized the uniqueness of individual learning paths. This recognition helped them to expand their self-concept as language teachers: They reflected on the tension in their own language learning biography between language learning in institutional contexts and the strategies they used to take their learning beyond the classroom. However, they also acknowledged that, as professionals in language teaching, they need to convey similar or different strategies to the learners of English that they will teach in the future.

Working with the participants both from Hong Kong and Berlin showed that, apparently, even for successful learners, becoming aware of one's own experience of learning and transforming this into a reflective and thus autonomous learning practice is a task that is far from easy. Still, what can be learned from almost all LHHs from the *corpus* of this project is that autonomy in language learning and the motivation to learn and use a language (i.e. English) are linked in a mutually reinforcing manner. The narratives showed that this dynamic can be triggered by four different parameters, one of which is 'media'. In this chapter, we discussed cases in which students of English construct their learner identity by contrasting experiences of structured and unstructured language learning. Broadly speaking, the education system paved the way for both Hong Kong and Berlin students to enter higher education, but it is through English language popular culture that participants began to see that they were individuals in language learning. Be it video games, pop songs or TV and film cultures, the learners appeared to be more comfortable in sharing their experience of learning English through their chosen popular culture genres. They were also more motivated to reach out to these media texts in English.

The participants in this study were all highly motivated to gain a high level of proficiency. Yet, it is difficult to claim that they all achieved this through regular classroom learning alone. Rather, they all showed that they invested heavily in different aspects of popular cultural practices. What is clear is that the participants viewed their own use of English beyond the language classrooms to have influenced their identity as language learners. It was through the writing of LLHs that the learners on the project came to see their own preferences for English language popular culture over their native language texts. But, as Dörneyi (2009) suggested, a vivid imagination is required in crafting the L2 self, and these learners would have benefited from a more explicit vocalization of this possible L2 self early on in their learning journey. By the same token, it is also beneficial to encourage learners to find their popular culture favorites earlier in life. The incorporation of LLH writing at an earlier age could help learners cultivate a stronger L2 identity and teachers mobilize additional learning resources.

Owing to the small scale of the project, there are certain limitations to the extent that we can generalize the findings. While the small number of participants on the exchange project enjoyed the experience, facilitating LLHs exchange among learners from different cultural backgrounds is not an easy task, particularly in terms of organization. The institutional constraints included the number of students in our courses, which was a major issue with our project, and the differences in semester schedule, which might have contributed to a certain degree of inactivity in the exchange. With an unequal number of participants, it was difficult to match exchange partners, as would have been suggested in tandem exchange, and some students were much quicker to respond than others. Also with different semester schedules, Hong Kong students found it more difficult to backtrack and sustain their interest. Another point raised by the Hong Kong participants was that they were quite unused to exchanging with graduate students. Their own experience of exchanging with overseas internet surfers was mostly based on a shared interest, i.e. overseas gaming partners, fan fiction writers, fellow photography lovers, etc. Pennycook (1998: 162) argues that language teachers 'need to see English language teaching as located in the domain of popular culture as much as in the domain of applied linguistics'. The use of learners' LLHs provided mosaic glimpses of learners' English worlds beyond the classrooms with arrays of popular culture activities and texts, and different degrees of consumption and participation. Future research collaboration in LLHs exchange will arguably benefit from addressing shared interests in popular culture as a common starting point for the exploration of the participants' English learning journeys.

References

Benson, P. (2001) *Teaching and Researching Autonomy in Language Learning*. London: Longman.

Benson, P. and Nunan, D. (eds) (2005) *Learners' Stories: Difference and Diversity in Language Learning*. Cambridge: Cambridge University Press.

Black, R.W. (2008) Digital design: English language learners and reader reviews in adolescent fan fiction. In M. Knobel and C. Lankshear (eds) *A New Literacies Sampler* (pp. 115–136). New York: Peter Lang.

Cheung, C-K. (2001) The use of popular culture as a stimulus to motivate secondary students' English learning in Hong Kong. *ELT Journal* 55 (1), 55–61.

Davis, J. (2007) Display, identity and the everyday: Self-presentation through digital image sharing. *Discourse, Studies in the Cultural Politics of Education* 28, 549–564.

Dörnyei, Z. (2005) *The Psychology of the Language Learner: Individual Differences in Second Language Acquisition*. London: Routledge.

Dörnyei, Z. (2009) The L2 Motivational Self System. In Z. Dörnyei and E. Ushioda (eds) *Motivation, Language Identity and the L2 Self* (pp. 9–42). Bristol: Multilingual Matters.

Duff, P.A. (2001) Language, literacy, content, and (pop) culture: Challenges for ESL students in mainstream courses. *The Canadian Modern Language Review* 58 (1), 103–132.

Duff, P.A. (2002) Pop culture and ESL students: Intertextuality, identity, and participation in classroom discussions. *Journal of Adolescent & Adult Literacy* 45 (6), 482–487.

Duff, P.A. (2004) Intertextuality and hybrid discourses: The infusion of pop culture in educational discourse. *Linguistics and Education* 14, 231–276.

Koolstra, C.M. and Beentjes, J.W.J. (1999) Children's vocabulary acquisition in a foreign language through watching subtitled television programs at home. *Educational Technology Research and Development* 47 (1), 51–60.

Lam, W.S.E. (2000) L2 literacy and the design of the self: A case study of a teenager writing on the internet. *TESOL Quarterly* 34 (3), 457–482.

Lam, W.S.E. (2004) Second language socialization in bilingual chat room: Global and local considerations. *Language Learning and Technology* 8, 4–65.

Lieblich, A., Tuval-Mashiach, R. and Zilber, T. (1998) *Narrative Research: Reading, Analysis and Interpretation*. Thousand Oaks, CA: Sage.

Marsh, J. (ed.) (2005) *Popular Culture, New Media and Digital Literacy in Early Childhood*. London: Routledge.

Meyer, M.A., Kunze, I. and Trautmann, M. (2007) *Schuelerpartizipation im Englischunterricht. Eine empirische Untersuchung in der gymnasialen Oberstufe*. Opladen, Farmington Hills: Verlag Barbara Budrich.

Moffatt, L. and Norton, B. (2005) Popular culture and the reading teacher: A case for feminist pedagogy. *Critical Inquiry in Language Studies: An International Journal* 2 (1), 1–12.

Murray, G. (2008) Pop culture and language learning: Learners' stories informing EFL. *Innovation in Language Learning and Teaching* 2 (1), 2–17.

Norton, B. and Vanderheyden, K. (2004) Comic book culture and second language learners. In B. Norton and K. Toohey (eds) *Critical Pedagogies and Language Learning* (pp. 201–221). Cambridge: Cambridge University Press.

Nunan, D. (2003) The impact of English as a global language on educational policies and practices in the Asia-Pacific Region. *TESOL Quarterly* 37 (4), 589–613.

Pennycook, A. (1998) *English and the Discourse of Colonialism*. London: Routledge.

Schön, D.A. (1987) *Educating the Reflective Practitioner: Toward a New Design for Teaching and Learning in the Professions*. San Francisco, CA: Jossey-Bass.

Chapter 11

Natural Talent, Natural Acquisition and Abroad: Learner Attributions of Agency in Language Learning

STEPHEN RYAN and SARAH MERCER

Introduction

In this chapter, we consider learners' beliefs concerning the roles of talent and the language learning environment, with a particular focus on how learners accommodate images of 'abroad' with classroom learning in their home country. Our discussion revolves around the central issue of how an emphasis on the 'natural' in language learning – either natural aptitude or natural acquisition outside the classroom – may deprive language learners of a sense of agency in classroom settings. If a learner believes successful language learning requires either – or both – natural talent and an extended period of time in a country where the language is spoken, then to what extent is it possible for learners to feel truly agentic about their learning in classroom settings? Our aim is to reflect on how learners' core assumptions may affect their motivation to take responsibility for their learning and their ability to construct an identity as autonomous language learners within different language learning contexts. We discuss these issues with reference to the concept of language learning mindsets (Mercer & Ryan, 2010) and explore how deeply held beliefs about the nature of language learning may, in fact, be disempowering and demotivating some language learners by stressing the primacy of natural acquisition contexts and natural talent over directed effort from the learner.

This chapter is not a research chapter per se, but rather a discussion of ideas that have emerged from ongoing analyses of data obtained from various studies looking at English learners at universities in Japan and Austria. The primary focus of the studies was on issues related to learners' beliefs about the relative roles of talent and effort in language learning, with a further area of inquiry being learners' self-related beliefs. However, a recurring theme apparent across the different data sets was the importance of beliefs about learning a foreign language 'abroad'. Our aim here is to suggest possible directions for future studies, which stem from our consideration of this recurrent theme. The chapter represents our attempt to take up White's (2008: 127) call to 'explore how learners' beliefs assist or constrain them in exercising their agency in particular contexts for language learning and use'.

The data extracts used throughout the chapter are intended to show what has caused us to reflect on this topic and the reasons for our current line of thinking. The data are not intended to serve as the basis for any concrete research-based claims, but rather they should merely serve to illustrate why we consider this line of thinking worthy of further specific research that would empirically explore the ideas proposed and discussed in this chapter.

We begin the chapter by considering the potential implications of learners' beliefs about language learning abroad and the effects of these on their sense of agency. We then outline a theoretical framework that we hope may be helpful in illustrating how learners' beliefs about 'abroad' may be conceptualised in relation to other key beliefs and learning behaviours. We conclude by offering practical pedagogic considerations for incorporating notions of 'abroad' into language learning programmes in a way that enhances learner motivation and agency.

Language Learning and Abroad

> ... there has evolved a popular belief, one shared by students and teachers, parents and administrators, that students who spend a period abroad are those who will ultimately become the most proficient in the use of their language of specialization. Consequently, hundreds of thousands of students depart annually for education abroad experiences with the expectation that they too will "pick up" if not become "fluent" in the target languages they have chosen to study, returning home with greatly enhanced language skills. (Freed, 1998: 31)

In many respects, spending time in a country where the target language is widely spoken represents the ultimate autonomous, independent learning experience (see Amuzie & Winke, 2009; Malcolm, this volume), and it is not our intention to question the veracity of the widespread and often deeply held belief that going abroad represents the optimum language learning experience (for a critical overview, see Ellis, 1994) nor the efficacy of study abroad programmes. In fact, we would agree that for many language learners an extended period of time spent in an environment where the target language is spoken is likely to be a highly effective way to learn the language (Wilkinson, 1998) and positively affect their motivation and interest in the language (Freed, 1995, 1998). However, we would like to hypothesise that strong beliefs in the efficacy of acquisition in naturalistic settings abroad may lead to some learners attributing the learning environment as the true agent of successful learning. A further attendant danger is that such beliefs may lead to the construction of learner identities based on a highly passive role for the learner.

We are particularly keen to explore how assumptions about acquisition processes affect learners' feelings of agency. For many learners, the opportunities to spend time in a country where the target language is spoken are limited, and the majority of their language learning occurs in classrooms in their home country. It may be the case that holding beliefs that emphasise language acquisition in naturalistic settings as opposed to formal, classroom-based learning disempowers learners; learners may defer effort and engagement by looking forward to time spent abroad, which they assume will effortlessly give them improved language skills. In stressing the advantages of an environment that facilitates acquisition without focused learning, learners and educators may be, often inadvertently, devaluing purposeful classroom effort. In this way, classroom instruction is positioned as a second-class, inferior form of language learning.

An emphasis on the acquisition dimension to language learning in a country where the target language is widely spoken may encourage learners to take an overly passive approach to learning while abroad. If learners come to believe that merely being in the country where the language is spoken is sufficient, then there is little incentive for them to approach language learning in an active or strategic manner. In order for learners to act as true agents of their language learning, they need to believe that successful learning occurs through their own efforts and actions; they need to believe that they have the power to determine their own learning outcomes through the application of strategic learning behaviour. As Miller and Ginsberg (1995: 243) point out, learners' beliefs about the nature of language learning can have a considerable impact on their behaviour, particularly in a stay abroad context: 'outside the classroom, during study abroad in particular, it is the learner's views that matter, for they shape the learning opportunities that arise and the learning strategies that will be employed'. Theories of language learning that elevate the role of the learning environment over directed, purposeful effort are unlikely to facilitate an active strategic approach to language learning in a stay abroad context; learners are unlikely to make conscious efforts to learn the language given their belief that such opportunities will occur 'naturally'.

In the next section, we present a theoretical framework that we believe may help to understand how deeply held beliefs about the value of time spent abroad may relate to other beliefs about the role of natural talent in language learning and how both sets of beliefs may affect learners' motivation and actual learning behaviour, particularly in terms of the diminished sense of agency that they may imply.

Language Learning Mindsets

Theoretical foundations

The concept of mindsets derives from the established psychological construct of implicit theories of intelligence (Dweck, 2000; Dweck & Leggett, 1988; Dweck & Molden, 2007; Hong *et al.*, 1999;), which Dweck (2000) employs in her social-cognitive model of motivation. In her more popular work, Dweck (2006) eschews the theoretically precise 'implicit theories' terminology in favour of the more accessible 'mindsets'. In respect to intelligence and learning, people tend to hold certain core assumptions concerning the respective roles of innate talent and effort. Some individuals believe their talents and abilities are fixed, not open to change or development, and by contrast, others may believe that their abilities can be nurtured through hard work or effort (Blackwell *et al.*, 2007). Employing the mindsets nomenclature, the belief that talents and abilities are innate or predetermined becomes a 'fixed' mindset, and the belief that talents and abilities are malleable is known as a 'growth' mindset.

Mindsets are best understood as a framework of core beliefs that operates as a constant backdrop to the construction of 'a larger system of allied beliefs and goals' (Molden & Dweck, 2006: 201). Mindsets connect and influence a range of key variables that 'work together as a motivational self-regulatory system' (Robins & Pals, 2002: 315). The broad consensus in the psychology literature (Blackwell *et al.*, 2007; Good *et al.*, 2003) is that a growth mindset is more conducive to positive academic achievement. Holding a growth mindset enables learners to become more motivated, autonomous and self-regulated by setting more challenging goals, making them more willing to take risks, persist and adapt in the face of difficulties, and approach work or study in a purposeful strategic manner.

The important role played by mindsets has already been established within domains readily associated with natural talent, such as sport and music (Martin, 2008; Ommundsen, 2001). Given the widespread tendency to attribute a prominent role to natural talent in the form of aptitudes in successful language learning (Fisher, 2001; Mori, 1999; Robinson, 2005; Sternberg, 2002), it is somewhat surprising that these ideas have yet to be applied to the field of language learning.

Outlining the framework

In this section, we present some of the key characteristics of language learning mindsets. The framework provided here (Figure 11.1) needs to be qualified with the caveat that this model is not intended to represent a generalisable, abstract model that ignores individual learners and their unique situated contexts (Ushioda, this volume). But rather, we hope that it may facilitate an understanding of potentially related learner beliefs and behaviours.

We need to take great care that we do not slip into over-simplification in the use of our model. Firstly, we do not intend to imply a simplistic, dichotomous relationship between the two mindsets. We prefer to conceive of language learning mindsets as lying on a continuum stretching from fixed to strong growth, with individuals having a tendency towards one mindset or the other, rather than a simple dichotomous division.

A second area of complexity that needs to be kept in mind is that it may not be appropriate to conceive of language learning as a single, monolithic domain. Indeed, it appears as if separate mindsets may occur at the skill level, e.g. learners may hold a relatively fixed mindset about speaking in a foreign language, while tending towards a growth mindset for another skill, such as writing (see Mercer & Ryan, 2010).

Furthermore, it is important to consider the situated and socially constructed nature of an individual's belief systems (Barcelos, 2003). As such, the model should not imply a static, generalisable set of beliefs that an individual would hold in all contexts, but is rather intended as a framework to help facilitate understandings of how learners may conceptualise language learning and their own role in the process.

Finally, it is not intended that the diagram should suggest uniformity across all the belief sets. Indeed, learners may hold seemingly contradictory and ambiguous beliefs within the framework. At this stage of our

Fixed Language Learning Mindset		Growth Language Learning Mindset
CORE BELIEFS ABOUT LANGUAGE LEARNING		
to be a successful language learner requires natural talent	*aptitude for language learning*	anybody can learn a language if they work hard at it
successful language learning occurs naturally	*the nature of language learning*	language learning requires long-term purposeful/strategic effort
languages can be learnt best in countries where the language is widely spoken	*the site of language learning*	language learning can take place anywhere the learner chooses to make the effort
a passive vessel	*the role of the language learner*	an active participant
LANGUAGE LEARNING BEHAVIOUR		
avoid challenges	*approach to challenge*	seek challenges
give up easily	*reaction to setbacks*	persist
regard effort as pointless	*attitudes to effort*	regard effort as rewarding
ignore or avoid negative feedback	*response to feedback*	welcome and learn from feedback
fear errors	*errors*	admit mistakes and work to overcome them
feel threatened by the success of others	*comparisons to other people*	feel inspired by the success of others

Figure 11.1 Core beliefs about language learning (Adapted from Holmes, 2007)

thinking, our immediate purpose is not to examine the exact nature of the relationships between these different behaviours and beliefs – although this is a possible future direction – but simply to outline possible tendencies and consider how these dimensions may be interlinked.

Incorporating abroad

The basic premise underlying the mindset framework is the relationship between beliefs and behaviour; an area that has been extensively discussed within the second language acquisition (SLA) literature (Barcelos, 2003; Benson & Lor, 1999; Cotterall, 1999; Horwitz, 1987; White, 2008). Working from Miller and Ginsberg's (1995) observation that it is not so much the validity of beliefs as their consequences that are of interest, our conceptualisation of language learning mindsets focuses on certain core assumptions that individuals make concerning the role of natural talent in language learning and the possible effects of these on learners' behaviour. However, here we hypothesise that, in addition to beliefs about the role of natural talent, a further unique feature of mindsets in the language learning domain may relate to beliefs about the importance or necessity of time spent in a country where the language is widely spoken and the relative 'naturalness' of the language learning process.

In many respects, a country where the target language is spoken remains a constant background presence in foreign language learning. Learners' evaluations of the value of spending time abroad may undermine strong beliefs in the central role of aptitude, since learners may believe that time spent abroad can compensate for any perceived talent deficit, and it may also weaken their beliefs in the efficacy of effort, as 'natural' acquisition abroad renders purposeful effort redundant. Learners may believe that this naturalistic setting represents the optimum environment in which to effortlessly acquire a language; in extreme cases, this may even extend to a belief that this naturalistic setting is, in fact, the only place where genuine language acquisition can occur and that gains achieved in this 'natural' setting can never be replicated in the language classroom through conscious strategic learning.

Ushioda (2008: 27) argues that, 'Failure to recognize the self as agent in controlling thought and thus motivation can lead learners to become trapped in negative patterns of thinking and self-perceptions, with detrimental consequences for their motivation', and we would concur, pointing out that beliefs which stress the primacy of natural talent and acquisition in naturalistic settings over individual efforts may diminish a sense of individual agency, thus being highly demotivating and negatively affecting approaches to classroom-based instruction. Our concern in this chapter is with the potentially disempowering nature of strong beliefs about the necessity and primacy of a stay abroad in order to learn a language.

Discussion

In order to illustrate our current thinking, we would like to present examples of data obtained from a series of studies exploring the language learning mindsets and self beliefs of English learners in Japan and Austria. However, it is vital to reiterate that we are not presenting conclusions or claims deriving from this research, but simply offering hypotheses and directions for future investigation suggested by our work. Since this chapter represents a series of reflections triggered by our research experiences, rather than a report of a specific programme of research, and given that there is neither the space nor need to describe the individual studies in detail, we will limit our description of the various data to a simple identification of the means of data elicitation – open-ended questionnaire response, semi-structured interview, written narrative, autobiography or interview-based case study – and the focus of the particular study that generated the data, either mindsets or self-beliefs. (For fuller accounts of the data collection and principal findings of these studies see Mercer, 2011; Mercer & Ryan, 2009 and Mercer & Ryan, 2010.)

Learners' beliefs about language learning in a study abroad context were not a consideration at the initial research design stage of any of the studies, yet the saliency of this dimension across all the data sets in both countries has persuaded us to re-evaluate our research and consider a possible link between learners' beliefs about 'naturally acquiring' a language while abroad, the role of natural talent and mindsets. It is this link that we would like to illustrate in this chapter and propose as an area worthy of further focused research.

The role of natural talent

Some of the data suggest that a number of learners may hold strongly 'fixed' mindsets that emphasise the primacy of natural talent, while others seem to display evidence of more 'growth' mindsets, which highlight the importance of hard work and effort:

S: And it's not something you think you can achieve with hard work?
E: No.
S: No. So, you think it's something you just have to have?
E: Yes, and I mean we're all exposed to the same, and if he writes a one[1] and I don't, then something is wrong with me and not with the system. Because why does he understand it and is able to apply the rules. Maybe I do understand but I'm not able to apply the rules

like somebody else. Or maybe I just don't have the ability. Or he can make the logical conclusions, I can't so you know... (Mindsets interview)

I think everyone is able to become a great athlete, musician or even translator. The effort is much more important than anything else, so if you learn or train hard enough, you can do everything. (Mindsets questionnaire)

However, a more typical pattern was for learners to assess the relative importance of innate talent and purposeful effort and fall at some point on a continuum between the two extremes:

I think some kind of talent is a good base on learning a foreign language, but if you try as hard as you can, you'll be able to make it. (Mindsets questionnaire)

Confirming the existence of a strong belief in the role of natural talent in language learning and exploring those beliefs has justified our concern that some language learners may regard the allocation of natural talent as the agent of success, not the active self. However, across the data, another set of beliefs appeared to threaten learners' constructions of the self as the agent of learning. These beliefs related to the perceived need to spend time abroad and the nature of language learning in such a context.

The importance of time abroad

The perception that an extended period of time abroad is essential to successful language learning permeated all the data that were generated across the series of studies. Many participants strongly emphasised a belief in the central role of time spent abroad in developing speaking skills:

And for becoming really good in speaking a language it is absolutely necessary to stay every year a few weeks in a country where the language you want to learn/improve is spoken. (Mindsets questionnaire)

Additionally, learners often appeared to make a distinction between aspects of the language that they feel have to be consciously studied in an explicit, analytical way, in contrast to aspects of the language that they suggest can be acquired through unconscious use, especially while abroad:

I wouldn't call natural ability the capacity to study a language through studying vocabulary and grammar, but rather the ability to acquire a language while staying in the country for some time and being in touch with the locals. (Mindsets narrative)

A key concern emerging from some of the data was that learners appear to believe that formal classroom-based learning can only take you so far and that, at some point, it becomes necessary to go abroad:

Rather than studying grammar forever, it is better to go out to the place where the language is spoken. (Mindsets questionnaire)

It's very difficult to acquire a second language. You really have to go and live in the country and go and speak and write naturally. Of course, grammar and learning how to write is important but I don't think anyone can really acquire a language just doing that. (Mindsets questionnaire)

It is important to stress that we are not challenging the validity of these beliefs, but merely questioning how they may affect approaches to learning. It may be the case that a strong belief in the value of time spent abroad encourages learners to give up when faced with difficulties in their home setting, in the belief that they have outgrown the language classroom and only time abroad can improve their language skills. Rather than reflecting on their learning and developing strategies to overcome challenges, learners may prefer to believe that any difficulties can be overcome by simply going abroad.

An extension of this logic concerns some learners' beliefs that excellence, however they choose to define this, can only be achieved in the context of a stay abroad:

What seems difficult for me right now is to exceed the level I have reached and to oust remaining insecurities. I think the best way to achieve this goal is to study abroad. (Self-beliefs autobiography)

The implication of this is that you can only get so far with conscious classroom learning and formalised instruction, but in order to reach a genuinely high level of proficiency, you need to spend an extended period of time abroad. The following student suggests that even at the end of her academic studies in English at university, she still needs to go abroad to truly 'perfect' her English:

I dream of working somewhere abroad for the first couple of years after graduating from university because I really want to reach a very high level of English before I start teaching at school. (Self-beliefs autobiography)

An unfortunate consequence of such beliefs may be that learners who have developed their language abilities exclusively in their home country feel that these abilities lack legitimacy because they have not been tested or authenticated in the context of a target language country. It also suggests that learners may be setting lower goals in their home country to reflect the perceived lower levels of attainment that they believe can be achieved in this context.

A short cut to success

Another key perception that some learners appear to have about learning the language in a stay abroad context is that progress will occur more rapidly compared with classroom learning in the home country:

> The best thing to do for everybody, who is aiming to learn a foreign language, is spend time abroad. When the language is used and heard every day for some months or years, the learning progress will proceed faster. (Mindsets narrative)

Indeed, although learners may be correct that increased exposure to second language (L2) input will help them to learn the language more quickly, this belief was often coupled with a more worrying belief, namely, that simply 'acquiring' the language naturally and unconsciously in a stay abroad context was an 'easier' way of learning the language, requiring less effort:

> As soon as I was there, as I was spending five months there and just learning without noticing it consciously that I was learning and getting better without really putting obviously hard work into it. (Self-beliefs case study)

There seems to be the idea among certain learners that by going abroad, you simply acquire the language effortlessly without any hard work, that spending time abroad, in effect, represents a short cut to successful language learning. Some learners seem to believe that you simply unconsciously acquire the language without the need for any purposeful behaviour during a stay abroad:

> During Australia, I was just acquiring language like a child. (Mindsets interview)

A strong belief in language learning as a natural process that is best achieved abroad situates the learner as a passive vessel absorbing language rather than as an active agent; if the learner can go abroad to this perceived 'perfect' language learning environment, then learning should occur naturally without the need for any effort or conscious reflection on the part of the learner.

Origins of beliefs about abroad

The contribution of teachers

Worryingly, beliefs about the primacy of effortless language acquisition in a stay abroad context often appeared to stem from and be perpetuated by teachers:

> We were and are always told that the only way to truly sound as native-like as possible is to spend some time in an English-speaking country and I think that's absolutely true. (Self-beliefs autobiography)

Some teachers may be conveying the message, implicitly or explicitly, that the only way to enhance your speaking skills and become fluent or achieve native-like pronunciation, which may be a goal for some learners, is to go abroad for an extended period.

Social comparisons

As is to be expected, learners' beliefs derive from their own experiences and may vary depending on whether the learner has or has not yet been abroad (Amuzie & Winke, 2009; Tanaka & Ellis, 2003):

> But then I have travelled a bit and spent one year as an exchange student in Ireland, where I learned that with producing and speaking a language a lot, people who don't have much talent or were too lazy to study, can also learn it. (Mindsets questionnaire)

A key element of their study abroad experience is the observations they make of other learners and the comments from this particular learner reveal the role of social comparisons in the formation of beliefs about language learning. The comment also illustrates how the availability of abroad as an optional site for language learning affects learners' perceptions of the role of effort and talent through the idea that natural acquisition overcomes any deficits a learner may have in terms of natural talent or effort.

Pedagogic Implications

The pedagogic challenge is how to harness the power of learners' images of abroad in a way that reinforces the role and importance of classroom learning while situating individuals as active agents in their own learning. There is also an accompanying need to address learners' conceptions of natural talent and the relative role it may play in successful language learning to ensure that learners develop a 'growth' mindset.

Although changes to deeply held beliefs do not occur readily, one of the most important and encouraging aspects of the mindset framework is the possibility that learner mindsets may be open to pedagogic intervention (Blackwell *et al.*, 2007). In this next section, we offer suggestions as to how educators may try to raise learners' awareness of mindsets and their effects on approaches to language learning.

Teachers and implicit messages

Our discussions suggest that explicit comments from teachers may serve to promote a belief in the need to spend time abroad in order to become a successful language learner. However, it is possible that language teachers may also be communicating such messages implicitly through their words and actions, such as choice of materials, models and interactions with learners (cf. Marshall & Weinstein, 1984).

One particular area in which teachers need to take care is in the form of praise or encouragement they offer to students (Dweck, 2002; Lam *et al.*, 2008). Teachers need to take care that their attempts to encourage learners do not inadvertently reinforce beliefs about the importance of natural talent, such as by applauding the relative ease or a particular outcome of an individual's learning, or over-emphasise the value of going abroad, such as by expressing admiration for the mere act of having been abroad. Teachers need to focus on praising effort, hard work and a sense of personal progress, thereby promoting a growth mindset in their learners and helping learners to feel agentic about their learning in the classroom context.

Another concern relates to the selection of role models that are – explicitly or implicitly – presented to learners. A familiar figure from language learning mythology is the unsuccessful classroom learner who, after spending a period abroad, suddenly makes a dramatic, even miraculous, improvement: the failed classroom student emerges as a successful natural language learner. It may be a useful strategy for teachers to counter some of the implicit messages contained in such myths through presentations of successful classroom learners who have achieved success through hard work and conscious effort. Teachers could try to incorporate models, through readings and other teaching materials, of excellent language learners who have not spent an extended period abroad, but who have achieved a high level of proficiency; explicit discussions of such materials may help to raise learner awareness of the value and possibilities of the language classroom and the learner's own role in and responsibility for their learning and self-directed behaviours.

Authentication of learning in the home environment

A disheartening implication emerging from our discussion is that learners who study exclusively in their home country may feel that their language learning achievements lack validity; they may see themselves as the second-class citizens of the language classroom and their abilities as somehow inferior to those whose language learning has been authenticated by an extended period overseas. This seems to be highly undesirable as it may demotivate or alienate those learners lacking either the means or opportunity to go abroad. Learners need to see that there are ways of enhancing their linguistic skills in the formalised learning environment, even if they cannot go abroad, and that their abilities, in line with a growth mindset, can be developed within their home study context through conscious, purposeful learning inside and outside the classroom setting. Teachers need to work towards dispelling those debilitating myths that may prevent learners from realising their potential or limit the goals that learners set in the home study environment.

Integration of study abroad

For numerous reasons – often administrative – study abroad programmes are often completely divorced from classroom learning in the home country. In many cases, the institution in the home country simply hands over responsibility for students' language learning to the overseas institution. Similarly, the students themselves may also delegate responsibility for their learning to the overseas context. Although programmes often offer courses on intercultural communication and dealing with cultural differences prior to the sojourn, very little is offered in terms of learner training to help students to consciously harness the language learning opportunities offered by a stay abroad (for a notable exception see Cohen *et al.*, 2005); the expectation seems to be that such preparation is unnecessary since the act of going abroad in itself takes care of the language learning dimension. It would seem desirable to aim for a greater integration of language learning in the home country and study abroad programmes in order to encourage learners to actively seek to enhance their language skills during a stay, thereby making the most of the linguistic opportunities such a stay can offer.

Conclusion

Young people especially are often extremely interested in spending time in another country as it can represent a major life experience, something far more significant than simply learning a language. As educators, we should welcome and encourage this, but we also need to take care not to send the message to our learners that a stay abroad is the only way, or necessarily even the best way to enhance one's language skills. In promoting the value of a sojourn abroad, educators ought to put more emphasis on the role of autonomous, strategic learning behaviour rather than passive acquisition; the agent of successful language learning should be the individual learner not the learning context. We need to empower our learners by helping them to recognise their own agency and support beliefs that indicate the power to learn consciously both in formalised contexts through strategic hard work and effort, as well as during stays abroad through active purposeful behaviour.

Examining learners' beliefs about language learning through the lens of mindset theory has caused us to reflect on how these may affect their behaviour both in more formalised learning contexts and in more naturalistic settings abroad. We have suggested ways in which core beliefs in language learning as an essentially natural process may demotivate or disempower learners. Attributing agency to the learning environment or natural ability rather than purposeful learning behaviour may hinder the construction of autonomous language learner identities. The challenge now remains to research explicitly the ideas put forward in this chapter concerning the nature of learners' mindsets and their effects on an individual's sense of agency, motivation and identity within different language learning contexts.

Note

1. In Austria, students are graded from 1 to 5: 1 = the best grade; 5 = fail.

References

Amuzie, G.L. and Winke, P. (2009) Changes in language learning beliefs as a result of study abroad. *System* 37 (3), 366–379.

Barcelos, A.M. (2003) Researching beliefs about SLA: A critical review. In P. Kalaja and A.M. Barcelos (eds) *Beliefs about SLA: New Research Approaches* (pp. 7–33). Dordrecht: Kluwer.

Benson, P. and Lor, W. (1999) Conceptions of language and language learning. *System* 27 (4), 459–472.

Blackwell, L.S., Trzesniewski, K.H. and Dweck, C.S. (2007) Implicit theories of intelligence predict achievement across an adolescent transition: A longitudinal study and an intervention. *Child Development* 78 (1), 246–263.

Cohen, A.D., Paige, R.M., Shively, R.L., Emert, H. and Hoff, J. (2005) Maximizing study abroad through language and culture strategies: Research on students, study abroad program professionals, and language instructors. Final Report to the International Research and Studies Program, Office of International Education, DOE. Minneapolis, MN: University of Minnesota. On WWW at http://www.tc.umn.edu/ ~ adcohen/documents/2005-Cohen-Paige-Shively-Emert-HoffMAXSAResearchReport.pdf.

Cotterall, S. (1999) Key variables in language learning: What do learners believe about them? *System* 27 (4), 493–513.

Dweck, C.S. (2000) *Self-Theories: Their Role in Motivation, Personality, and Development*. Philadelphia, PA: Psychology Press.

Dweck, C.S. (2002) Messages that motivate: How praise molds students' beliefs, motivation, and performance (in surprising ways). In J. Aronson (ed.) *Improving Academic Achievement: Impact of Psychological Factors on Education* (pp. 39–58). Amsterdam: Academic Press.

Dweck, C.S. (2006) *Mindset: The New Psychology of Success*. New York: Random House.

Dweck, C.S. and Leggett, E.L. (1988) A social-cognitive approach to motivation and personality. *Psychological Review* 95 (2), 256–273.

Dweck, C.S. and Molden, D.C. (2007) Self theories: Their impact on competence motivation and acquisition. In A.J. Elliot and C.S. Dweck (eds) *Handbook of Competence and Motivation* (pp. 122–140). New York: Guilford Press.

Ellis, R. (1994) *The Study of Second Language Acquisition*. Oxford: Oxford University Press.

Fisher, L. (2001) Modern foreign languages recruitment post-16: The pupils' perspective. *Language Learning Journal* 23 (1), 33–40.

Freed, B.F. (1995) Language learning and study abroad. In B.F. Freed (ed.) *Second Language Acquisition in a Study Abroad Context* (pp. 3–33). Amsterdam: John Benjamins.

Freed, B.F. (1998) An overview of research in language learning in a study abroad setting. *Frontiers, The Interdisciplinary Journal of Study Abroad*, 4, 31–60.

Good, C., Aronson, J. and Inzlicht, M. (2003) Improving adolescents' standardized test performance: An intervention to reduce the effects of stereotype threat. *Journal of Applied Developmental Psychology* 24 (6), 645–662.

Hong, Y., Chiu, C., Dweck, C.S., Lin, D.M-S. and Wan, W. (1999) Implicit theories, attributions, and coping: A meaning system approach. *Journal of Personality and Social Psychology* 77 (3), 588–599.

Horwitz, E.K. (1987) Surveying student beliefs about language learning. In A.L. Wenden and J. Robin (eds) *Learner Strategies in Language Learning* (pp. 119–132). London: Prentice Hall.

Lam, S., Yim, P. and Ng, Y. (2008) Is effort praise motivational? The role of beliefs in the effort and ability relationship. *Contemporary Educational Psychology* 33 (4), 694–710.

Martin, A.J. (2008) Motivation and engagement in music and sport: Testing a multidimensional framework in diverse performance settings. *Journal of Personality* 76 (1), 135–170.

Mercer, S. (2011) *Towards an Understanding of Language Learner Self-Concept*. New York: Springer.

Mercer, S. and Ryan, S. (2009) Talented for languages? Describing the mindsets of advanced language learners. In E. Schwarz and S. Mercer (eds) *Das Spiel der Sprachen: Impulse zu einer translationsbezogenen Sprachdidaktik. Working with Language: Insights into Language Teaching for Translators* (pp. 11–31). Graz: ITAT.

Mercer, S. and Ryan, S. (2010) A mindset for EFL: Learners' beliefs about the role of natural talent. *ELT Journal* 64 (4), 436–444.

Marshall, H.H. and Weinstein, R.S. (1984) Classroom factors affecting students' self-evaluations: An interactional model. *Review of Educational Research* 54 (3), 301–325.

Miller, L. and Ginsberg, R.B. (1995) Folklinguistic theories of language learning. In B.F. Freed (ed.) *Second Language Acquisition in a Study Abroad Context* (pp. 293–316). Amsterdam: John Benjamins.

Molden, D.C. and Dweck, C.S. (2006) Finding "meaning" in psychology: A lay theories approach to self-regulation, social perception, and social development. *American Psychologist* 61 (3), 192–203.

Mori, Y. (1999) Epistemological beliefs and language learning beliefs: What do language learners believe about their learning? *Language Learning* 49 (3), 377–415.

Ommundsen, Y. (2001) Students' implicit theories of ability in physical education classes: The influence of motivational aspects of the learning environment. *Learning Environments Research* 4 (2), 139–158.

Robins, R.W. and Pals, J.L. (2002) Implicit self-theories in the academic domain: Implications for goal orientation, attributions, affect, and self-esteem change. *Self and Identity* 1 (4), 313–336.

Robinson, P. (2005) Aptitude and second language acquisition. *Annual Review of Applied Linguistics* 25, 46–73.

Sternberg, R.J. (2002) The theory of successful intelligence and its implications for language-aptitude testing. In P. Robinson (ed.) *Individual Differences and Instructed Language Learning* (pp. 13–44). Amsterdam: John Benjamins.

Tanaka, K. and Ellis, R. (2003) Study-abroad, language proficiency, and learner beliefs about language learning. *JALT Journal* 25 (1), 63–84.

Ushioda, E. (2008) Motivation and good language learners. In C. Griffiths (ed.) *Lessons from Good Language Learners* (pp. 19–34). Cambridge: Cambridge University Press.

White, C. (2008) Beliefs and good language learners. In C. Griffiths (ed.) *Lessons from Good Language Learners* (pp. 121–130). Cambridge: Cambridge University Press.

Wilkinson, S. (1998) Study abroad from the participants' perspective: A challenge to common beliefs. *Foreign Language Annals* 31 (1), 23–39.

Chapter 12

Future Selves, Motivation and Autonomy in Long-Term EFL Learning Trajectories

MARTIN LAMB

Introduction

One area of recent educational theorising in which the concepts of identity, motivation and autonomy intersect is the study of future-oriented components of the self. The basic premise is that 'the selves we strive to become focus motivational attention, guide behaviour, and are an important source of positive self-regard' (Oyserman, 2008: 269). In other words, the self-identity we wish for in the future can be a source of motivation to engage in self-regulated, or autonomous, learning, which will help us achieve that identity. This configuration is of course only one 'take' on these much-studied concepts (there are many other possible sources of motivation besides 'identity', for example), but the tripartite relationship has inspired research in the fields of general education (e.g. Oyserman, 2008) and management (e.g. Boyatzis, 2006), and has begun to be applied to the field of language learning (Dörnyei & Ushioda, 2009). In this chapter, I will present evidence from a longitudinal study of Indonesian adolescents, which indicates the presence of future-oriented components of the self in their motivation to learn English, and is suggestive of a link between this and long-term autonomous learning of the language.

Literature Review

Links between personal identity and second language (L2) motivation have been studied for several decades, being salient in the work of social-psychologists such as Gardner and Lambert (1972) and Giles and Byrne (1982). Based on Tajfel's (1974) social identity theory, these theories proposed that individuals' motivation to learn a particular L2 would be influenced by, for example, their own ethnic identity, how strongly they identified with the L2 community, and the perceived ethnolinguistic vitality of the L2 speaker group. In this body of work, a person's identity was conceived as a stable trait, one shaped largely by birth and the structuring experiences of early life. The emphasis was on what a person had become, rather than on what they might become. It was the advent of poststructuralist views of identity during the 1990s that first introduced notions of future identities to the field of L2 motivation, for example in the work of McKay and Wong (1996) and Norton (2000). In this view '[i]dentities are about negotiating new subject positions at the crossroads of the past, present and future' (Block, 2007: 27); individuals are perceived to be agents in the construction of their own multiple, dynamic identities, and the futures they imagine for themselves are perceived to influence their behaviour. The evidence for this may often be found in the stories they tell; to take two recent examples, Murray (2008) recounts the experiences of a Japanese woman called 'Mable' who derived motivation to learn English from her love of western films and TV programmes and her imagined participation in the world portrayed on screen, while King (2008) attributes the strong investment in English of his Korean informants partly to their efforts to construct gay identities in expatriate communities.

These ethnographic and narrative-based studies have provided colourful portraits of individuals involved in 'identity work' while learning an L2, work that involves making imaginative projections of the future as well as making sense of past and present experiences of learning/using the language in their various communities. However, such studies do not make specific claims about the origins and effects of future-oriented language-related components of the self. This is the aim of new lines of inquiry that have their basis in 'self-psychology' and, in particular, in the notions of 'possible selves' (Markus & Nurius, 1986) and 'self-discrepancy' (Higgins, 1987). Dörnyei's (2009) L2 Motivational Self System proposes that a major part of motivation to learn an L2 is derived from a person's view of their own possible future self, especially where there is a discrepancy between a person's current condition and an 'ideal L2 self'. Dörnyei argues that the power of imagination is crucial in initiating and sustaining self-regulatory (autonomous) learning. By contrast, the 'ought-to L2 self' represents the future identity one feels one *should* have, but because it reflects other people's motives rather than one's own, it is less likely to promote autonomous learning and may instead encourage a focus on avoiding failure. Early empirical work in diverse international settings (e.g. Taguchi *et al.*, 2009; Ryan, 2009; Yashima, 2009), as well as among different age groups (Kormos & Csizér, 2008), is furnishing evidence that the ideal L2 self is an important component of learners' motivation to acquire an L2, and in global contexts where English is mainly conceived of as an international lingua franca rather than as an identity marker of particular Anglophone communities, a better predictor of motivated learning behaviour than the traditional concept of 'integrativeness'.

The causal link to self-regulated learning behaviour is hypothesised, but is not yet established. Indeed, Dörnyei (2009) makes clear that several conditions need to be fulfilled for a strong ideal L2 self to translate into effortful learning. The image of the future needs to be strong and vivid, and for a long-term endeavour like language learning, it has to be sustained through regular and often mundane activity. Referring to the even longer-term enterprise of becoming a British Wimbledon men's champion, tennis player Andy Murray recently commented:

> I've thought about serving for the title – but the closer you get to a grand slam the less you think about it. In the gym is the time I think about those things – to find a reason for putting in the hard work – and when you're going through it on the running track. (Mail Online, 2009)

Moreover, as Dörnyei (2009: 37) explains, for an athlete 'the coach and the training plan are just as much a part of the complete vision as the image [of winning]' and 'virtually all the researchers in the area of possible/ideal selves point out in one way or another, that future self-guides are only effective if they are accompanied by a set of concrete action plans', such as creating proximal subgoals and managing one's time effectively.

There is plenty of agreement, therefore, that the 'future self', 'motivation' and 'autonomy' of language learners are related in interesting and potentially important ways. But, as Ushioda (2009) has pointed out, there are basic ontological differences in the approach taken by researchers to understanding and describing their relationship. On the one hand, there are those, just described, who continue a positivist tradition of uncovering causal relations between key variables, in this case building on findings in self-psychology to identify the key future-related components of the self-concept that contribute to the growth of motivation and, under specified conditions, to self-regulated learning behaviour (the preferred term to 'autonomy'), with the ultimate aim of creating a predictive model of the processes involved. On the other hand, there are those who eschew such ambitions, preferring instead to do justice to the complexity of relations of 'person-in-context' (Ushioda, 2009) by producing holistic descriptions of individual learners over time, usually through analysis of their narrative accounts. For them, the focus is more on 'identity' than the 'self', since the interest is in actual people 'relating the self to the world... through cycles of perception, action and interpretation' (Van Lier, 2007: 58), while motivation may be more appropriately conceived as 'investment' (Norton, 2000) or 'agency' (Sealey & Carter, 2004) to recognise its fluctuating and contingent nature.

The study I present here is in the spirit of the latter approach, in that my aim is to describe the way individual language learners talk about their futures at different points in time, and relate that to their apparent investment in English over the period. But I also use concepts from the former approach, such as ideal L2 self, on the understanding that their precise connotation is still being negotiated in the field and that the study may, therefore, inform the way the constructs are delineated and their operating conditions hypothesised, in future research (Dörnyei, 2009; MacIntyre *et al.*, 2009).

Research Methodology

From 2002 to 2004, I conducted a small-scale, mixed method study of young Indonesians' motivation to learn English during their first two years of junior high school, from ages 11/12 to 13/14, in a Sumatran town I will call Ajeng, a provincial capital of 300,000 people with a rapidly developing local economy based on palm oil and logging industries. The study found high levels of motivation and autonomous learning behaviour among some pupils and I argued that the motivation:

> gained its strength and character from identification processes not with native-speakers of the language but with a future self whose competence in English provided access to academic and professional opportunities as well as to diverse forms of entertainment, to state-of-the-art technology and high status international social networks. (Lamb, 2007: 759)

I also argued that for many learners with middle-class family backgrounds, their state school English lessons appeared to be less significant in sustaining their motivation and effecting progress in the language than private courses and other contextual supports.

In 2008, I returned to Indonesia to track down the same 12 learners who had formed the focal group in the above study. They were originally selected to represent a cross-section of motivational profiles, with eight regarded as highly motivated and four as apparently unmotivated, based on their initial questionnaire responses and on teachers' comments about them. The learners were now aged 17/18 and either in their last year of school (9) or the first year of university (3). Once located, I interviewed them in either Indonesian or English, according to their choice, about their current motivation to learn English, learning experiences in the intervening four years and their hopes for the future. Many of the prompts were similar to those I had given in the three interviews I had conducted with them in the years 2002–2004. I also asked each one to write a short 'language learning history' (LLH), which covered some of the same ground as the interview, but asked them to comment specifically on:

- learning experiences in each institution they had attended;
- positive and negative experiences in the learning of English;
- resources, material or human, which had helped or hindered their learning;
- their plans for future learning of English, if any;
- where they would be in 10 years' time.

All 12 learners were interviewed, and the recordings (average 27 minutes) were fully transcribed. Ten of the learners completed LLHs, written either in English or Indonesian (or a mixture), varying in length from one to four A4 pages.

The main method of data analysis was to compare responses to prompts *across learners* and *across times for individual learners*. These responses were also compared to relevant sections in the written 'histories'. While each individual's learning trajectory was unique, distinct patterns emerged in the way that the two broad groups of learners – those originally identified as 'more' or 'less' motivated – talked about the role of the language in their present and future lives. To exemplify this pattern, while also conveying a sense of individuality, I will present data from four of the learners, two (with pseudonyms Dico, male, and Marlina, female) from the 'more motivated' group and two (Krisna and Widya – both male) from the 'less motivated'.

Results

First of all, I present evidence concerning the proportion of English used in the interviews by the learners, and relate this to their self-reported autonomous learning of English over the four years since I had last seen them. I shall make the case that the gap between those originally identified as more or less motivated learners had in many ways widened during this period. This will be followed by a comparison of the way the two pairs talk about their future and the place of English within it.

Contrasting learning trajectories

At each of the four interviews, the learners were given the choice of using English or Indonesian with me. Considering they had been studying English for at least three hours a week throughout this time, it is not surprising that there was a trend in the interviews towards more use of English, but this was *only* among the eight learners previously identified as 'motivated'. Figure 12.1 shows the number of turns started in English for the four learners described in this chapter. Dico and Marlina used more English in successive interviews, and by 2008 over 90% of their turns started in English, though about a quarter also included some code-switching back to Indonesian. The change for Marlina was the most dramatic and she was also able to sustain her turns in English with minimal code-switching. The upward trajectory of these learners is typical of those originally identified as 'more motivated'. Meanwhile, learners Widya and Krisna used no English in any of their interviews (beyond perfunctory greetings).

Admittedly, counting turns in a single (and singular type of) interaction is a crude measure of L2 proficiency, but the divergence between the two groups is striking. Opportunities to use English with a foreigner in

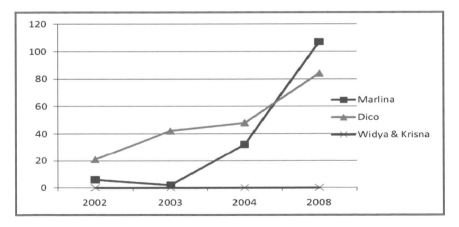

Figure 12.1 Number of utterances begun in English during the four interviews, for four learners

this context are rare, and the increased willingness and capacity of Marlina and Dico to take the opportunity could be seen as evidence of an emerging 'English-mediated identity' (Block, 2007: 144). Conversely, for those who turned down such a rare opportunity it is perhaps even stronger evidence of a lack of such an identity.

Evidence of autonomous learning

From the more successful learners' perspective, the development of their English has been and continues to be a personal struggle, demanding a high level of autonomy and access to relevant resources. Both of them talk with detachment about their learning of English in school, and express a degree of frustration with their experiences there. Fortunately, they have been able to express their agency using learning resources outside school.

Like several of the more motivated learners, Marlina compares her school English lessons unfavourably to her private school (LIA – *Lembaga Indonesia Amerika*):

> because in LIA I have to speak but in school it just about grammar grammar grammar and grammar. [M, 6]

In her younger days, she was much more forthright in her criticism of her English teachers, as well as of her classmates who were poorly motivated and whose unruly behaviour in class disturbed her. In 2008, she appeared to have found a satisfying identity as a relatively expert English user, one who was on good terms with her teacher and was a resource for her floundering classmates:

> in the final exam there is a listening section, I know that my friend cannot get it so when there was "try-out" *kemarin* [yesterday] my friend is told me "M M M, help me I cannot hear what they said I don't know anything" so [I said] "yeah I will help you". [M, 7]

Through all my interviews with her, she related the learning of English primarily to her private course, and she was proud to have now reached 'Higher Intermediate 3' level. Moreover, she is aware of having access to many other resources outside school, notably English-using, internationally minded Indonesian relatives and friends, including the daughter of an Indonesian ambassador currently staying in her house 'who very motivate me to learn English' [M, 11].

Dico was already in the first year of university in Jakarta when I met him in 2008, studying computer science, having been placed in an elite 'acceleration' class early in junior high school. In all his interviews over the six years, he consistently presented himself as a 'lazy' language learner, taking pride in his progress but not deriving particular pleasure from the process. In 2008, he repeated 'I think I'm lazy because when something hard to finish I become lazy but if that was simple I want to finish it' [D, 6]. Despite his professed lethargy, he attended a private course twice a week almost uninterrupted from the age of 11 to 17, and wrote in his LLH, 'I felt the English I got in course better than in school, maybe because in school I prefer to play with my friend than study'. Now he said he learned English incidentally while studying, as he was having to process IT material in English on a daily basis – he disliked using Indonesian language software because 'I feel it's better in English' – and also while rehearsing for his amateur rock band who had decided to sing in English. Perhaps because he was already out of the school system, he had an even more detached view of his school English classes than Marlina. He distinguished between the teachers who had motivated him and those who had not:

> The teachers that... didn't use English outside class... maybe they just think English is just a school subject, not for using, whereas maybe Miss R and Mr B for them English is really a means of communication for the future. [D, 26, part translation]

Marlina and Dico's descriptions were not dissimilar to the other six 'motivated' learners, who all gave a sense of trying to take personal control of their learning and exploiting the nexus of resources that were at their disposal, from variable quality school English classes through private courses to synchronous online chatting. Murphey and Carpenter (2008: 32) point out in relation to their own use of LLHs that 'the act of asking is itself a way of stimulating reflection and scaffolding agency', and on this fourth visit I became aware that participation in my research may have been one factor that contributed to this autonomy. As one learner put it in her LLH, 'it's really interesting when you came to SMP 7, it was my first experience, to see, meet, and speak with the native speaker of English'. On the other hand, my intervention did not seem to have the same beneficial effect on Krisna or Widya, neither of whom had reported much autonomous learning behaviour in my earlier interviews, and were not particularly active learners in their school classes. In 2008, they both quickly indicated a preference for speaking in Indonesian, and while similarly critical of some school practices, neither indicated that they had invested effort in learning English over this period beyond what they were compelled to do for school.

Widya shared the relatively prosperous background of Dico and Marlina and had well-educated parents. In the past, he had studied at the premier private English institute in the town, but in 2008 he was unequivocal about his English:

I: So have your skills in English developed?
W: No, they've got worse [laughs]. No progress.
I: No progress?
W: The problem is, it's all about school now. There are no private lessons outside.[W, 1, transl.]

He says that his parents still encourage him to learn English and that if his school schedule was not so full, 'maybe I'd be sent to a private English course' [W, 15, transl.]. Despite the fact that he is not developing his language skills, he finds school English lessons enjoyable, liking the teacher and materials, and he regards the examination result as 'very, very important' for his future. In his LLH, he reported that 'friends, girlfriend and family' were a source of motivation for him to learn English, but when questioned about this in his interview, he related it again to performance in class quizzes – 'I don't want to be below them, I want to get above them!' He offered no evidence of having tried to learn or use English outside school.

Unlike Widya, Krisna is determined to project a *changed* identity, as somebody who had grown into a serious student of English compared to his younger self, who, in his words, sat at the back of the class and 'didn't really concentrate'.

I've started to like English now because each time I hear it I can hear new words, words which are really er, in my opinion, English sounds... mature, I mean, when you use the words you sound like an adult even though you're still young. [K, 3, transl.]

Although he still only sits in the middle of the class – he is 'not brave enough' to try sitting at the front, where he is much more likely to get nominated by the teacher – and his speaking skills have not developed as he would have wished, he does feel his grammar and vocabulary knowledge has increased, and he was striving to get a high enough score in the school-leaving examination (UAN) to gain entry to his desired university in West Sumatra. He attributes his change to a former girlfriend, who persuaded him of the importance of English and 'always made an effort to push me, so I wasn't afraid'. Nevertheless, apart from increased concentration in school, and occasional use of English in

Karaoke parties, Krisna was not apparently making any other autonomous efforts to learn the language.

It is probably true that a conventional written test of English would have found a smaller gap in language proficiency between the two sets of learners than Figure 12.1 suggests. Nevertheless, I hope to have shown in this section how the stark contrast in their willingness to use the language in the interview is mirrored in their differing levels of investment in the language outside school.

Future self-guides of more autonomous learners

I turn now to what the four learners say about their futures, in their interviews with me and in their LLH. The main evidence about their self-guides comes from those sections of the interview where I ask them where they think they will be in 10 years' time (also a prompt for the LLH); however, I also use data from other parts of the interview where they spontaneously talked about the future (e.g. in response to my question about how important they think English is). As I had used similar prompts in my 2003 and 2004 interviews, it was possible to make a direct comparison of their responses.

Throughout my interviews with her, Marlina consistently stressed the importance of English for her future life. However, there are interesting contrasts in the way she responded to my question about the importance of English, as seen in these extracts:

> 2003
> What's clear is the most important thing is not to forget religion. After that, we have to know English, because according to my mum, who knows what's going to happen in 10 years time, maybe the international language will be English. [M, 24, transl.]
> 2004
> My mother says English is important language, if you cannot to speak English you cannot to live in the... *jaman yang akan datang* [future times]. [M, 4]
> 2008
> For me English is the most powerful language in the world because with English we can go there, everywhere that we want and we can get a lot of information because, in internet for example all the information is in English so to get it we have to know about English and ... English is a must for me. [M, 1]

In her earlier interviews, she frequently invokes her parents' (usually her mother's) support for her views; in the later interview, they are presented as her own views. Moreover, in the earlier interviews the emphasis seems to be on having to prepare oneself for a threatening future, and an awareness of disadvantage if English is not mastered, whereas in 2008, she speaks of what English can enable her to do. Possibly, this signals a diminution of the ought-to L2 self and a strengthening of the ideal L2 self. Her own visions of the future have become much sharper over this period. In 2004, she was quite vague and again cited her mother – 'I'd like to go to university abroad but my Mum don't like it' – whereas in 2008 she spoke of her plans at length; they involved studying in the Communication Faculty at a specific university in Bandung ('[Ajeng] is not qualified to progress my education') then going on to do a master's degree abroad, thereafter earning enough money to pay for her parents to take the Haj.

Studying at a university in Jakarta, Dico has already made good his 2004 prediction that he would leave Ajeng to further his studies. Like Marlina, he was extremely vague about his future in earlier interviews, but by the age of 17 he seemed to have a much sharper vision of the future and the place of English:

> With what I'm studying now, my kind of job will be in the manufacturing and the use of computers, and even for that, if we buy or sell products, we take a risk, we need English because we buy them abroad... What I mean is, to get the precise thing we need, we usually make inquiries about the price with people from overseas, or search on the internet, they use English, rarely Indonesian. [D, 18, part transl.]

In his earlier interviews, as part of his 'lazy boy' persona, he had downplayed the importance of English, whereas in 2008 he is matter-of-fact about its value:

> [I]n my life now, many tasks I do using English. For the example, now I'm a college student, the subject book of the lesson, almost use English, beside that, using technological tools, usually it manuals books use English too (like computer parts). That's some of English uses in my life... I can't guess how useful English in my future, but I swear it is very useful... I think English still be useful in my life now and next day. [D, LLH]

Even more than for Marlina, English is already entwined in the daily life of Dico, and he literally cannot imagine a future without it.

Future self-guides of less autonomous learners

Widya's family background (his father is a Professor of Education) may help explain his early awareness of the value of English to his future. In my very first interview with him, aged 11, I asked him if he had any ambitions and he replied:

> To be good at English, because in the future, according to my parents, globalization is going to happen, western people are going to come to Indonesia and will get involved in every country. [W, 14, transl.]

Six years later, he reiterates the importance of English in almost the same words: 'English is really needed in this globalization era' [W, LLH, transl.]. The tense has changed – globalisation has arrived – but he does not elaborate and, as indicated above, he equates success in English to scoring good marks in school examinations. His immediate ambitions are modest:

> My plan is just to stay in [Ajeng], studying... and if I can, to take a course at the same time, computer course, English course, to advance my career. [W, 21, transl.]

Although at the very end of his interview, he adds that he would like one day to do postgraduate study abroad 'if I can... like my dad did'. He does not say what or where he might study, nor does he ask me if I can procure him a scholarship, like two of the other learners did (half-jokingly). It seems that this is a rather blurry future image, one that owes more to parental advice than his own imagination, and the repeated use of phrases like 'if I can' makes it sound very tentative. Interestingly, he becomes animated about the future when discussing a vision for alternative education. In his LLH, he wrote:

> If I become a success I have a dream to build a home school for poor or special needs children, and what's most important is that the curriculum will use a foreign language, mainly English. [transl.]

He also elaborated on the notion of 'home schooling', which he had heard about on Indonesian TV and read in magazines. His L2 ideals appear to be related to the next generation, rather than to his own future self.

As we have seen, Krisna was eager to assert a change in his orientation to English since I had last met him in 2004, thanks largely to the influence of a former girlfriend. In his 2008 interview, he emphasised the importance of English thus:

Maybe in the future I'll keep studying English because English has a really important role in many areas especially work and also communication. Because now every job has a connection with computers and English. So if I don't master English well then maybe I'll have difficulty doing my job, and also problems in accessing computers. [K, LLH, transl.]

What is interesting to note here is, firstly, the hedging of his intention to 'keep studying English', and secondly, the way he focuses on the dangers of *not* mastering English rather than emphasising the opportunities it brings, as Marlina and Dico do. He does have dreams of his own, but English does not appear to be strongly implicated in them, and he evinces great uncertainty about the future (e.g. repeated uses of 'maybe/perhaps') and a lack of agency (e.g. 'if it's up to me'). In the same rather sad way as Widya, he projects his dreams about English onto the next generation:

I don't really know yet [what I want to do] but if it's up to me, my desire is to become a computer expert in a company, and maybe also, in 10 years time, because perhaps I'll already have children, maybe I'll give some basic lessons in English, so that my children will understand English from the beginning of school, because now it's already the beginning of the global era. [K, 16, transl.]

Discussion and Implications

I will begin the discussion by briefly summarising my findings. On meeting my 12 focal learners again, I found that the gap in their oral proficiency – or at the very least their willingness to demonstrate their proficiency in authentic communication – had widened. The learners originally designated as 'motivated' were all able to sustain extended conversations in English now, whereas those originally designated as 'less motivated' still rejected the opportunity to demonstrate any competence. Although no conclusions can be drawn about how they have developed this proficiency, Dico and Marlina were typical of their motivated peers in continuing to ascribe a subordinate role to their school learning of English, though individual teachers *are* cited as inspirations, and they credited their growing ability to use English to various activities outside school, in which they engaged autonomously (in the sense of having chosen them themselves) and persistently. The learners who declined to speak in English acknowledge the potential importance of English in their lives, but did not claim to have engaged in any sustained effort to learn outside school.

Turning to evidence of the learners' future self-guides, there are noteworthy differences in those of the two groups. For Dico and Marlina, their imagined futures are very different, but each *assumes* competence in English. Both learners' vision of the future have become sharper, as would be expected by their late teens. In Marlina's case, she appears to have taken greater ownership over her imagined future, perhaps signalling a strengthening of her 'ideal' as against her 'ought-to' L2 self. But there is also evidence of consistency in their visions over the six-year period – Marlina's wish to study abroad, and Dico's need to move to Jakarta to continue his education. Apart from English, another element that features in the imagined futures of *all* the motivated learners is a move away from Sumatra, towards the metropolitan cities of Java or beyond. By contrast, the future visions of Widya and Krisna remain vague and tentative. A common feature of their talk about the future is frequent hedging, indicating feelings of uncertainty about what will happen and a lack of personal agency in securing favourable outcomes. Widya and Krisna both now view English as more important than they did in their early teens, and intend to study the language again in the future – but there is still a sense of obligation in their statements as if they are motivated more by fear of failure than a true vision of a future English-speaking self. Indeed, they seem to transfer their own aspirations for English from themselves to the next generation.

Among one pair of learners, then, we have an association between high initial motivation, autonomous learning of the language and increasingly sharp and confident visions of a future English-using self. This association is made more visible through comparison with the other pair of learners in the same context, who showed lower initial motivation to learn the language, a virtual absence of autonomous learning and much less obvious visions of a future English-using self (this pattern of difference is apparent in other individuals in the study too, though space does not allow me to exemplify it here). In this sense, the study offers encouragement to the current research initiatives exploring the links between the self, language identity and motivation to learn an L2 (Dörnyei & Ushioda, 2009). In particular, the study presents individualised descriptions of strong ideal L2 selves in learners who have invested considerable effort in learning English over their teenage years, 'operationalising the vision' (Dörnyei, 2009: 37) through various pathways of autonomous learning. The ideal L2 selves described are very much active users of the language, and because of its negative washback on school

English classes the school leaving examination does not function as a useful proximal subgoal, but instead is regarded more as a frustrating, if necessary, diversion.

As also predicted by the L2 Motivational Self System (Dörnyei, 2009), the ought-to L2 selves exhibited by the other learners appear to have much weaker motivational power over the long term and there is no apparent link with autonomous learning. In fact, they are each more satisfied with state school provision, and place great emphasis on the school leaving examination. It is also clear from the way they talk about the future that although the less successful learners view mastery of English as a valuable goal, they also view it as less likely to be achieved; and this, in turn, may make it less likely to promote self-regulated learning (MacIntyre *et al.*, 2009).

The consistency of the learners' future visions over the six years of contact is also encouraging, in that it argues for an element of coherence even during a period of life known for its experimentation with different identities (Harklau, 2007), and in an academic era when poststructuralist theorising on learner identity emphasises its hybrid and transitory nature (Pavlenko, 2002). What I have observed here among the more successful learners is a sharpening of their visions of themselves as future English users, which in the L2 Motivational Self System model would be predicted to enhance motivation, as 'the more elaborate the possible self in terms of imaginative, visual and other content elements, the more motivational power it is expected to have' (Dörnyei, 2009: 19). Nevertheless, I must concede that I only have insight into learners' identities as *represented* to me in their interviews and LLH – while this is reasonably consistent over the six years, there may well have been fluctuations to which I was not party, and whole other identities to which I had no access and which could conceivably have influenced their learning of English.

The evidence is less clear-cut about when ideal L2 selves may develop and influence motivation. Dörnyei (2009: 38) cites Zentner and Renaud (2007) as claiming that stable ideal-self representations do not emerge before adolescence, and therefore 'the self approach may not be appropriate for pre-secondary students', and Kormos and Csizér (2008) found that Hungarian university students' ideal L2 selves were stronger than secondary school students', whose motivation to learn English was more dependent on their language learning experience. The case of Marlina would seem to support this view. In her earlier interviews at age 11–13, her constant references to her mother indicate that she was more guided by an ought-to L2 self, and she was also much more affected by what was going on in her school (and private course) classroom. By the age of 17, her talk indicates that she has internalised her parents' ideals for her and she talks in a more animated way about opportunities to use English in her private life than about specific learning experiences. On the other hand, Dico appears to have developed an ideal L2 self at an earlier age and no such change is evident here. Clearly, there is a need for larger-scale investigations of the L2 Motivational Self System as it operates in early adolescence, i.e. near the beginning of secondary school.

Finally, this study highlights the potential importance of context, and especially immediate family context, in 'developing' and then 'priming' possible selves (Dörnyei, 2009). The learners who appear to have developed ideal L2 selves are from 'middle-class' backgrounds, in that their parents are educated and their families are relatively prosperous; they also have links with the world beyond Sumatra – i.e. Marlina's parents both got master's degrees abroad, while Dico's father worked in Jakarta and an older brother was at boarding school in Java. Frequent and early parental encouragement, available models of successful Indonesian learners, access to attractive multimedia English texts and paid-for supplementary learning in private courses (with other similarly minded young Indonesians) were all probably instrumental in helping these learners confidently imagine themselves as future users of English; and the denial of these opportunities to learners like Krisna must help explain why they could not so imagine themselves. The case of Widya perhaps warns us against simple deterministic explanations though, for he apparently shared some of the favourable background characteristics of Dico and Marlina. Meanwhile, there are suggestions in the data that I myself may have had a role in 'priming' the ideal L2 self, by giving them these rare opportunities to enact their emergent identities as English speakers. An awkward instance of researcher interference, perhaps, but also a reminder that one of the local school teachers' biggest challenges in such contexts is to supplement their learners' regular diet of L2 knowledge accumulation with activities that 'simulate a desired end-state' (Dörnyei, 2009: 20), i.e. authenticate their possible English-speaking selves through in-class and out-of-class communication. Motivating learners like Krisna, who probably form the vast local majority, may be an even greater challenge though, for it involves generating the very possibility of being a competent, active user of English.

Conclusion

Motivation, autonomy and identity are all important concepts in the study of L2 learning and teaching, and their potential interconnections have often been discussed (see Chapters 1 and 16, this volume). However, there have been surprisingly few attempts to directly address their possible relationships, and one of the reasons for this is that each has its own tradition of inquiry, with its own research methods and distinct ontological perspectives. In this chapter, I have explored the 'future selves' of four Indonesian teenage learners of English, in qualitative data generated over a six-year period, and found links between the growing strength and clarity of these future selves, the emergent L2 identities of the individual learners, their expressed motivation to learn the L2 and their actual level of autonomous learning. In so doing, I hope to have provided some encouragement both to ongoing quantitative research into the relationship between future-oriented components of the self and motivated learning behaviour, and also to complementary qualitative studies that analyse how they play out in actual human beings in specific contexts of learning.

References

Block, D. (2007) *Second Language Identities*. London: Continuum.
Boyatzis, R.E. (2006) An overview of intentional change from a complexity perspective. *Journal of Management Development* 25 (7), 607–623.
Dörnyei, Z. (2009) The L2 Motivational Self System. In Z. Dörnyei and E. Ushioda (eds) *Motivation, Language Identity and the L2 Self* (pp. 9–42). Bristol: Multilingual Matters.
Dörnyei, Z. and Ushioda, E. (2009) *Motivation, Language Identity and the L2 Self*. Bristol: Multilingual Matters.
Gardner, R. and Lambert, W.E. (1972) *Attitudes and Motivation in Second Language Learning*. Rowley, MA: Newbury House.
Giles, H. and Byrne, J. (1982) An intergroup approach to second language acquisition. *Journal of Multicultural and Multilingual Development* 3, 17–40.
Harklau, L. (2007) The adolescent English language learner: Identities lost and found. In J. Cummins and C. Davison (eds) *Handbook of English Language Teaching* (pp. 639–653). Amsterdam: Kluwer Academic.
Higgins, E.T. (1987) Self-discrepancy: A theory relating self and affect. *Psychological Review* 94, 319–340.
King, B.W. (2008) "Being gay guy, that is the advantage": Queer Korean language learning and identity construction. *Journal of Language, Identity and Education* 7 (3), 230–252.
Kormos, J. and Csizér, K. (2008) Age-related differences in the motivation of learning English as a foreign language: Attitudes, selves, and motivated learning behaviour. *Language Learning* 58 (2), 327–355.
Lamb, M. (2007) The impact of school on EFL learning motivation: An Indonesian case-study. *TESOL Quarterly* 41 (4), 757–780.
MacIntyre, P., MacKinnon, S. and Clément, R. (2009) The baby, the bathwater and the future of language learning motivation research. In Z. Dörnyei and

E. Ushioda (eds) *Motivation, Language Identity and the L2 Self* (pp. 43–65). Bristol: Multilingual Matters.

Mail Online (2009) 'Fancy seeing you here: Murray and Nadal come face to face at Wimbledon'. Mail Online, 19th June 2009. On WWW at http://www.dailymail.co.uk/sport/tennis/article-1193779/Fancy-seeing-Murray-Nadal-come-face-face-Wimbledon.html. Accessed 22.10.09.

Markus, H. and Nurius, P. (1986) Possible selves. *American Psychologist* 41 (9), 954–969.

McKay, S.L. and Wong, S.C. (1996) Multiple discourses, multiple identities: Investment and agency in second language learning among Chinese adolescent immigrant students. *Harvard Educational Review* 3, 577–608.

Murphey, T. and Carpenter, C. (2008) The seeds of agency in language learning histories. In P. Kalaja, V. Menezes and A.-M. Barcelos (eds) *Narratives of Learning and Teaching EFL* (pp. 17–34). Basingstoke: Palgrave Macmillan.

Murray, G. (2008) Communities of practice: Stories of Japanese EFL learners. In P. Kalaja, V. Menezes and A.-M. Barcelos (eds) *Narratives of Learning and Teaching EFL* (pp. 128–140). Basingstoke: Palgrave Macmillan.

Norton, B. (2000) *Identity and Language Learning: Social Processes and Educational Practice*. London: Longman.

Oyserman, D. (2008) Possible selves: Identity-based motivation and school success. In H. Marsh, R.G. Craven and D.M. McInerney (eds) *Self-Processes, Learning, and Enabling Human Potential* (pp. 269–288). Charlotte, NC: Information Age.

Pavlenko, A. (2002) Poststructuralist approaches to the study of social factors in L2. In V. Cook (ed.) *Portraits of the L2 User* (pp. 277–302). Clevedon: Multilingual Matters.

Ryan, S. (2009) Self and identity in L2 motivation in Japan: The ideal L2 self and Japanese learners of English. In Z. Dörnyei and E. Ushioda (eds) *Motivation, Language Identity and the L2 Self* (pp. 120–143). Bristol: Multilingual Matters.

Sealey, A. and Carter, B. (2004) *Applied Linguistics as Social Science*. London: Continuum.

Taguchi, T., Magid, M. and Papi, M. (2009) The L2 Motivational Self System among Japanese, Chinese and Iranian learners of English: A comparative study. In Z. Dörnyei and E. Ushioda (eds) *Motivation, Language Identity and the L2 Self* (pp. 66–97). Bristol: Multilingual Matters.

Tajfel, H. (1974) Social identity and intergroup behaviour. *Social Science Information* 13, 65–93.

Ushioda, E. (2009) A person-in-context relational view of emergent motivation, self and identity. In Z. Dörnyei and E. Ushioda (eds) *Motivation, Language Identity and the L2 Self* (pp. 215–228). Bristol: Multilingual Matters.

Van Lier, L. (2007) Action-based teaching, autonomy and identity. *Innovation in Language Learning and Teaching* 1 (1), 46–65.

Yashima, T. (2009) International posture and the ideal L2 self in the Japanese EFL context. In Z. Dörnyei and E. Ushioda (eds) *Motivation, Language Identity and the L2 Self* (pp. 144–163). Bristol: Multilingual Matters.

Zentner, M. and Renaud, O. (2007) Origins of adolescents' ideal self: An intergenerational perspective. *Journal of Personality and Social Psychology* 92 (3), 557–574.

Chapter 13

'Failing' to Achieve Autonomy in English for Medical Purposes

DIANE MALCOLM

Introduction

In the globalized context of greater opportunities and challenges for second language (L2) learning, it has become increasingly relevant for language learning researchers to examine how language learners create identities through exercising their agency outside the immigrant or English as a second language (ESL) settings. The Arab Gulf region is among the many places worldwide where post-secondary medical education is largely delivered through the medium of English, facing medical students with the task of upgrading their English language proficiency as a necessary precursor to academic success. Institutions vary in the amount of support provided for English improvement, and novice learners, underprepared by their secondary school English training for the demands of university level academic study, frequently fail. While, in general, academic failure may be seen as a demotivating factor, in this chapter I will consider how some Arabic-speaking students at a medical university derive from their experience of failure the impetus to exercise greater responsibility for their own English learning; in other words, according to Holec's (1981) classic definition, they exercise their autonomy as learners. The issue of how failure relates to motivation as it develops throughout the academic and life experiences of these students, and how this can be related to the concepts of learner agency and learner autonomy will also be addressed.

Motivation in Language Learning

Integrative or instrumental motivation

The foundations for any discussion of motivation in L2 learning are the terms 'instrumental' and 'integrative' motivation, based on the formulations derived from the seminal research of Gardner and Lambert (1972).

As contrasted with learners who are assumed to have a less sustainable instrumental motivation for a specific aim, such as fulfilling a language requirement at school or qualifying to get a better job, those with integrative motivation, associated with an interest in and desire to identify with members of a community of speakers of the language, were postulated to have better language learning outcomes and greater achievement. These theoretical concepts have had an abiding influence on theories of motivation in language learning, but the 'instrumental/integrative' divide has been criticized for focusing narrowly on language achievement as the most important underlying facet of motivation, while ignoring the other important motivational forces that play a part in a learner's lifelong language learning experiences (Ushioda, 1996). The term 'integrativeness', nevertheless, continues to have an important place in motivation research and theory, although interpreted more broadly than its original conception situated, as it was by Gardner and Lambert, in the particular socio-cultural setting of Anglo-Canadians learning French (Dörnyei & Csizér, 2002; Dörnyei, 2005, 2009; Lamb, 2004). Lamb (2004), for example, discusses the pervasiveness of English as part of the globalization phenomenon, relating motivation to bicultural identity (Arnett, 2002). A bicultural identity includes a local identity, which may be more related to instrumental aims, such as the need to pass school English courses, and a more integrative global one, in which language learners become part of a worldwide, English-dominant culture transmitted through the media and the internet.

Intrinsic or extrinsic motivation

Investigations of L2 learner motivation have also drawn on self-determination theory (SDT), associated with Deci and Ryan (1985), which distinguishes between intrinsic motivation, characterized as 'doing something because it is inherently interesting or enjoyable', i.e. learning for learning's sake, and extrinsic motivation, that which leads to a particular outcome, i.e. has an 'instrumental value' (Ryan & Deci, 2000: 60). According to their taxonomy, extrinsic motivation is made up of four categories, varying in their degree of autonomy, from external (the least autonomous) to integrated, the most autonomous form. In this latter type, 'identified regulations (i.e. when a person has identified the importance of a behavior and taken it on as his own) have been fully assimilated to the self' (Ryan & Deci, 2000: 62). This and the other, more autonomous types of extrinsic motivation, 'represent active, agentic states' (Ryan & Deci, 2000: 55).

Attribution theory and self-efficacy beliefs

In a review of autonomy and motivation, Dickinson (1995) also relates SDT to autonomy, pointing out that increased involvement in their own learning produces greater motivation in language learners, thus increasing the effectiveness of learning. He also discusses the relationship between autonomy and attribution theory, which attempts to link success or failure to stable or unstable internal or external causes. Personal ability is an example of a stable, internal cause, while putting in effort is an unstable internal cause. According to Ushioda (1996: 16), 'the ideal motivational scenario is one in which students attribute positive outcomes to personal ability and negative outcomes to temporary short-comings which can be remedied'. Success leads to greater motivation for students who relate it to factors under their own control, and for those who are focused on their learning goals, i.e. are more intrinsically motivated.

Motivational concepts can also be related to self-efficacy beliefs, which are defined as 'personal judgments of one's capabilities to organize courses of action to attain designated goals' (Bandura, 1977). These beliefs 'provide students with a sense of agency to motivate their learning through use of such self-regulatory processes as goal-setting, self-monitoring, self-evaluation and strategy use' (Zimmerman, 2000: 87).

Process and socio-cultural models of motivation

More recently, Dörnyei (2005) has elaborated a process model of motivation to take into account its fluctuating nature during the lengthy course of language learning. Three stages make up this model, a pre-actional, actional and post-actional stage, also referred to as choice motivation, executive motivation and motivational reflection, which account for how wishes are translated into goals and actions to achieve them, and how the process is evaluated. Dörnyei points out that this model has its limitations, notably neglecting the socio-cultural contribution to motivation, but does attempt to take into account 'the temporal progression of L2 motivation' (Dörnyei, 2005: 88).

Language learning motivation has also recently been related to socio-cultural theory, where learning is seen as a socially mediated phenomenon. As discussed in Ushioda (2007), in the Vygotskyan perspective, motivation to control situations in order to reach particular goals is mediated by others who transmit their knowledge about the goals approved by the culture. She also relates the concept of an 'optimal challenge' (derived from SDT), an undertaking that stretches personal abilities, to Vygotsky's 'zone of proximal development' (ZPD), personal development with the guidance and collaboration of more experienced peers. This scaffolding through the ZPD helps bring about self-regulation of mental processes, creating 'a sense of personal agency in formulating goals and intentions (which) is crucial to the development of the learner's capacity to regulate their own motivation and thus their own learning' (Ushioda, 2007: 22). Lately, Ushioda has presented a 'person-in-context relational view of motivation' (Ushioda, 2009: 215), foregrounding motivation and identity as organic processes co-constructed through social participation (see also this volume).

Investment and agency in learner motivation

With their call for a new (post-structuralist, socio-cultural) interpretation of the 'good language learner', Norton and Toohey (2001: 311) draw attention to the situated nature of language learning, and the need for a 'closer look at the activities, settings and learning that inevitably accompanies social practice'. Furthermore, they relate the notion of a learner's investment in an L2 to the importance of human agency in forming their identity in the contexts in which the language is learned. Much of the situated experience they describe relates to learner histories in immigrant settings, where, it might be argued, the notion of investment carries a higher significance than may be the case in English as a foreign language (EFL) settings.

The term 'agency' has been defined as 'the socio-culturally mediated capacity to act' (Ahearn, 2001: 112). Rather than being an inherent capacity, agency is seen as 'something that a person can achieve...only in transaction with a particular situation' (Biesta & Tedder, 2006: 19) and which can only be understood retroactively. Language learner identity has most recently been bound up with the motivational self-system (Dörnyei, 2005, 2009) and the notion of possible, 'ought to' and ideal selves. According to Dörnyei, if the ideal self, the person the learner would like to become, is a proficient user of the target language, the learner can be described as 'having an integrative disposition' (Dörnyei, 2009: 27). He also points out the need for an 'action plan', or a set of procedural steps that will lead the learner to the ideal self, similar to an elite athlete's training plan.

Autonomy and motivation in foreign-language settings

As discussed in Littlewood (1996), two essential components of autonomy are willingness and ability. Motivation, however defined, is insufficient for a successful learning outcome without opportunity and sustained practice. On the other hand, without clear goals and underlying purpose, it is difficult to keep on track with the often tedious and laborious task of language learning. Thus, motivation underpins both the short-term choices made by learners to enhance their learning and overcome their deficiencies as well as inspiring their vision of future competence.

In foreign language settings, tertiary-level learners may be highly motivated to succeed academically and have specific career goals in mind. However, their progress may be hampered by limited prior exposure to the language of study, inadequate resources and little formal support for their language learning. As a result, they must overcome a host of motivational challenges to their personal, academic and language development. In what follows, I explore the challenges faced by four foreign language learners in relation to the range of motivation theories summarized above.

Rationale for the Present Study

With the socio-cultural turn in language learning, there has been a shift in research focus to aspects of language learning beyond the cognitive-psychological framework that dominated much of the latter half of the 20th century. Within the field of learner autonomy, the focus of inquiry is also shifting away from the identification and classification of discrete manifestations of self-regulated learning, such as the description, categorization and classification of beliefs and strategies, and the concomitant interest in learner training. Palfreyman (2003: 246), for example, calls for more focus on the social networks that support language learning, and research into how personal identity as a language learner develops in the context of social mediation in 'arenas, such as the family, peer-group and educational institution'. Teachers in academic EFL settings who wish to help scaffold learner development can benefit by gaining a greater understanding of the factors beyond the classroom that support and impede a learner's path to autonomous learning. Nevertheless, our view of our students is often shaped by their performance in the immediate classroom setting, their test results and their apparent lack of progress. In this setting, failing students are often characterized as unmotivated, lazy and beyond help, a judgment I have also been guilty of pronouncing. My experience of teaching medical students who struggled to pass English courses, but who later went on to succeed in the upper years, made me wonder how they overcame initial failure and improved their English skills independently to deal with the demands of studying medicine in English. This small-scale exploration is therefore intended to describe how responsibility for language learning develops over time, through different life and study circumstances, and among some who may not initially seem very promising examples of autonomous learners.

Context of the Study

The medical university where I teach English to Year One medical students offers a six-year program leading to the MD degree. All students are Arabic-speaking nationals of Arab Gulf countries, mostly Bahrain, Saudi Arabia and Kuwait. Regardless of initial English proficiency level, students must take the same courses and are required to achieve a minimum grade point average (GPA) in Year One before progressing to the upper years. As this is the first time these Arabic-speaking students have studied academic content in English, those of low proficiency struggle with both English and science courses, failing in one or more of which may result in failing the year.

The specific impetus for this investigation was the response to my asking a former student how he was doing in Year Two. 'I failed', he replied, 'I failed because of English'. What he meant by this intriguing remark did not become clear until several months later when I was able to interview him. I subsequently interviewed three other students who I knew had overcome failure to pass into higher years. Some information about each of these students is given in Table 13.1.

Table 13.1 Some characteristics of students interviewed

Name	Year at time of interview	Year Repeated	Some actions taken to improve English
Ali	Year One	Year One	Has not taken any extra courses
Khalid	Year Three	Year Two	Took an English course abroad during the summer after failing
Omar	Year Three	Year One	Twice took English courses abroad in summer holidays, after Years One and Two
Mubarak	Year Four	Year One	Took an English course abroad after repeating Year One

Note: Pseudonyms have been used and any personal details modified

Each had been my student, two in regular classes meeting six hours a week, and the others in remedial classes that met twice a week. Thus, they were not chosen at random. I was well aware of the difficulties they had faced with English in Year One and curious to know how they had managed them. Semi-structured interviews of approximately 30 minutes duration were conducted in English in my office. Subsequently, their transcripts were examined for recurring themes using qualitative analysis software (NVIVO 8, 2008). All four participants willingly described their experience of failing, how much they attributed it to English proficiency, how they dealt with their English problems and how they felt about their English ability now.

Failing because of English: Beginning Stages of Studying In English

Year One students whose previous schooling was exclusively in Arabic undergo a kind of language shock when they realize that they are responsible for science content delivered in English. In this 'sink or swim' atmosphere, English classes are meant to offer students support for those areas of language use most appropriate for academic study in this particular setting. For stressed students, however, the most important aspect of English courses may be that each has five credits. Getting a good grade in English can compensate for poor grades in other courses with fewer credits. Therefore, some students with low English ability concentrate on English coursework in order to achieve the all important grade. When Khalid said he failed because of English, he meant that he spent his time on English assignments, not on science subjects like biology and chemistry. As a result, he passed English, and he achieved a good enough GPA to go on to Year Two. However, at this stage he realized he could not read English well enough to adapt to the study required in this demanding setting, which led to his failing the year:

> The second year was very bad for me...I can't know what does the writer mean. I was trying to manage. I was trying to read, read a lot. But I didn't success.[1]

The others, who did not pass Year One, attributed their failure to poor English ability in varying degrees. Mubarak stated that about 80% of the reason for his failure was related to English, while for Ali, English was only one of the reasons. Omar acknowledged his difficulties with English from the beginning, but managed to pass one English course. However, he had an overall GPA just below the requirement, so he resented having to repeat Year One.

> I think it's not fair because I thought about I passed from English . . . and there is biology the PG [GPA] is not over 2.3 or something like that.

Motivation in this initial stage appears to be purely instrumental, where getting a good grade is the main incentive to study English, in order to progress to the 'real' medical stage. Nevertheless, the students at this stage experienced inadequacy and confusion linked to their poor language skills. As Mubarak said:

> The first month I feel I'm stupid. I stay in the lecture and I don't understand anything. In school I am the best student but here I feel I'm the bad student. So that make psychological problems.

Khalid experienced frustration at not understanding anything when trying to read, so he stopped:

> When I close the book, I feel like something press on my chest . . . I feel very angry, like, "why I close the book?" I have to read because I want to pass, but . . . .

Ali compared himself to others in the class:

> In the English class I thought that many student was better than me. So that was a problem for me. I have some feelings that I am not so good as they and sometimes I be embarrassing because I couldn't speak like them.

In order to progress in their studies, at this early stage these students had to deal with a variety of emotions and threats to their self-esteem. To handle these new and unsettling feelings, they turned to trusted sources of advice and help.

Sources of help: Mediating agents

When I asked Omar whether his difficulties with English made him want to give up, he said:

> Uh, no. This I think, I have my friend he like me. He failed in first year and I saw him later and he are improved. And I told myself, 'why I don't speak English well?

Mubarak depended on his family's advice:

I don't have experience at that time. [I spoke] with my family. They said, "you must try." And "the life is ... experience. You can't decide at first without experience... You must take experience to know".

Khalid also had the example and support of a family member:

[I didn't give up] Because I think my family is looking at me. And my relative, he's now in sixth year. He was looking at me and he said, "Work hard, you will do it." ... I didn't tell anybody the problem was English. Just I told myself it's English and I have to work hard.

In the socio-cultural view of language learning, the Vygotskyian concept of mediation is a crucial one (Donato & McCormick, 1994). As the realization grew that they had to take steps to improve their English ability, these failing students reached out to the more experienced sources, or mediators, in their immediate setting: family members and friends. Khalid asked his older, more experienced relative for advice, as well as his best friend, and they responded by giving him books that they had used when studying English abroad. Mubarak also got advice from a brother who had studied in the UK, while Omar's father pushed him to improve:

My father, he graduated from United States, he lived there for about seven years. He speak English. He want me to speak English like him before I came to this uni. But I don't have the reason to speak. When I came here now there is the reason. I should if I want the MD to speak, I should do everything to improve...to get the MD.

Ali also had a relative of the same age who studied medicine in a different college:

And sometimes we talk about the object [subjects] that we have. And he's take courses in English more than me, but I think there is no different in us, because he's understand me and I understand him and we try to improve our English.

With the encouragement and mentoring provided by supportive individuals who had faced and overcome similar problems, the students were able to make plans to improve their English and regain their confidence.

Steps to Becoming Autonomous English Learners

As time went by, each student took specific steps to improve his English. For example, Ali took advantage of a library near his house to set up a reading plan:

Near my house there is a library and they have newspapers in English and I try to read the headings and if the headline has something that I like to read, I try to read the object [subject]. Always sports.

He also tried to read some old medical books that he had collected from a secretary in the medical faculty. Mubarak made textbook reading a daily action, and read signs written in both Arabic and English to increase his vocabulary as well as reading skills:

Because I take a long time to read in English every day I read... I read everything. Any words written in Arabic and English, I read the English and the Arabic. In [the hospital] "outpatient" /kharijia/, "clinic", I try to understand.

Khalid, who had failed because of his difficulties with reading, read children's books, even though he felt embarrassed at what he did:

I took some books, small stories and I just read. I didn't tell anyone, because I thought someone would make a joke or something, because these kind of books seemed to be silly. It's for children, 30 or 40 pages.

Perhaps because of his resentment at having to repeat the year, Omar took longer to put into action a plan to improve his reading for the upcoming medical phase:

In about ...second semester I told myself I should to read. I should to improve myself or I will face bigger problem in the second year.... Then I start to study. I bought some books about grammar...but not too much. I don't spend all my time. I will liar if I told you this. I bought some books, grammar and vocab.

Study Abroad

Although all these students took steps to improve their English reading, probably the most important skill for academic study, they also felt a need to improve their listening and speaking skills. As opportunities to speak English are limited in the immediate Gulf context, especially in Saudi Arabia, the home country of three of the students, they all took summer courses in different English-speaking countries. For example, after repeating and passing first year, Mubarak realized:

Still I have problems with talking, because you know I not discuss with native speakers of English. I deal with Arab... So I tried to improve my speaking skills by travel one month and half just to take time with native speakers of English and to talk with them, to improve my speaking skills.

At the time of our interview, several years after his study abroad, he struggled to find the English words to express himself, and regretted how he had lost the ability to speak spontaneously, as he had been able to after his summer course. This he put down to 'the long time dealing with Arabs' in his home and school setting:

That affect me, because now I talk with you I must remember some words and I put it and like that. But after one month [abroad] I spontaneously I speak.

When Khalid came back from his summer abroad, he noticed:

There is a big change. Maybe the words doesn't change. I know a lot of words, vocab. [before going abroad]. But the grammar and talking, speech. It's now I think I'm better than before.

Omar appeared to have the most life-changing experience in his study abroad, through improving his speaking confidence by talking to the host father about the culture in his country, as well as with Mexican students in his class:

I learn from them a lot. Especially the Mexican I search about the word to speak with them. I want to explain to them what I want. So it's good for me.

However, the positive effects of this experience wore off quickly when he returned to the academic environment of medical school:

When I came back really I was interested in a lot of thing, in tv, movies, really I don't want subtitle. I was interested the first two weeks, then I feel bored, oh I feel bored. Atmosphere is different, in every country is different. Here in uni. just study, study, study. They don't think about sport, they don't think about anything. So I don't push myself hard to learn English when I came back.

He also resented having to repeat the year because of missing out on the needed GPA by so little, and felt that he was wasting his time. Nevertheless, his first trip abroad spurred an interest in traveling, and Omar gained the confidence to make all the arrangements by himself, in

English, for another study abroad session the following summer. Since then, he has also traveled around Europe, and uses his English everywhere. As he put it:

> I feel confident, I have self-esteem now. I go anywhere, I can speak with anyone.

Amuzie and Winke (2009) found that study abroad experiences led to the development of greater independence in language learning and brought about a belief that improvement depended more on the learner's own efforts than the teacher's efforts. Similarly, while the language gains noted by the students in the present study might not have been great, their experiences abroad also appeared to contribute greatly to their growing sense of responsibility for improving their own English and the conviction that they could find ways to do so.

Evaluation of Progress in English

Being autonomous implies having the ability to monitor and evaluate learning strategies and experiences, in order to plan future efforts. While these learners all feel they have benefitted from the steps taken so far, they have a realistic assessment of the current state of their English skills. For example, Mubarak is now convinced of his ability to study medicine in English:

> Reading I improved, and it's every year better than before. Listening also. For my study I am good. I don't have any problem.

Nevertheless, he does not feel confident about dealing with any situation in English, particularly in speaking. He explains why he needs to improve his speaking skills in English both for future goals and current needs:

> You can't as a doctor improve yourself without English. You must deal with books and patients in English. So from that I think I have to improve my language. I must improve my speaking skill to deal with doctors, students, in lectures, demonstrations, and in professional skills. I have to deal with English speakers.

Omar is confident that he can use English in all settings, but he also feels a need to improve his speaking, as he has no chance to improve it except when he travels. However, he has noticed that he now takes a more active role in his learning:

Now everything I don't understand it, I ask about it. Especially the word on the street or... shop. What's this word? It's strange for me.

His reading for medical study has improved to the point where, he states:

I don't have dictionary now, just [a medical dictionary] for meaning in English. I don't translate any word from Arabic. Maybe some word is strange or I don't know what's mean, I understand it from the sentence.

Ali, who was still in first year at the time of the interview, assessed himself as 'better than before'. He still sometimes felt shy and embarrassed in class, but 'I work to improve this shy-ing'. Although he did not go abroad to study, he found ways locally to overcome his hesitancy about using English. His relative advised him to:

do things in English more than Arabic...speak English in everywhere, in supermarket, or with the seller man, or when you order some meal from anywhere.

He found this difficult, however:

Sometimes I see children talk to the seller man in English and I feel shy for myself because they are better than me. Not because I don't know English, but how to talk to him.

Of the four, Omar is the only one who said he was actively looking for a way to improve his English skills in future:

I still need to improve my English but I face problem, I don't know how to. I always travel but there is no [course] specially [for medical purposes] for just tourist. But I think after MD, after I graduate, I think if I take specialized, there, resident in US or Canada, I think I will improve. So much.

His remarks make it clear that he associates English proficiency with advancement in the medical profession. When asked if he thought it was important for a medical student in the Gulf to speak English, since most of his patients would be Arabic speakers he replied:

I'm not talk about [how to deal with] patients. I'm talk about how to get the professor or specialized without English. If I'm not good, how? It's something that come with doctor I think.

Ali, still in first year, sees a more restricted purpose for English for future doctors:

> Sometimes you have patients who don't speak Arabic. So you have to talk to them in English. I think it is not necessary to know everything in English, just the easiest or just the English to communicate with others.

Discussion

In this section, the actions taken by these initially unsuccessful learners are related to the motivational theories discussed above. Clearly, their two identities of English language learner and medical student are intertwined, more intimately at some times than others. In Year One, they concentrated on English as a school subject to be passed at all costs, leading some to concentrate on the English course while neglecting other courses. The growing realization that competence in English was vital to future success both in upper years and in their professional future spurred these students to actively seek out ways to compensate for and upgrade their language deficiencies. In accordance with the Vygotskyan concept of scaffolding, their subsequent actions were initially mediated by advice and assistance from more experienced student peers, friends and family members. Study abroad experiences acted as 'optimal challenges' (Ushioda, 2007), stretching them to improve their speaking ability and bolstering their confidence in using English. The steps that they have taken so far seem to define them as autonomous learners: they have identified their needs, sought out ways to improve, regulate and evaluate their language learning. All are also motivated by their future visions of the 'ideal L2 self' (Dörnyei, 2009), competent medical doctors whose facility with English is an essential element of their professional makeup. In SDT terms, they appear to have moved towards the more autonomous end of the extrinsically motivated continuum, *identified regulation*, in which learners see the usefulness and value of learning (Ryan & Deci, 2000). Only Omar displays some evidence of integrative motivation in the original sense proposed by Gardner and Lambert, i.e. interest in learning a language to identify with members of its community:

> I want to learn Spanish . . . because I like Spanish, I like their talking, their language. I think there is something interesting in their language. Spanish it's good. There are beautiful girls there.

Omar also has a more realistic assessment of his abilities and competence than he did on entering the university. Although he acknowledges that he is more mature than when he began, he also said that he was not very mature yet:

> Because nobody told himself, "I'm very mature." There is [always] something to learn, something to know about the life.

He thinks his English ability has improved, but 'not too much', and laments the loss of the fluency that he experienced after returning from his stimulating, language-enhancing summer abroad. While he, like Mubarak, regrets his lost spontaneity in using English, both readily attribute the cause to their current life circumstances, where English is rarely used in the immediate context except for study purposes.

These students also preserve their self-esteem by attributing their failures, in part, to external factors (as discussed in Dickinson, 1995), while acknowledging the role of personal effort and maturity (i.e. self-efficacy beliefs, as elaborated by Zimmermann, 2000). For example, Mubarak lays the blame for student failure on the medical college not providing enough English language training for underprepared students in Year One.

> A lot of students [have] problems, just in this university. Students coming here have good scores in their [high school]. The majority are so good. From this, we know the mistake in the system.

The feelings of inadequacy, confusion and resentment expressed by these students as they make the transition from studying in Arabic-medium high schools to an English-medium medical college are common to many Year One students, not only those who fail. Undoubtedly, the immense cultural prestige invested in becoming a doctor in the Gulf cultural setting, as well as family pride and expectations help these students to persist through the many setbacks they face. The counter-balancing effect of a positive possible self, the future doctor, with the feared self (Oyserman & Markus, 1990), a medical school failure, also adds to the impetus to succeed. However, the consequences of failure in this high-stakes setting add to the pressures on each individual. Contrary to teachers' initial impressions, failing students in this setting are far from unmotivated and passive. With the scaffolding of experienced others, establishing plans of action and persisting in their efforts, they are able to progress towards their life goal of English-competent future medical professionals.

Conclusion

The present study is intended as a preliminary and exploratory description of a few individuals' responses to academic failure, attributed at least in part to deficiencies in English language ability. From shaky beginnings, these learners have exercised their agency to overcome this obstacle on the way to their desired future identity. Failing may have served as a 'wake-up call', making these students recognize the importance of English for their academic success, and forcing them to find ways to improve. For their teachers, it may be heartening to consider that failure may not mark the end of the road for some students, but rather act as a spur that sets them on the path to becoming more autonomous and successful learners. For those interested in learner development, these students' accounts may serve to underline the importance of taking a long-term perspective on motivation, agency and autonomy as they relate to language learning.

Note

1. Extracts from the interviews are transcribed as they were spoken by participants, including their grammatical inaccuracies in English.

References

Ahearn, L.M. (2001) Language and agency. *Annual Review of Anthropology* 30, 109–137.

Amuzie, G.L. and Winke, P. (2009) Changes in language learning beliefs as a result of studying abroad. *System* 37 (3), 366–379.

Arnett, J.J. (2002) The psychology of globalization. *American Psychologist* 57 (10), 774–783.

Bandura, A. (1977) Self-efficacy: Toward a unifying theory of behavioral change. *Psychological Review* 84, 191–215.

Biesta, G. and Tedder, M. (2006) How is agency possible? Towards an ecological understanding of agency-as-achievement. *Working Paper 5, Learning Lives: Learning, Development and Agency in the Life Course*. University of Exeter: Teaching and Learning Research Programme. On WWW at http://www.tlrp.org/project%20sites/LearningLives/papers/working_papers/Working_paper_5_Exeter_Feb_06.pdf. Accessed 17.7.08.

Deci, E.L. and Ryan, R.M. (1985) *Intrinsic Motivation and Self-determination in Human Behavior*. New York: Plenum.

Dickinson, L. (1995) Autonomy and motivation: A literature review. *System* 23 (2), 165–174.

Donato, R. and McCormick, D. (1994) A sociocultural perspective on language learning strategies: The role of mediation. *The Modern Language Journal* 78 (4), 453–464.

Dörnyei, Z. (2005) *The Psychology of the Language Learner: Individual Differences in Second Language Acquisition*. Mahwah, NJ: Lawrence Erlbaum.

Dörnyei, Z. (2009) The L2 motivational self system. In Z. Dörnyei and E. Ushioda (eds) *Motivation, Language Identity and the L2 Self* (pp. 9–42). Bristol: Multilingual Matters.

Dörnyei, Z. and Csizér, K. (2002) Some dynamics of language attitudes and motivation: Results of a longitudinal nationwide survey. *Applied Linguistics* 23 (4), 421–462.

Gardner, R.C. and Lambert, W.E. (1972) *Attitudes and Motivation in Second Language Learning*. Rowley, MA: Newbury House.

Holec, H. (1981) *Autonomy in Foreign Language Learning*. Oxford: Pergamon.

Lamb, M. (2004) Integrative motivation in a globalizing world. *System* 32 (1), 3–19.

Littlewood, W. (1996) "Autonomy": An anatomy and a framework. *System* 24 (4), 427–435.

Norton, B. and Toohey, K. (2001) Changing perspectives on good language learners. *TESOL Quarterly* 35 (2), 307–322.

Oyserman, D. and Marcus, H.R. (1990) Possible selves and delinquency. *Journal of Personality and Social Psychology* 59 (1), 112–125.

Palfreyman, D. (2003) Expanding the discourse on learner development: A reply to Anita Wenden. *Applied Linguistics* 24, 243–248.

QSR International Pty Ltd. (2008) NVivo 8, Qualitative research software.

Ryan, R.M. and Deci, E.L. (2000) Intrinsic and extrinsic motivations: Classic definitions and new directions. *Contemporary Educational Psychology* 25, 54–67.

Ushioda, E. (1996) *Learner Autonomy 5: The Role of Motivation*. Dublin: Authentik.

Ushioda, E. (2007) Motivation, autonomy and sociocultural theory. In P. Benson (ed.) *Learner Autonomy 8: Teacher and Learner Perspectives* (pp. 5–24). Dublin: Authentik.

Ushioda, E. (2009) A person-in-context relational view of emergent motivation, self and identity. In Z. Dörnyei and E. Ushioda (eds) *Motivation, Language Identity and the L2 Self* (pp. 215–228). Bristol: Multilingual Matters.

Zimmermann, B.J. (2000) Self-efficacy: An essential motive to learn. *Contemporary Educational Psychology* 25, 82–91.

Chapter 14

Crucial but Neglected: English as a Foreign Language Teachers' Perspectives on Learner Motivation

NEIL COWIE and KEIKO SAKUI

Introduction

Motivation to learn a second language (L2) has long been a focus of research in second language acquisition (SLA) and sophisticated models of motivation have been developed. These models include various social, psychological, contextual and temporal aspects. However, the perspectives of language teachers on learner motivation have played little role in motivation theory. This is unfortunate because teachers can have a strong influence on their learners and what they believe motivates students is worthy of investigation. This chapter examines the perceptions that experienced English as a foreign language (EFL) teachers in Japanese universities hold about learner motivation. It highlights strategies that the teachers use to motivate students, discusses views that the teachers have on learner identity and autonomy in relation to motivation, and suggests implications for both classroom practice and motivation research.

Motivation Research

The nature of language learner motivation has been extensively investigated for a considerable period of time. The concept is a complex one that has been conceptualised through a variety of approaches: social psychological (Gardner & Lambert, 1972; Gardner, 1985), cognitive situated (Crookes & Schmidt, 1991; Dörnyei, 2005; Ushioda, 2003; Williams & Burden, 1997) and process (Dörnyei & Otto, 1998). These approaches have measured and defined a number of factors that have contributed to ever more sophisticated models of learner motivation.

These models describe general motivational orientations, such as integrative, instrumental, intrinsic and extrinsic; or, they include psychological variables such as self-efficacy, attribution or expectancy. Recent research has added a more political dimension to the motivational debate, including Norton's (2000) feminist and post-structuralist approach putting forward the alternative concepts of investment and identity. These ideas are appealing to many researchers seeking to reconcile large-scale group surveys with a more individual examination of learner motivation. Dörnyei (2005, 2009) acknowledges the potential of Norton's approach and links it with his own most recent theory of motivation – the L2 Motivational Self System and the three associated constructs of ideal L2 self, ought-to L2 self and L2 learning experience.

These studies on motivation as a collective have attempted to answer *why* students are motivated to learn; however, there are relatively few that have investigated *how* and to what extent learners can be motivated to learn in classrooms. The classroom realities are that many learners are reluctant to study a foreign language and are not necessarily motivated to learn (Brophy, 2004; Sakui & Cowie, 2008); a limiting factor that is not fully addressed in the motivation literature. Woods (1996) argues that in applied linguistics, initial studies focused on pedagogy, then on learners and, finally, on teacher cognition. We can detect a parallel picture in motivation studies in which relatively few studies are available on the topic from language teacher perspectives; that is, studies of how teachers understand learner motivation and how they try to influence it in order to facilitate the language learning process.

Two studies that have addressed these *how* questions are provided by Dörnyei and his co-researchers, who carried out large-scale surveys of language teacher practices in specific cultural contexts. In a study of Hungarian EFL teachers, Dörnyei and Czisér (1998) aimed to empirically verify which of a list of intuitive strategies would be seen as most useful by teachers and to link it with a three-part framework of motivation (language, learner and learning situation level). The chosen strategies, called 'Ten Commandments', include the following examples: 'create a good atmosphere and personal relationships', 'familiarise learners with the target culture' and 'promote learner autonomy'. In a second major study, Guilloteaux and Dörnyei (2008) researched teacher motivational practices in South Korean schools by examining the link between teachers' motivational practice and student behaviour. The researchers demonstrated a correlation between teachers' overall strategy use and students' levels of motivation

One common feature of both studies was their conclusion that further research is needed in other settings to verify if the suggested strategies are culturally transferable. A second common feature is that both studies made an explicit attempt to link motivation theory and classroom practice. However, these theories were predetermined by the motivation researchers themselves, who wanted to estimate how far teachers' practices fitted with theory. What was not examined was the teachers' own perspectives on motivational theories and how these can influence their pedagogy. Borg (2006: 40) claims that 'teacher cognition research has affirmed the active role which teachers play in shaping classroom events and highlighted the complex nature of classroom decision-making'. If we are to take this claim seriously, it is essential to investigate further how teachers understand and respond to learner motivation, in particular to find what links there might be between motivation theories and pedagogical practice. With this in mind, two research questions have guided this study:

(1)   How do classroom EFL teachers understand learner motivation?
(2)   What motivational strategies do teachers employ?

Participants and Research Context

In order to gain an understanding of teacher cognition and strategies in a culturally and socio-politically specific context, it was decided to focus on teaching in Japan. Thirty-two EFL teachers working in Japanese universities responded to an e-mail survey conducted in early 2009. The survey asked for basic data regarding age, gender, qualifications and teaching context. It then asked open-ended questions reflecting the two research questions above. After an analysis of the e-mail responses, three teachers (David, Alan and Noriko) who gave particularly thorough replies were each interviewed for a more in-depth examination of their perspectives.

Table 14.1 and 14.2 summarise the salient features of the respondents. The teachers were from six different countries: USA (9), UK (8), Japan (7), Canada (4), Australia (3) and China (1). The average age of the 14 women and 18 men was 45.96. As can be seen from the tables, the teachers were experienced and highly educated. Twenty-one of the teachers (68.8%) had more than 10 years experience of university teaching. This figure actually underestimates the total amount of English language teaching (ELT) experience that the teachers had, as very few would have started their teaching career working at the university level. Twenty-five teachers (78%) had ELT master's degrees and seven had a doctoral

Table 14.1 Respondent teaching experience

Years of experience at university level	n	%
Less than 5 years	5	15.6
5–10 years	5	15.6
11–15 years	13	40.6
Over 15 years	9	28.2
Total	32	100.0

Table 14.2 Respondent qualifications

Highest qualification	n	%
Master's in ELT	25	78
PhD/EdD in ELT	7	22
Total	32	100.0

qualification (22%). It was assumed that these were the kinds of teachers who, in theory, would have had some level of exposure to SLA and motivation theories.

Japanese university teaching context

Eighteen of the teachers were full-time and 14 were part-time teachers working at different universities. Almost all the teachers (27) taught 'general English' classes, reflecting the nearly universal requirement in Japan for such classes for first-year university students. The next most common types of classes were academic writing (16), English for special purposes (ESP) (13) and examination preparation (7). The number of students that each teacher taught ranged from 5 to 50; the average class size was 28.09. Such classes may be streamed according to some kind of placement test, but they may also contain students with a wide range of ability levels and attitudes towards English learning.

Data analysis

The e-mail survey responses and interview transcripts were analysed separately by the two authors; each analysis was then compared and a composite interpretation produced. Using a qualitative approach, teacher responses were coded into common topics and then abstracted into overall categories to be used as the basis of interpretation (Richards & Morse, 2007). The frequency of categories was noted, but interesting outlier responses were also included. In the following results, quotations from participants are coded with a number from 1 to 32 (which was assigned to each participant in order to protect their anonymity), their nationality, gender and highest qualification.

Results

Results are divided into two sections reflecting the two research questions. The first section presents how the teachers understand motivation in terms of how familiar they are with common motivation concepts and what kinds of definitions of motivation they gave. The second section describes teacher strategies to enhance student motivation.

Teachers' understandings of motivation

Examples of references in the e-mail survey to L2 motivation concepts were examined to find out to what extent the respondents were familiar with research, and to what extent these concepts guided their understanding of learner motivation. It is important to note that our original survey questions did not directly refer to or ask about motivation research. This is for two reasons: firstly, we wanted to give teachers as much freedom as possible to describe their thoughts and strategies on learner motivation. Secondly, we did not want to scare some teachers away by asking about specific aspects of motivation theories. Therefore, the data described here emerged naturally from the teachers' voices and linguistic repertoire.

Some of the teachers explained that they had read about motivation theory and some had even carried out research on motivation: 'I've just done a dissertation on teacher motivation, and realised that motivation was not at all the simple thing that we think it is' (T17: British, M, EdD). Some teachers referred to well-known researchers and studies:

> Unlike Gardner, I include desire to learn without relevant behaviour as motivation. (T8: Australian, M, PhD)

> I have read Zoltan's [Dörnyei] and Ema's [Ushioda] books and chapters, and any articles my friend sends me on motivation. (T15: American, F, Master's)

The three interviews with David, Alan and Noriko echo this tendency of participants to be familiar with motivation research at some level:

> Alan: I don't remember [regarding his master's program] a lot of hard science involved in it, there was some issues of psychology I think. But nearly everything was dealing with whether motivation was intrinsic or extrinsic, that I recall reading about and of course everyone wants intrinsically motivated students but that's not always possible.

A further way to explore what familiarity teachers have with motivation theories is to identify the kinds of jargon that they use. Table 14.3 shows the five most common terms that the teachers used, which are found in the motivation literature: goal, intrinsic, extrinsic, desire and attitude. In the left column is a count of how often the terms were used by the teachers and on the right side is an example of the term in context. This is some evidence of the impact of motivational theory on teacher understanding of learner motivation.

Table 14.3 Common motivation terms used by respondents in the e-mail survey

Term and frequency	Example
Goal – 24	Promoting an awareness of the value of a learning goal. (T7: American, M, Master's)
Intrinsic – 8	The intellectual, emotional, or psychological impetus to learn more about something. I suppose it can be extrinsic or intrinsic, but I personally feel that real "motivation" comes from inside. (T13: American, M, Master's)
Extrinsic – 8	I have had the pleasure of reading quite a bit about motivation, and while there is no end to definitions being offered, it basically is divided into two basic: intrinsic and extrinsic motivation. (T26: Canadian, M, Master's)
Desire – 7	Learner motivation means learners coming to class with a desire for improving their English abilities in ways relative to their own objectives. (T1: British, M, Master's)
Attitude – 6	I see learner motivation as a positive attitude that a learner has toward learning. (T3: British, F, PhD)

As well as these five terms, teachers used other motivational terms to a lesser extent; e.g. drive (5), instrumental (5), autonomy (2), flow (2) and integrative (1).

Having described how familiar the teachers are with motivation concepts we would now like to show how they defined learner motivation. Only three of the teachers (9.4%) expressed any doubts that they could define learner motivation: 'The more I read... the less I feel I understand motivation' (T15: American, F, Master's). Overall, it seems clear that most teachers were confident that they knew what learner motivation is and could articulate a definition of the concept:

> Students feeling an internal drive to acquire knowledge. (T7: American, M, Master's)

> I think learner motivation is a kind of desire, hope, need or interest to learn English. (T18: Chinese, F, Master's)

A further examination of the data suggests that a majority of these teachers reported that students' motivational behaviours were an important part of their definition of learner motivation:

> Learner motivation is the desire, duration and effort students invest in learning English. For me as a teacher, this means when tasks are given to students, how much, how long, and how hard they are on-task as opposed to off-task. (T6: British, M, Master's)

> There is extrinsic motivation, however for my purpose I see learner motivation as what motivates my students in a particular class to take an interest, participate, and make an effort in their studies. By extension, it is also intrinsically what motivates each individual student. (T22: American, M, Master's)

> A learner is motivated when she is eager to learn in and out of the classroom. She will take it upon herself to ask questions to the teacher if she doesn't understand something or wants to know more about the topic being discussed. She will also participate readily in class by making an effort to talk to other students in pair or group discussions. She asks the teacher for more help and support outside of the class, such as asking how she can improve her English skills on her own. (T25: American, F, Master's)

These excerpts show how much value the teachers placed on actually witnessing students' motivational behaviours and how important these are considered to improve language skills. In addition, the notion of motivational behaviours does not seem to exist alone, but was usually expressed in tandem with other concepts such as desire (as in T6's report) or interest (T22). As shown in the previous section, the most common motivation term that teachers used was goals and this too was reported in conjunction with the need for students to demonstrate motivational behaviours:

> If they [students] are hard-working, diligent, and faithful to task, they can put in their efforts to achieving their goals. They also need to have concentration and a firm determination to fulfil their personal or pedagogical goals. (T21: Japanese, F, Master's)

A composite understanding of how the teachers conceptualise learner motivation can be expressed in terms of three main features that motivated students consistently display. Motivated students demonstrate a set of specific *behaviours* in the classroom, such as showing enthusiasm and effort, working on task and working independently. In order for them to do so, they need to have a positive *attitude* towards English in which they reveal some interest or enjoyment in the subject, or a strong desire to learn, and/or have clear *goals* or reasons to learn English, such as to improve their skills or to get a good grade.

The following quotation is a succinct expression of these three features:

> I see learner motivation as a positive attitude that a learner has toward learning. This means that they should be fairly clear about what it is they want to learn or achieve, and have the commitment and self-discipline to take steps to move toward or realise that goal. (T3: British, F, PhD)

Motivational strategies employed by teachers

Most teachers believed strongly that they could enhance their learners' motivation through employing various strategies:

> Definitely, the teacher has a major role to play in motivation... the teacher has a major influence on the mood of the class. (T14, Australian, F. Master's)

> Yes, I think I can influence students because I can show them how fun and interesting learning English can be. (T25: American, F, Master's)

The large number of motivational strategies that the teachers reported can be classified into four categories: high-quality teaching, affect, personal relationships and goals. Firstly, the teachers mentioned using a large number of teaching techniques in order to provide their students with varied and thoughtful lessons. These strategies cover a number of areas of teaching, such as developing the curriculum, material selection, setting up learning situations that suit learner interests and levels, and expressing clear expectations of classroom roles and norms:

> I'm big on the idea that a teacher, through considering curriculum situations, carefully preparing a syllabus for a specific group of learners and then bringing this home with stimulating materials at the classroom level, can and should set up conditions that will motivate students. We can influence student interest, make things relevant and create conditions where students can feel satisfied when we prepare our lessons. (T27: Canadian, M, Master's)

In order to ensure quality teaching, teachers also try to influence their students' learning process by modelling enthusiasm and effort in the lessons. They focus on the learning process, such as making sure that students play a central role in learning, give students opportunities for success in their learning and encourage them to make mistakes and experiment.

A second group of strategies reported by the teachers were ones to influence student affect. Many of the teachers tried to influence their students' attitude towards learning English by making them feel more positive about it. They would try to decrease anxiety and build confidence by praising students, and use humour and jokes in lessons to try to lighten the classroom atmosphere. Within the next quotation are several strategies that were frequently mentioned by many of the teachers:

> By helping to overcome negative feelings or habits related to studying English (e.g. learned helplessness). By giving students an enjoyable experience of studying English, by helping them to feel that they can actually communicate in English, and that their English can improve. By giving them an experience of using English to achieve something useful which they otherwise couldn't. (T4: British, M, Master's)

This excerpt shows that teachers used strategies to alter how students feel about studying English. A number of teachers pointed out that many students do not have confidence in learning English and have a negative self-image as language students. The teachers believed that they could change these perceptions by making lessons both enjoyable and satisfying so that students could have a positive attitude about themselves and their learning.

A third strategy area, and one strongly linked with affective strategies, was the development of a positive personal relationship between a teacher and his/her students. Strategies to do this included using student names, remembering what students talk about from one lesson to the next, sharing stories of the teachers' own learning experiences and being respectful of student concerns:

> I try to learn what *already* motivates students: hobbies, clubs, areas of interest at university, etc. By showing an interest in what interests them, I think I can make them try harder to relate those interests to me, of course through the medium of English. (T13: American, M, Master's)

The final group of strategies were those that teachers used to encourage students to have clear goals:

> I believe that as a teacher one of my main roles is to try and enhance learner motivation. This includes trying to help students assess where they are now, set learning goals, and suggest strategies to achieve them. This is something I try to do at the level of the whole class (needs assessment, syllabus design and implementation) and of the individual (learning strategies, learning logs, self-assessment and reflection). (T3: British, F, PhD)

This excerpt shows how teachers wanted to help refine student goals and support them in their learning. They also wanted to encourage their students to be positive in trying to achieve their goals, to learn from their mistakes and to experiment and evolve.

Discussion

The responses from the teachers reveal an interesting picture of their perceptions of learner motivation in EFL classes in Japanese universities. We would now like to explore in more detail two facets of this picture: firstly, to discuss what motivation means to the teachers, especially their emphasis on external evidence of motivational behaviour; and secondly, we would like to compare the results of this study with Dörnyei and Ciszér's (1998) research on motivational strategies to explore whether teacher strategies can be transferrable across cultural differences.

What does 'motivation' mean to these language teachers?

The vocabulary and concepts these teachers use to show their understanding of motivation touches on diverse attested definitions and relates to theory. To list some examples, they include 'attitudes', 'instrumental', 'integrative' from socio-cultural approaches (Gardner & Lambert, 1972; Gardner, 1985); the importance of having 'goals' from goal-setting theory (Locke & Latham, 1990); 'extrinsic and intrinsic motivation', which are so often connected to self-determination theory (Deci & Ryan, 1985, 2002) as well as 'autonomy' (Benson, 1997).

Having been exposed to different theories in motivation, what these teachers seem to value most is witnessing motivational behaviours in the classroom. In addition, they recognise that in order for students to exhibit motivational behaviours, students also need to have reasons to learn, such as desire, interest or goals. In other words, if students show desire, interest or goals and then transfer them to motivational behaviours, the teachers consider that learners are motivated. This picture of motivation seems closest to the model of Williams and Burden (1997: 121), which consists of three stages: (1) reasons for doing something; (2) deciding to do something; and (3) sustaining the effort, or persisting. The model claims that initial interest is not sufficient by itself, but needs to be transferred to motivational behaviours that, in turn, need to be sustained in order to attain some satisfactory outcome. This reveals quite an overlap with the findings of the current study in which the teachers recognise that 'why' students are motivated is important, but they perceive that this is not enough to be classed as motivation. More important is to what extent learners demonstrate motivational behaviour in the classroom and how persistent they are both in and outside the lesson.

Another reason for these teachers' definition being similar to Williams and Burden's model is that since motivation, as with many psychological constructs, is a difficult concept to 'witness' from outside, classroom teachers may tend to consider that what students actually do matters far more than what kinds of reasons or goals students might have. Also, individual attitudes and goals are different from student to student, so although knowing about them is important, as practitioners it can be very difficult to keep track of every student's psychological orientation towards language learning. Teachers might want and need to focus on what they can witness.

Williams and Burden's model is one of the clearest to explain motivation, and the teachers' definition reflects its clarity. We would argue that such clarity is due to the fact that these teachers have a great deal of knowledge and expertise in language classrooms, which enables them to conceptualise a complex phenomenon such as motivation. Many studies on teacher cognition show that experienced teachers have craft knowledge that is not expressed consciously or explicitly, but in automatic and tacit ways (Eraut, 2000).

How do the ways these teachers foster motivation compare with previous studies?

In this section, we will discuss what strategies the teachers in the present study employ in order to influence their students' motivation, and we will compare them with Dörnyei and Csizér's (1998) previously mentioned study of key strategies that EFL teachers most frequently use.

The teachers in the Japanese cohort use four main groups of strategies to increase learner motivation: (1) strategies to ensure high-quality lessons; (2) strategies to improve affect; (3) strategies to promote good relationships with students; and (4) strategies to positively impact on goals. In Table 14.4, the left-hand column shows the Ten Commandments of Dörnyei and Csizér. The right-hand column shows whether the teachers in the current study use these strategies (√) or not (×), and which of the four types was used.

Table 14.4 A comparison of strategy use across studies

Ten Commandments	*Current study*
1. Set a personal example	√ (1)
2. Create a pleasant atmosphere	√ (2) (3)
3. Present tasks properly	√ (1)
4. Develop a good relationship with students	√ (2) (3)
5. Increase students' linguistic self-confidence	√ (1) (2)
6. Make classes interesting	√ (1)
7. Promote learner autonomy	×
8. Personalise the learning process	√ (1)
9. Increase goal orientedness	√ (4)
10. Familiarise learners with the target language culture	×

The strategies identified in the study match well with the Ten Commandments, which suggests that the strategies proposed in the Hungarian context are also relevant to a Japanese one, and might be part of a strategy repertoire that can be applied across different cultural contexts. Many of these strategies also reflect the fact that the teachers view their learners as *people*, rather than just students. They do this through setting a personal example, creating a pleasant atmosphere, promoting personal relationships and increasing self-confidence. The uses of these types of strategies imply that the teachers value what Ushioda (2009, this volume) terms learner's 'transportable identities' (after Zimmerman, 1998 and Richards, 2006). Many teachers in this study take an active interest in their learners' emotions and feelings, trying to find out who they are and understand what their lives are like beyond the classroom. This adds further evidence to support Ushioda in viewing motivation as an entity incorporating an individual learner's identity, life goals, self-image and emotions in a complex social setting; rather than treating motivation as an abstract construct based on psychometric measurements that ignores a learner's invaluable individuality.

Although the evidence for overlap in strategy use between the Ten Commandments and the current study is strong, the results also show two commandments that are not frequently represented in the data – the seventh (to promote learner autonomy) and the tenth (to familiarise learners with the target language culture). Regarding autonomy, two teachers used the general term, autonomy, in relation to motivation, and other teachers described encouraging specific behaviours, such as students working independently, taking an active role, asking questions and setting their own tasks. These descriptions of autonomy seem closest to what Benson (1997) categorises as autonomy from a psychological aspect. Within this approach there is an emphasis on 'broader attitudes and cognitive abilities which enable the learner to take responsibility for his/her own learning' or 'general mental dispositions and capacities' (Palfreyman, 2003: 3), rather than a technical perspective focusing on skills and strategies, or a political one to empower learners.

Teachers in the study did not state that fostering autonomy was a motivational strategy; however, this does not mean that they consider autonomy is unnecessary for motivation. Instead, many expect autonomy to be a pre-requisite for motivation and it is not their role to try to promote it: 'Motivation for L2 learners implies that they have the autonomy to deal with their own language learning' (T12: Canadian, M, PhD).

There are several possible factors that could explain the differences between this study and that by Dörnyei and Csizér (1998), one of which is student age. Teachers in the current study teach at the tertiary level, whereas Dörnyei and Csizér's research included secondary school learners. Depending on learner ages, teachers might have different expectations in terms of the level of autonomy that learners bring to classrooms and a teacher's role in fostering autonomy. Another factor might be that school culture and ethos in Hungary and Japan are different, resulting in diverse views of autonomy.

A second difference between the Dörnyei and Csizér study and the current study is that the teachers in Japan did not make particular references in the survey to any particular target community. This could reflect the fact that the participants did not have a special interest in any one target culture, or that they view 'culture' from a slightly different perspective, as the three interviewees revealed. Two of the three interviewees spoke about how they saw their role as one of increasing awareness in their students of specific cultural issues, or of encouraging students to reflect on their own culture in Japan:

> David: Looking at your own culture, I'm from Canada, I was thinking about what is bilingualism, what is multi-nationalism? But not culture-things like "in Canada we...[or] how to tap maple syrup from a tree" or anything, nothing like that. Immersion, education in Canada, talking about things like that. I'm interested in gender and, er anything. It can be anything I guess.

Here, David is explaining that he teaches about culture in connection with broad topics such as gender, rather than it being specifically related to one country such as Canada. We feel that the teachers in this study viewed learner identity as being situated within a global context rather than being linked to one geographical or target culture. This view of learner identity related to culture supports findings in recent research. Ryan (2006), for example, claims a general trend in ELT focusing on a less well defined and more global view of English that is moving away from concern for a specific target culture. Yashima (2009) similarly identifies that motivated Japanese students tend to position themselves as international English users. These studies collectively suggest that learner motivation to learn English reflects the ever-changing influence of global trends on individuals.

Our study has shown only a glimpse of the relationship between motivation and related constructs such as autonomy and culture. Further investigation of teacher perceptions should shed light on these complex matters and could include questions such as: Do teachers view the development of learner autonomy as being closely related to the age of learners? Do teachers believe that autonomy is mediated by interaction between the cultural expectations of teachers and learners? How do teachers perceive autonomy as being related to teacher and learner identities?

Conclusion

There have been relatively few studies of motivation in EFL that take account of teacher perspectives. These experienced and educated teachers had a wealth of insightful views on learner motivation embedded in years of practice. Their definition of motivation is a practical one based on students showing a positive attitude, having clear goals and acting out behaviours to achieve those goals. Further, they use a wide variety of strategies to try to impact on motivation.

One important aspect of this study is the way in which it highlights the interdependence of theory and practice in education. McNamara (2008: 302), reflecting on being exposed to theories in his training years, remembers how, 'theory broke up a lot of old concrete in my head' and that exposure to theory clarified the complexities he faced in the classroom. We would hope that the constantly evolving motivation theories will continue to play a similar role for practitioners and clarify the complexities of the classroom. However, there is a danger that theory may not always do so. Theorising motivation, particularly based on psychometric measurements, may have become too complex to comprehend and apply in real situations, as one of the participants in the study questions:

> Recently with the advancement in learner motivation studies, I feel the motivation framework is getting more and more intricate (or the motivation researchers… are getting too meticulous). (T24: Japanese, M, Master's)

This teacher's comment points out the limits of abstract motivation models in traditional research (Ushioda, 2009, this volume). We acknowledge that such abstract models are valuable and necessary to gain theoretical insights into motivation, but what these teachers also need are comprehensible explanations for motivation that make sense in and can be applied to their teaching contexts. We would suggest that one way to gain a wider picture of motivation is that theories of learner motivation include teacher perspectives, as this study has done. The participants in this study have been consumers, and some of them are producers, of motivation theories, and they are at the interface between language and learners. We hope that their voices and the voices of other teachers will be heard in order to foster the development of knowledge about motivation in the language classroom.

References

Benson, P. (1997) The philosophy and politics of learner autonomy. In P. Benson and P. Voller (eds) *Autonomy and Independence in Language Learning* (pp. 18–34). London: Longman.

Borg, S. (2006) *Teacher Cognition and Language Education: Research and Practice.* London: Continuum.

Brophy, J. (2004) *Motivating Students to Learn* (2nd edn). Mahwah, NJ: Lawrence Erlbaum.

Crookes, G. and Schmidt, R.W. (1991) Motivation: Reopening the research agenda. *Language Learning* 41, 469–512.

Deci, E.L. and Ryan, R.M. (1985) *Intrinsic Motivation and Self-Determination in Human Behavior.* New York: Plenum.

Deci, E.L. and Ryan, R.M. (2002) *Handbook of Self-Determination Research.* Rochester, NY: University of Rochester Press.

Dörnyei, Z. (2005) *The Psychology of the Language Learner: Individual Differences in Second Language Acquisition.* Mahwah, NJ: Lawrence Erlbaum.

Dörnyei, Z. (2009) The L2 motivational self system. In Z. Dörnyei and E. Ushioda (eds) *Motivation, Language Identity and the L2 Self* (pp. 9–42). Bristol: Multilingual Matters.

Dörnyei, Z. and Czisér, K. (1998) Ten commandments for motivating language learners: Results of an empirical study. *Language Teaching Research* 2, 203–229.

Dörnyei, Z. and Otto, I. (1998) Motivation in action: A process model of L2 motivation. *Working Papers in Applied Linguistics* 47, 173–210.

Eraut, M. (2000) Non-formal learning, implicit learning and tacit knowledge in professional work. In F. Coffield (ed.) *The Necessity of Informal Learning* (pp. 12–31). Bristol: The Policy Press.

Gardner, R. (1985) *Social Psychology and Second Language Learning: The Role of Attitudes and Motivation.* London: Edward Arnold.

Gardner, R. and Lambert, W. (1972) *Attitudes and Motivation in Second-Language Learning.* Rowley, MA: Newbury House.

Guilloteaux, M. and Dörnyei, Z. (2008) Motivating language learners: A classroom-oriented investigation of the effects of motivational strategies on student motivation. *TESOL Quarterly* 42 (1), 55–77.

Locke, E.A. and Latham, G.P. (1990) *A Theory of Goal Setting and Task Performance.* Englewood Cliffs, NJ: Prentice Hall.

McNamara, T. (2008) Mapping the scope of theory in TESOL. *TESOL Quarterly* 42 (2), 302–305.

Norton, B. (2000) *Identity and Language Learning: Gender, Ethnicity and Educational Change.* Harlow: Longman/Pearson Education.

Palfreyman, D. (2003) Introduction: Culture and learner autonomy. In D. Palfreyman and R. Smith (eds) *Learner Autonomy Across Cultures* (pp. 1–19). Basingstoke: Palgrave Macmillan.

Richards, K. (2006) 'Being the teacher': Identity and classroom conversation. *Applied Linguistics* 27 (1), 51–77.

Richards, L. and Morse, J. (2007) *Readme First for a User's Guide to Qualitative Methods* (2nd edn). Thousand Oaks, CA: Sage.

Ryan, S. (2006) Language learning motivation within the context of globalisation: An L2 self within an imagined global community. *Critical Inquiry in Language Studies* 3 (1), 23–45.

Sakui, K. and Cowie, N. (2008) 'To speak English is tedious': Student resistance in Japanese university classrooms. In P. Kalaja, V. Menezes and A.M. Barcelos (eds) *Narratives of EFL Teaching and Learning* (pp. 98–112). Basingstoke: Palgrave Macmillan.

Ushioda, E. (2003) Motivation as a socially mediated process. In D. Little, J. Ridley, and E. Ushioda (eds) *Learner Autonomy in the Foreign Language Classroom: Teacher, Learner, Curriculum and Assessment* (pp. 90–102). Dublin: Authentik.

Ushioda, E. (2009) A person-in-context relational view of emergent motivation, self and identity. In Z. Dörnyei and E. Ushioda (eds) *Motivation, Language Identity and the L2 Self* (pp. 215–228). Bristol: Multilingual Matters.

Williams, M. and Burden, R. (1997) *Psychology for Language Teachers*. Cambridge: Cambridge University Press.

Woods, D. (1996) *Teacher Cognition in Language Teaching*. Cambridge: Cambridge University Press.

Yashima, T. (2009) International posture and the ideal L2 self in the Japanese EFL context. In Z. Dörnyei and E. Ushioda (eds) *Motivation, Language Identity and the L2 Self* (pp. 144–163). Bristol: Multilingual Matters.

Zimmerman, D.H. (1998) Discoursal identities and social identities. In C. Antaki and S. Widdicombe (eds) *Identities in Talk* (pp. 87–106). London: Sage.

Chapter 15

A Dynamic Account of Autonomy, Agency and Identity in (T)EFL Learning

JING HUANG

Introduction

For many learners, identity construction is at the center of their language learning processes. While many relevant studies have been conducted in second language settings (e.g. McKay & Wong, 1996; Morita, 2004; Norton, 2000), there is a lack of research on identities of language learners in foreign language contexts. In the long-term learning process in institutional contexts, both identity and agency play an important role in shaping the development of autonomy. The complex relationship among the three constructs of autonomy, agency and identity has been described by Benson (2007: 30) in these terms: 'agency can perhaps be viewed as a point of origin for the development of autonomy, while identity might be viewed as one of its more important outcomes'. However, observations of this kind need to be supported by more empirical evidence. This chapter foregrounds the development of identity and autonomy in relation to a particular teaching English as a foreign language (TEFL) context, that of Chinese trainee TEFL teachers in a mainland Chinese university. It addresses the following research question:

What roles do agency and identity play in the development of autonomy among students in a Chinese social and institutional context?

Autonomy, Agency and Identity in Foreign Language Education

Benson (2001: 47) defines autonomy as 'the capacity to take control of one's own learning'. He further argues that an adequate description of autonomy in language learning should at least recognize the importance of three inter-dependent levels of control: control over learning management, control over cognitive processes and control over learning content. Benson (2001: 99–100) also links different levels of control over learning to the idea of proactive and reactive autonomy proposed by Littlewood (1999). Proactive autonomy is the form of autonomy in which learners determine learning objectives, select learning methods and techniques, and evaluate what they have learned. Reactive autonomy is 'the kind of autonomy which does not create its own directions but, once a direction has been initiated, enables learners to organize their resources autonomously in order to reach their goal' (Littlewood, 1999: 75). In terms of the three levels of control, Benson (2001: 100) suggests that reactive autonomy might be described as control over the levels of learning management and cognitive processes without control over learning content. By contrast, proactive autonomy implies learner control over all three levels.

As mentioned above, autonomy in language learning closely relates to the notions of agency and identity. To social theorist, Giddens (1976, 1984), agency is concerned with the capacity to 'act otherwise'. Candlin and Sarangi (2004: xiii) conceptualize agency as 'the self-conscious reflexive actions of human beings'. In the broad field of applied linguistics and language education, Lantolf and his colleagues' perspectives on agency represent 'neo-Vygotskyan' approaches, which emphasize that agency arises out of individuals' engagement in the social world (Lantolf & Thorne, 2006; Lantolf & Pavlenko, 2001; Lantolf, 2002; Morita, 2004). For the current study, I would like to propose that agency, including learner agency, entails action, and often suggests action that arises from deliberation and choice (Allison & Huang, 2005). While this is not strictly a definition of agency, I use this conceptualization to guide the data analysis. For example, such a conceptualization enables a close scrutiny of language learners' responses to the constraints and opportunities in the particular research context, which in turn offers a useful way to problematize and look critically at actual language and teaching situations.

The concept of identity may simply refer to 'our sense of who we are and our relationship to the world' (Kanno, 2003: 3). Norton's work (1995, 2000, 2001) conducted in the North American context has been influential in identity research. She is primarily concerned with interactions between native speakers and non-native speakers of the target language, and the social context in which these interactions occur. Therefore, the issue of power relations between language learners and target language speakers becomes the most salient. There has been little research on identity conducted in the foreign language context. However, a study conducted in the Chinese university context by Gao *et al.* (2002) has relevance for the current study. Their study relates the question of 'who am I' to a range of specific questions regarding discourse style (e.g. preference for an English or Chinese way of speaking and thinking) and selection/construction of a social role (a writer/reader/speaker), career directions, self-perceptions of talents and competencies, person-alities, values and beliefs, cultural belongings, external images and inner pursuits. These conceptualizations of identity find support in Chik's (2007) study in the Hong Kong context, which links identity to academic and career promotional aspects, and in Murray and Kojima's (2007) study in the Japanese context, which defines identity in terms of personal pursuit and fulfillment.

Research Context

The study was conducted in a teacher-education university in mainland China. The major research participants were students in a four-year BA TEFL degree program in the English Department (around 200 for each year grouped in 5–6 classes). I considered myself as more an insider than an outsider due to my status as a former teacher in the research context. In the past decade, the pass rate in high-stakes external examinations (examinations not in the regular curriculum) and 'employment rate' (the proportion of students being employed on graduation) have been the priority agendas for the department and the students. The external examination, which enjoys special status at the university level is *kaoyan* – the Chinese shortened form for '(taking) the postgraduate entrance examination'. About 20–30% of fourth-year TEFL students take this examination in order to pursue their postgraduate studies in a university of their choice. Kaoyan preparation usually takes around two years. In addition to kaoyan, other high-stakes external examinations are TEM-4 and TEM-8 (Test for English Majors, Band-4 and Band-8) scheduled, respec-tively, in the second and fourth years. Both are national proficiency tests for all English majors. Students must pass TEM-4 to secure the BA degree. Therefore, the participants in the study were generally pragmatic learners whose priority agendas were to pass important examinations and to find a job on graduation.

Methodology

The research study followed an interpretative qualitative approach. Data for the study were collected during five fieldwork trips over two academic years (2005–2007). Data sources included autobiographies in English or Chinese of 150 fourth-year students; 100 pages of autobiographical learning accounts in English of third-year students; 73 group/pair/individual semi-structured Chinese interviews with students at different years; 26 group/pair/individual semi-structured interviews in Chinese or English with teachers; classroom observation, field notes and administrative and other relevant documents.

Data analysis was ongoing, along with data collection, and thus could partly inform enquiry scheduled at subsequent stages. The following procedures were used cyclically to analyze the word-processed data (based on Palfreyman, 2001: 79):

- Annotate each dataset, highlighting themes that seem significant in light of previous data or that indicate possible new directions.
- Look for recurring themes in the annotations of each dataset.
- Combine and compare data from different sources, and regroup the data under headings corresponding to themes in the annotations and text.

Since fieldwork for this study extended over two years and the amount of data increased steadily and rapidly, the procedures described above were followed iteratively. After data collection (and the embedded ongoing data analysis) had finished, a content analysis of the whole dataset was conducted. Content analysis procedures included grouping verbal responses into categories and comparing category judgments at different times by the researcher.

Findings: Students' Four-Year Learning Experiences in University

This section presents students' four-year learning experiences in university, highlighting influential events and connecting them to the notions of autonomy, agency and identity in learning English.

'Having no goal' and 'not knowing what to do' in the first year

A dominant and recurrent theme for a majority of first-year students was 'having no goal' and 'not knowing what to do'. They said that they felt lost, confused and puzzled in their first year, because of this, although there were other contributing factors. (In data extracts quoted hereafter, '®' refers to the researcher, while initials only recognizable to the researcher are used for participants except in Extracts 3, 9 and 10 in which the pseudonym 'Mark' is assigned to a student whom I want to identify for a particular purpose in the final discussion.)

Extract-1: Interview, WQ(W)-CBX(C)-LXF(L)-DXF(D)-HX(H)-2005cohort (translation)

®: Just now you mentioned you felt confused and puzzled. Why?

H: We had little knowledge of university life, so we had no goal.

C: After we entered university, we hadn't made any plan or set any goal.

[. . .]

W: We had this kind of feelings because our exclusive goal in senior secondary school was to do well in the college entrance exam. After entering university, we had no goal, no will to fight, so we felt confused and didn't know what to do.

[. . .]

C: We had fewer courses in the first semester. We had to manage our learning most of the time.

Many students did not have a clear life goal and could not find meanings at the initial stage of their tertiary education. This may indicate that they were unclear about their self-identity. These general feelings of loss, confusion and puzzlement expressed by the majority are counter-balanced by the perspectives of a minority of students, as illustrated below:

Extract-2: Interview, XJH-ZYR-2003cohort (translation)

XJH: At the beginning, I thought I shouldn't come to this university as I could have done better in the entrance exam, but since I was here [...]. Before coming here, I had made necessary psychological adjustments. Now I have discussed this problem with teachers and classmates here. Therefore, I didn't feel confused. I had a goal-kaoyan-in Year 4. I also wanted to become a teacher very much, so I knew building a solid language foundation was very important.

Comments of another first-year student, Mark, further illustrate why he did not feel lost and confused, unlike the majority.

Extract-3: Interview, Mark-2003cohort (translation)

My tertiary education in the past three years was full of "meaning and fulfillment" (*chongshi*). [. . .] I had goals [. . .]. I had no problem in adapting to university education. [. . .] I had started to think about how to use library resources in year 1 [. . .]. When I was in senior secondary school, although I needed to work hard for the college entrance exam, I still bought newspapers to read to know more about the society. I was thinking then I would have a deeper understanding of social issues when I entered university. University education offers chances for personal development and I think this university has met the necessary learning conditions. So, I didn't feel confused in year 1. [...] Whenever I had time, I went to the library. Sometimes I couldn't understand things I read, but if I considered them useful in my future studies, I would make copies and put them in a folder.

Mark's comments confirmed my observations of his behavior in a short course I was teaching. In addition to his capacity to set personally meaningful goals, he differentiated himself from a majority of others in that he held a broader rather than purely pragmatic-oriented vision regarding tertiary education and personal development. His learning also extended beyond foreign language learning to social issues in which he could find personal meanings and relevance. He was among the few in his class who showed strong interest in theoretical learning (see more discussion on theoretical learning in the following section). Despite his relatively 'humble' background (in a low-ranking university emphasizing pragmatic learning), Mark's identity development at the level of thinking and the extent of personal agency was comparable to that of three English majors at a prestigious Chinese university (Gao *et al.*, 2002), who developed 'reader', 'writer' and 'public speaker' identities. It might even be suggested that he had developed a 'thinker' identity in his university education (he was admitted into a master's program on international law in a prestigious university on graduation). This self-identity formation process seemed to start from his first year in university or even earlier.

Learning for and in external examinations throughout the BA program

Students held mostly positive views toward the high-stakes external examinations, especially TEM-4 in the second year and kaoyan in the final year. Thus, they exercised great agency to benefit from them.

Gains in TEM-4 and Kaoyan

TEM-4 was considered by almost all students as necessary for English majors. The imminent approach of the test helped focus their English learning from the state of 'having no goal' and feeling 'lost, confused and puzzled', which had characterized their first-year learning. In addition, the intensive preparation process over a long period of time helped sharpen their target language skills. Many considered the test as 'unforgettable', generating a sense of 'meaning and fulfillment' (*chongshi*).

Extract-4: Autobiography, 2002C2-24LY (translation)
I didn't realize how much time I had idled away until the approaching of TEM-4. [...] My life was full of "meaning and fulfilment" when I was working hard at TEM-4. I immersed myself totally in going over English lessons and exercises every day. [...] I eventually passed the test, which was one of the most joyful and meaningful things I have done in university.

Throughout their four-year university education, students stated they had gained the most from studying for TEM-4, in that their capacity to take control over their learning, especially control over learning management, had developed in the process of preparing for this examination. For example, they stated TEM-4 stimulated self-reflection and learning management, which were not much evident in their first-year learning. Many said that they worked harder studying for the test than the college entrance examination. Of course, pressure from the need to pass the test to secure the BA degree was also a major reason for their hard work.

Throughout their four years in university, students also took a number of other external examinations, including TEM-8, kaoyan and various professional certificate tests. Their views and attitudes toward these tests and actions taken in response to them were similar, i.e. they used external tests to motivate and pressure themselves in their language learning, and felt gains from preparing for them. Participation in kaoyan and other tests could be considered proactive rather than reactive autonomous behaviors because, unlike TEM-4, students could choose whether or not to enroll in these tests.

Extract-5: Interview, CDF-2003cohort (translation)
I think kaoyan is also a means to motivate yourself. You have a goal there, and you won't be satisfied with only finding a job. With a goal, you'll spend more time on studying. It doesn't mean you must succeed in the exam. Even though you fail, you can learn a lot from the process.

Students tended to regard kaoyan, TEM-4 and teaching practicum (TP) (see discussion on TP in a following section) as the most meaningful and unforgettable events throughout the BA TEFL program. All three entailed hard work, yet usually brought about a sense of gains and achievement to participants.

TEM-4 and English-Major Identity

Students' hard work for and sense of gains from TEM-4 were also grounded in their conceptualization of the English-major identity. Passing the test constituted evidence of success as an English-major student. Being a successful English-major student was mainly a matter of proficiency. In the extract below, XD linked her experience of learning for TEM-4 to the threat to her English-major identity and face, her current position as a student leader, her sense of 'meaning and fulfillment' and 'having learned a lot' from TEM-4:

> Extract-6: Interview, XD-2002cohort (translation)
> X: My TEM-4 experience was a blow to me. The preparation process was painstaking. I've never had to bear such pressure [...]. I am a person with strong self-esteem. As a student leader, I was once warned of possible failure in TEM-4. This was really a threat to face.
> ®: How do you think of TEM-4 when you are looking back...?
> X: TEM-4 is important. From a practical point of view, how can I say I am an English-major without passing TEM-4? Although I got only 61, a horrible pass, I gained a sense of meaning and fulfillment from the process.

Generally speaking, students in the study invested much more time and energy in preparing for TEM-4 than TEM-8. There were several reasons for this. For example, since these students were studying in a non-prestigious local university usually with the relatively modest goal of finding a teaching job in a primary or secondary school, TEM-8 was not considered as indispensable as TEM-4. Passing TEM-4 was considered as the hallmark of an English-major identity while TEM-8 did not usually threaten the English-major identity, although passing it would be advantageous in job-hunting. In addition, passing TEM-8 was not necessary for the BA degree as TEM-4 was.

Kaoyan also presented an opportunity for identity development and fulfillment. Many kaoyan students claimed that the university provided them with limited opportunities and space for personal development. When talking about their first-year experiences, some students said that they had come to a 'wrong' university and they deserved a better one. Interestingly, many of these students claimed that they used kaoyan to re-orient their personal development and to change their future lives.

'English for practical purposes' in the third and fourth years

From the third year onwards the curriculum focus shifted from the exclusive emphasis on language proficiency of the first two years, to a greater emphasis on pedagogical theory learning and other areas of advanced learning, such as British and American literature (hereafter 'theoretical-advanced/theoretical-oriented/theoretical learning'). The third year was also a time when students began to consider more seriously their future careers. The term 'English for practical purposes' (EPP) is used to describe students' practical (pragmatic) orientation to language learning. Theoretical learning and oral English development constituted two illustrative cases for EPP. In this connection, it might also be argued that students' great investment in studying for high-stakes external examinations explored above was partly grounded in their EPP conceptualization and orientation.

Theoretical Advanced Learning

Students were generally passive and lacked agency in theoretical learning. Their reasons included the relatively high language demand to understand learning materials, the perceived boringness of theoretical-oriented learning, insufficient opportunities for putting knowledge into practice, and course assessment emphasizing memorization. The data suggest that the most important reason was their conceptualization of the usefulness of theoretical-oriented learning.

Extract-7: Interview, XD-2002cohort (translation)
The *Lexicology* course is useful, because it concerns every aspect of our English learning, and will be applicable in our future teaching. But as for those abstract theories, we think they are useless, or we can't relate them to our current learning or future work. Take [British and American] literature for example. Most of us think it is useless. Actually, what other purposes can it serve except for your self-cultivation in literature? What can you use it for in the future?

The comments above foregrounded the practicality of learning English. Students tended to emphasize the immediate application of what was taught and admitted their utilitarian orientation toward English learning: 'Our utilitarianism is strong. We think spending time on learning theoretical things won't produce any actual benefits'. Lack of investment in theoretical-advanced courses was also due to students' conceptualization of their limited applicability to secondary teaching:

Extract-8: Interview, LY-CXQ-2002cohort (translation)
LY: Sometimes doing well in theoretical learning doesn't necessarily mean you can teach well. Those theories are sometimes too profound,

yet secondary English teaching doesn't need those profound things
at all.

Students' passivity in theoretical learning might also result from a
tension between their life goals and their conceptualization of the
usefulness of theoretical learning. Peer comments might help us better
understand students' modest life goals and self-positioning and subsequent passivity in theoretical-oriented learning. The following extract
from Mark, the third-year student quoted in Extract 3, shows that most
students only wanted an ordinary job after graduation. However, he
distinguished himself from his peers.

Extract-9: Interview, Mark-2003cohort (translation)
For them, they can stop at finding a job. I think I will probably do
various things in the future. So, why don't I take the opportunity of
tertiary education to learn more to broaden my vision, and to read
works by famous experts [...]? In this way, you can benefit a lot, and
reach a greater depth of thoughts.

Mark was one of a minority of students who showed a particular
interest in theoretical-oriented learning. The following remarks further
illustrate why students were generally not interested in theoretical-
oriented learning.

Extract-10: Interview, Mark-2003cohort (translation)
I think it's relatively difficult to pursue theoretical-oriented teaching
in our university. Students are not from well-to-do families. Their
parents and relatives tell them, "You should find a job after
graduation." This is their direction. It's fixed at the beginning, and
very difficult to change.

Oral English (speaking)

Students were more willing to establish their personal agendas
through taking the initiative in improving speaking rather than other
language skills, especially in the third and fourth years when finding a
job became a priority for most. Similarly, students also displayed
initiative and enthusiasm in the six-week TP (see more discussion in
the next section). They stated that both English speaking and TP involved
practical skills and directly affected their daily lives.

In the following extract, the student cited 'practicality', 'applicability' and 'practice-orientation' toward learning, as well as possibilities
for quick results as the major reasons for their being more engaged in
the processes of acquiring oral English and in teaching–learning in TP

(see the following section for other reasons for TP). While the result of investment in speaking and in TP was tangible and predictable, theoretical-oriented learning, which was characterized by 'passively absorbing knowledge', was unlikely to produce quick results.

> Extract-11: Interview, XD-2002cohort (translation)
> TP and speaking are skill-based and characterized by high applicability and practicality. [...] In theoretical courses, we only absorb knowledge, which is passive and boring. The practicality of speaking and TP is obvious. For example, in job hunting, you have to speak, so you must practise your oral English. But theoretical courses are different. You can't see their results. [...] Or, it takes a long time to see any progress.

Another interesting view of speaking in the data was that speaking represented the image – the 'front' (*menmian*) of English majors. This view was arguably related to students' conceptualization of practicality and usefulness of oral English. According to them, oral English performance might affect one's self-efficacy and motivation for learning, due to its image-projecting function. This speaking self-image also led to awareness of and individual effort to exploit the 'comparative advantage' of English majors in their future careers in comparison with non-English majors (whose written English might be as good as English majors).

> Extract-12: Interview, LSY-YJ-LQY-2002cohort (translation)
> LSY: For students in subsequent grades, they should know what they expect. [...] Oral English represents the front (*menmian*), so they must practise it. In job hunting, your written English may also be tested, but if your oral English is good, you'll be able to get much more "impression credits". So, they must improve their oral English to defeat students in other disciplines.

Because speaking affected how an English learner was viewed and judged by others, students established proactive agendas to take initiatives in improving it. Many described their efforts in practicing oral English, including speaking to themselves when they could not find partners. Some even paid to attend private speaking courses. By contrast, few students reported taking actions in developing reading and writing skills.

Teaching practicum and informal teaching-learning

As mentioned above, students were particularly active and took the initiative in TP (and in speaking development). This was partly grounded in their EPP orientation toward English learning. However, there were other reasons to account for their self-initiation and self-direction in TP. The one-off six-week TP in the final year provided a rare and valuable chance for students to put knowledge acquired from theoretical courses into practice. More importantly, in TP, student teachers acted on and were driven by a sense of 'teacher responsibility' and a feeling of being needed, both of which enhanced their confidence in combating difficulties in their own teaching.

> Extract-13: Interview, ZX-LQY-2002cohort (translation)
> ®: Students were all active in TP, and didn't need teachers to press them. Why?
> L: Because [...] there was a chance for practice [...].
> Z: For me, TP was fun. Because you had learned something, you wanted to share with your pupils, and this would inspire you to learn more. If they had questions, they would ask you, so you had a feeling of being needed, and a sense of responsibility. [...] No matter what difficulties you might encounter, you had the confidence to overcome them.

These comments seem to show that, during the TP, students began to develop a teacher identity. Students' attitudes toward TP and their acceptance of a school-teacher identity are further demonstrated by comments in the following extract. Differences in the nature of the two processes of English learning and TEFL learning, and their comparative strengths and weaknesses in each process, led students to different degrees of personal investment.

> Extract-14: Interview, PSY(P)-LT(L)-YH(Y)-2002cohort (translation)
> P: Even though many students were not outstanding in the university, they had a sense of superiority and achievement in TP, because their own pupils worshipped them [...]. But rivals were many here, and if you couldn't beat others [...], you wouldn't have much enthusiasm for doing things [...].
> L: During TP, when those pupils asked you questions and you helped them solve their problems, they would begin to like you and adore you. You would see yourself as a useful person.
> ®: But if you put in so much enthusiasm in your study here, you'll also make great progress.
> P: Being a teacher gives you a different feeling from being a student, because there are differences in the two processes in terms of responsibility and work nature. In university, you live a study life.

What you need to do is to work hard [...] and get high marks in the final exam. [...] But TP is different. [...] Secondary teaching doesn't demand high academic achievement. However, it involves one's social and communicative abilities, and ability to build a relationship with pupils. In fact, most of us are not too bad in these aspects.

These insights into the two learning processes help to further explain why students were more active in TP (and TEFL learning) than in general English learning. In their views, students who were not particularly strong in English learning and thus not considered as excellent students in university could still excel in their teaching or become good teachers in TP and in their future teaching.

Prior to TP, students who wanted to become teachers had been engaged in various forms of extracurricular teaching-learning, such as tutoring school pupils, volunteering to teaching in economically under-developed areas, attending teacher-development associations, teaching short English courses and tutoring non-English majors in other faculties. Although students participated in these activities to make pocket money or enrich their university life, in their dual identities as language learner and prospective language teacher, students assigned their informal TEFL learning experiences a learning-to-teach purpose. Many of them con-cluded that their confidence and success in their own teaching in TP could be attributed substantially to their extracurricular teaching-learn-ing prior to TP. Furthermore, students were generally willing and able to take greater control over their TP and their informal teaching-learning than their learning of English in general (as discussed in Huang, 2009, Chapters 4 and 7).

Discussion and Conclusions

This section summarizes and discusses students' four-year learn-ing experiences in university presented above and examines the interrelatedness between agency, autonomy and identity in the long-term TEFL learning process in the Chinese social and institutional context.

In the first year in university, students are unsure of what to do, reactive, examination-oriented and not autonomous. Later, they develop greater autonomy as they experience the practical phases of their English learning and TEFL training, as language learners and student teachers. At the same time, their identity shifts from 'lost-at-sea' aimless first-year students, to more confident future teachers as a result of their interaction with their own students in the TP. In the long-term TEFL learning process, prospective-teacher identity stimulated the exercise of strong personal agency, thus promoting the development of 'student-teacher autonomy', or 'teacher-learner autonomy' in the terms of Smith and Erdoğan (2008). This student-teacher autonomy is more 'proactive' in that their TEFL learning is more purpose-directed, more individualized, more self-initiated and more self-directed (see Huang, 2009).

The overall findings show that learner agendas and agency are closely related. In a broad sense, agendas can be understood as 'things to do', agency 'entailing actions arising from deliberation and choice', and autonomy 'the capacity to do'. As the 'raw material' for autonomy, agency is more concrete, specific and observable, while autonomy is a capacity that entails long-term development. What can further distinguish agency from autonomy is perhaps the degree of control that learners are able to exercise in a specific context, which relates to the broad definition of autonomy in language learning.

The findings reported here demonstrate that a personally relevant and meaningful agenda might lead to the exercise of agency, which, in turn, might lead to greater autonomy (taking greater control of own learning and personal life) in the long term. Learner agendas and agency might be affected by students' conceptualization and construction of future development, such as career orientation as well as other factors such as their general conceptions of English learning. The students' different responses to theoretical-oriented learning, oral English and TP, and their greater agency and investment in TEFL learning as a whole than in English learning, illustrate this point. A simplified relationship among identity (and conceptions of language learning grounded in identity), agency (and agendas substantiating agency) and autonomy might be shown as in Figure 15.1.

However, the findings reported above indicate that there is potentially an interaction between these factors and that the interaction is embedded in a learning context that can be relatively large or small. Diagrammatically, relationships among identity, agency and autonomy might be indicated as in Figure 15.2.

Figure 15.1 A simplified relationship among identity, agency and autonomy

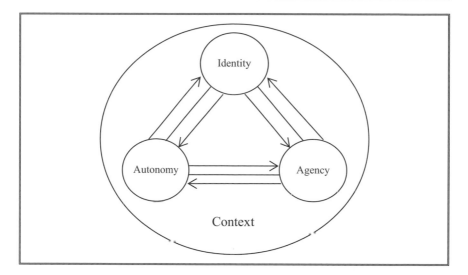

Figure 15.2 (diagrammatical): Relationships among identity, agency and autonomy

These findings, therefore, offer support for the proposal by Benson (2007: 30) that 'agency can perhaps be viewed as a point of origin for the development of autonomy, while identity might be viewed as one of its more important outcomes'. It might also be reasonable to suggest that self-identity conceptualization and construction might be both an origin and an outcome of autonomy in learning English.

Conceptualizing these constructs longitudinally, I propose a model to describe individual differences in the development of autonomy for the Chinese learners of this study (Figure 15.3).

This model illustrates differences in the development of autonomy among individual students (represented as the distance between Line C and Line D) in relation to the combined impact of self-identity conceptualization and construction, personally relevant agendas and the exercise of individual agency (the vertical axis), and time (the different learning stages through four different academic years in university and beyond; the horizontal axis). In this model, Student X may achieve greater autonomy (represented as Point C-1) than Student Y (Point D-1), although Student X is at an earlier educational stage than Student Y. Point A-B is an imaginary intersecting point from which autonomy grows, not a point of 'zero' autonomy. The dashed and wavy

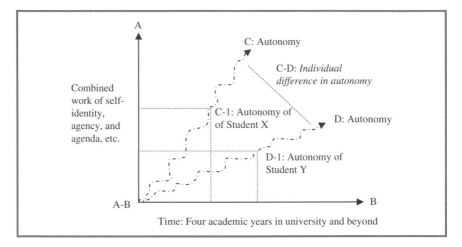

Figure 15.3 (longitudinal): Individual difference in autonomy in relation to identify, agency and agendas

lines (C and D) imply that long-term development of autonomy is usually unstable and 'wavy'.

This model may be applied to the Chinese English language learners of this study, who were grouped in class (*ban*) units, taking roughly the same courses in the same curriculum taught by the same teachers. Although they displayed similar learning characteristics in a homogeneous learning context throughout the four academic years, there were individual differences. These differences related to their 'capacity to take control over their learning' (Benson, 2001: 47), which was conditioned by their learning purpose or sense/direction of personal development (i.e. their self-identity conceptualization and construction), whether they were able and willing to establish their personally relevant agendas and to exercise their individual agency to achieve their learning and life goals.

Since the current study focused on group characteristics without an in-depth analysis of the behavior and learning conceptions of individual students through a case study approach, over the years, this model remains an assumption. Nevertheless, the brief description of a few individuals as counter-exemplars (e.g. Mark, as discussed above), as well as my long-term participant observation as a teacher and researcher in this context, offer evidence that self-identity, learner agency and learner agendas are among the most significant factors affecting an individual student's development of autonomy and simultaneously his/her learning in the longer term.

References

Allison, D. and Huang, J. (2005) Accommodation, resistance, and autonomy: Evidence from Chinese EFL learning diaries. Paper presented at the 14th World Congress of Applied Linguistics, University of Wisconsin-Madison, 24–29 July 2005.

Benson, P. (2001) *Teaching and Researching Autonomy in Language Learning*. Harlow: Pearson Education.

Benson, P. (2007) Autonomy in language teaching and learning. *Language Teaching* 40 (1), 21–40.

Candlin, C.N. and Sarangi, S. (2004) Preface. In A. Sealey and B. Carter (eds) *Applied Linguistics as Social Science* (pp. xiii–xv). London: Continuum.

Chik, A. (2007) From learner identity to learner autonomy: A biographical study of two Hong Kong learners of English. In P. Benson (ed.) *Learner Autonomy 8: Teacher and Learner Perspectives* (pp. 41–60). Dublin: Authentik.

Gao, Y.H., Li, Y.X. and Li, W.N. (2002) EFL learning and self-identity construction: Three cases of Chinese college English majors. *Asian Journal of English Language Teaching* 12, 95–119.

Giddens, A. (1976) *New Rules of Sociological Method: A Positive Critique of Interpretative Sociologies*. London: Hutchinson.

Giddens, A. (1984) *The Constitution of Society: Outline of the Theory of Structuration*. Berkeley and Los Angeles: University of California Press.

Huang, J. (2009) Autonomy, agency and identity in foreign language learning and teaching. PhD thesis, University of Hong Kong.

Kanno, Y. (2003) *Negotiating Bilingual and Bicultural Identities: Japanese Returnees betwixt Two Worlds*. Mahwah, NJ: Lawrence Erlbaum.

Lantolf, J.P. (2002) Sociocultural theory and second language acquisition. In R.B. Kaplan (ed.) *The Oxford Handbook of Applied Linguistics* (pp. 104–114). Oxford: Oxford University Press.

Lantolf, J.P. and Pavlenko, A. (2001) (S)econd (L)anguage (A)ctivity theory: Understanding second language learners as people. In M.P. Breen (ed.) *Learner Contributions to Language Learning: New Directions in Research* (pp. 141–158). Harlow: Pearson Education.

Lantolf, J.P. and Thorne, S.L. (2006) *Sociocultural Theory and the Genesis of Second Language Development*. Oxford: Oxford University Press.

Little, D. (1991) *Learner Autonomy 1: Definitions, Issues and Problems*. Dublin: Authentik.

Littlewood, W. (1999) Defining and developing autonomy in East Asian contexts. *Applied Linguistics* 20 (1), 71–94.

McKay, S. and Wong, S-L. (1996) Multiple discourses, multiple identities: Investment and agency in second-language learning among Chinese adolescent immigrant students. *Harvard Educational Review* 66 (3), 577–608.

Morita, N. (2004) Negotiating participation and identity in second language academic communities. *TESOL Quarterly* 38 (4), 573–603.

Murray, G. and Kojima, M. (2007) Out-of-class language learning: One learner's story. In P. Benson (ed.) _Learner Autonomy 8: Teacher and Learner Perspectives_ (pp. 25–40). Dublin: Authentik.

Norton Peirce, B. (1995) Social identity, investment, and language learning. _TESOL Quarterly_ 29 (1), 9–31.

Norton, B. (2000) _Identity and Language Learning: Gender, Ethnicity and Educational Change_. London: Longman.

Norton, B. (2001) Non-participation, imagined communities and the language classroom. In M.P. Breen (ed.) _Learner Contributions to Language Learning: New Directions in Research_ (pp. 159–171). Harlow: Pearson Education.

Palfreyman, D. (2001) The socio-cultural construction of learner autonomy and learner independence in a tertiary EFL institution. PhD thesis, Canterbury Christ Church University College.

Smith, R. and Erdoğan, S. (2008) Teacher-learner autonomy: Programme goals and student-teacher constructs. In T. Lamb and H. Reinders (eds) _Learner and Teacher Autonomy: Concepts, Realities, and Responses_ (pp. 83–102). Amsterdam: John Benjamins.

Chapter 16

Identity, Motivation and Autonomy: Stretching our Boundaries

GAROLD MURRAY

Introduction

The chapters in this volume represent a concerted effort by educators working in the area of learner autonomy in language learning to explore empirically their increasing awareness of the links that exist between identity, motivation and autonomy. In the opening chapter, Ushioda convincingly establishes that these constructs are interconnected as she demonstrates how insights from work investigating learner autonomy and identity can inform our understanding of language learner motivation. She concludes that classroom practices that promote language learner autonomy are likely to contribute to the development of learners' identities and motivation by enabling them to engage their 'transportable identities' (Richards, 2006) and to 'speak as themselves' in the target language. On the other hand, Ryan and Deci (2003: 254), whose self-determination theory (SDT) of motivation places great importance on autonomy as a psychological need, contend that 'identities can also fulfil the need for autonomy, for they can provide a forum through which people develop and express personal interests, values, and capacities'. While Ryan and Deci's thinking supports Ushioda's views on the links between identity, motivation and autonomy, as well as the implications for practice, the juxtapositioning of their ideas highlight the need for a closer examination of the interrelatedness of these constructs. Although researchers and theorists have already begun to explore the connections between identity and motivation in educational psychology (see a special issue of the *Educational Psychologist* edited by Kaplan & Flum, 2009) and in language education (Dörnyei & Ushioda, 2009; Norton, 2000), learner autonomy has not figured prominently in their analyses.

This volume moves autonomy to the fore in the discussion on identity and motivation in language learning. The authors have explored the links between these three constructs in a number of different cultural contexts and learning environments, including classroom, out-of-class and self-access settings. In addition to this, they have employed a range of research methods, such as survey, ethnographic and narrative inquiry, and analysed their data from a variety of theoretical perspectives. This concluding chapter focuses on themes emerging from these chapters with a view to synthesising how the insights they provide might advance theory development, inform practice and point to directions for future research.

Implications for Theory Development

Taking the perspective that links do exist between identity, motivation and autonomy, as well as exploring the commonalities of these three constructs can have important implications for theorising. The chapters presented in this volume support the notion that identity, motivation and autonomy share three noteworthy traits: they change over time, they depend on context and they are socially mediated. Somewhat ironically, to the casual observer in everyday life, identity, motivation and autonomy give the illusion of residing within the individual. This apparent attribute has served to mask what might be perceived as a duality inherent in all three, which has recently generated a great deal of discussion in academic literature: to what extent and in which ways are they cognitive or social phenomena?

In the area of learner autonomy, as Benson (2007) notes, this dichotomy has been evident from the outset, reflected in early definitions that either viewed autonomy as residing within the learning situation (Dickinson, 1987) or within the learner as a capacity, i.e. 'the ability to take charge of one's learning' (Holec's, 1981: 3), or a set of capacities, such as critical reflection, decision making, etc. (Little, 1991). This dichotomy is potentially problematic for theorising, research endeavours and practical applications. For example, as Benson goes on to point out, although Holec (1981) defines autonomy as an attribute of the learner, implying certain cognitive capacities, he describes taking charge of one's learning in terms of taking responsibility for various elements of the learning situation, e.g. setting goals, selecting materials and activities, monitoring progress and assessing outcomes. Holec's definition explained 'WHAT autonomous learners are able to do', rather than 'HOW they are able to do it' (Benson, 2007: 23). In other words, while Holec's definition has served as a model for operationalising learner autonomy in learning situations, it has not established autonomy as a cognitive construct. Elsewhere, Benson (2008: 25) observes that autonomy in language learning theory seems to have resolved the cognitive-situational duality 'by focusing on the learner's capacity for autonomy at the expense of a focus on freedom in learning'. Benson (2008: 30) sees this as an imbalance that needs to be addressed by a shift 'towards a more complex view of the requirements for autonomy and of the relationship between autonomy in learning and autonomy in life'.

The work of Menezes (this volume) suggests that a means of redressing this imbalance may lie in theorising autonomy in language learning from the perspective of complexity theory. As Larsen-Freeman and Cameron (2008) point out, in complexity theory the context is viewed as part of the system and not a backdrop against which the action is played out. Applying this notion to learner autonomy in language learning, Menezes (this volume: 63) writes:

> In Paiva (2006), I argue that autonomy is a socio-cognitive system nested in the SLA system. It involves not only the individual's mental states and processes, but also political, social and economic dimensions. It is not a state, but a non-linear process, which undergoes periods of instability, variability and adaptability. It is an essential element in SLA because it triggers the learning process through learners' agency and leads the system beyond the classroom.

Menezes's conceptualisation of autonomy as a socio-cognitive system nested in the second language acquisition (SLA) system enables the discourse to move beyond the dual nature of autonomy as either primarily a cognitive or situational phenomenon, and at the same time provides an avenue for the exploration of the relationship between autonomy in learning and autonomy in life.

Furthermore, Menezes's comments point to a broader issue, suggesting that it is time to revisit fundamental aspects of learner autonomy in language learning not only from the perspective of constructivist and sociocultural theories of learning (Little, 2007a), but also from other ecological perspectives (Kramsch, 2002), including complexity theory (Larsen-Freeman & Cameron, 2008) and semiotics (van Lier, 2004). Reflecting on autonomy in language learning thirty years after he proposed his classic definition, Holec (2009) observes that a lack of conceptual unity has impeded the comparability of research results and consequently diminished the contributions that educators are making to the field. He appeals to practitioners and researchers 'to give further consideration to the "real" meaning of autonomy, thus reappraising their "theory" on the basis of their "practice"' (Holec, 2009: 22). Menezes's experience suggests that viewing our practice from other theoretical perspectives can yield insights that can help us refine our understanding of autonomy and further the development of theory.

Sade (this volume) illustrates how employing complexity theory in the analysis of language learners' narratives has provided her with insights that have implications for theorising in the areas of identity and motivation. These insights have led her to challenge the post-structuralist notion of fragmented identities and propose in its stead the concept of 'identity fractalisation', interrelated multiple identities that form a whole. The concept of identity fractalisation offers a potential means of addressing an issue that has concerned theorists working with SDT. Noels (2009) notes the need for a 'rapprochement' between the constructivist view of self as 'dynamic, multiple, and relational' and the SDT notion of the self that calls for assimilating various identities into 'their integrated sense of self' - a process that connotes the existence of 'a true, authentic self' (Noels, 2009: 308). Sade's construct of identity fractalisation, which enables theorists to view identities as multiple yet forming a whole, could offer a means of bridging the gap between these two divergent conceptualisations of self.

Another line of inquiry revealing the links between identity and motivation in language learning has prompted Dörnyei (2005, 2009) to introduce the L2 Motivational Self System. Most of the empirical work exploring his model has been quantitative in design (for examples, see Dörnyei & Ushioda, 2009); however, several qualitative studies in this volume have employed the L2 self construct in their analysis. These inquiries offer insights that enhance our understanding of the L2 self as well as the interplay of identity, motivation and autonomy. For example, Lamb's longitudinal study of Indonesian adolescents reveals an association between high initial motivation, autonomous learning of the language and an increasingly refined vision of an L2 self. In another study, Malcolm illustrates how, over time, male medical students in the Arab Gulf region developed L2 selves by taking responsibility for their learning, indicating the importance of taking a long-term perspective on motivation and autonomy in language learning. In another longitudinal study, Murphy, investigating how learners sustain motivation in a distance language learning course offered in the UK, concludes that learners' visions of an L2 self can come in conflict with other ideal selves arising from various life contexts. Murphy found that, in the face of multiple and possibly conflicting identities, those learners who exercised their capacity for autonomy by making conscious decisions and choices regarding their learning, enhanced their motivation to realise their vision of an L2 self. In a study exploring plurilingual learning in self-access centres in Mexico, Castillo Zaragoza notes that the relationship that learners have with each language enables them to discover different aspects of who they are as a person, suggesting the potential to develop an L2 self for each language being studied. In a second study focusing on self-access language learning, Murray illustrates the mutually supportive roles imagination and metacognition play as learners' work to realise their visions of an L2 self. Each of these qualitative studies adds to our understanding of how L2 selves can serve to motivate learners and the role learner autonomy can play in this process.

In several of the chapters, as the authors explored the links between identity, motivation and autonomy, a fourth component emerged: agency. This raises two questions: What exactly are we referring to when we talk about agency in language learning and what are its connections to identity, motivation and autonomy? Work on agency in the field of sociology (notably, Giddens, 1984) and education (e.g. Biesta & Tedder, 2006) suggests that definitions and interconnections are extremely complex and will provide topics for research and reflection for some time to come. In her discussion of agency in relation to language, Ahearn (2001: 112) has provisionally defined agency as 'the socio-culturally mediated capacity to act'. The implicit parallels between this definition of agency and Holec's (1981) definition of autonomy hint at the close connection between the two constructs and underlying issues of power and control. Van Lier (2997: 48) refers to autonomy as 'the feeling of being the agent of one's own actions' and goes on to state that 'ultimately, motivation and autonomy are but two sides of the same coin of agency'. Reflecting on the relationship between agency and identity and autonomy, Benson (2007: 30) cautiously observes that 'agency can perhaps be viewed as a point of origin for the development of autonomy, while identity might be viewed as one of its more important outcomes'. These comments foreshadow the need for an in-depth exploration of agency and its relationship to autonomy, motivation and identity in the field of language education.

Two of the chapters in this volume directly address the issue of agency. In their chapter, Gao and Zhang examine the interrelatedness of agency and metacognition, contending that these contructs, reflecting the duality of sociocultural and cognitive approaches to inquiry, should be viewed as complementary to each other in the study of learner autonomy. In another chapter, Huang investigates the relationship between autonomy, agency and identity. While his study supports Benson's (2007) observation that agency may be a point of origin for the development of autonomy and identity one of its outcomes, it also suggests that identity conceptualisation and construction can also be a point of origin for autonomy, thus drawing attention to the possibility of a non-linear relationship between the constructs. These two studies indicate that the role of agency in language learning and its relationship to identity, motivation and autonomy provide a number of themes for future investigations whose outcomes are certain to have an impact on practice.

Implications for Practice

Practice has always figured prominently in the literature on learner autonomy. In fact, learner autonomy theory has largely emerged from the work of practitioners, and 'theoretical perspectives on learner autonomy have thus been continually tested and refined as they have been brought up against hard realities of language learning and language teaching' (Little, 2007b: 2). In keeping with this tradition, practice has a central place in this volume as educators explore how autonomy, identity and motivation are related. Recent research in the area of motivation suggests the focus on pedagogical practice is not misplaced. Although large-scale studies have confirmed the role of the L2 self in determining learners' motivation, there is empirical evidence to suggest that the work of teachers must not be overlooked. Reporting on a study involving Hungarian secondary school and university students, Csizér and Kormos (2009) found that language learning experiences had a stronger influence than an ideal L2 self on the secondary school students' motivation, while both played an equally important role in motivating the university students. This finding led Csizér and Kormos (2009: 108) to conclude that 'it is largely the teachers' responsibility to motivate students'.

Addressing the issue of teachers' responsibility to foster learners' motivation, Ushioda (this volume) calls on teachers to engage with students as individuals who bring multiple identities to the learning context and who may not identify themselves as language learners. In order to do this, she suggests that teachers create learning opportunities for classroom talk that engage students' transportable identities - latent identities that they bring with them to the classroom context (Richards 2006), such as football fan, club member or romantic partner. In her chapter depicting the language learning experiences of a young Brazilian male whose identities of football fan and rock musician were paramount,

Sade illustrates the alienation and demotivation that can result when teachers fail to value and support the expression of these identities. According to Ushioda (this volume), classroom practices likely to foster the engagement of learners' transportable identities are those that enable learners to 'speak as themselves'.

Ushioda further contends that the practice of engaging students' identities is not new to experienced language teachers and suggests that motivational theory has been lagging behind classroom practice. Cowie and Sakui's (this volume) study examining teachers' perspectives on motivation supports Ushioda's observation. In a revealing comment, one teacher defines motivation as 'learners coming to class with a desire for improving their English abilities in ways relative to their own objectives'. In addition to recognising learners as people with their own objectives, Cowie and Sakui report that many of the 32 teachers in their study took a genuine interest in their students, trying to discover who they were and what their lives were like. Ushioda (this volume) would urge teachers to continue in this vein and to implement classroom practices fostering learner autonomy that enable students' motivations and identities to develop as 'co-constructed processes'.

In another study documenting teachers' perspectives, Reinders and Lázaro interviewed educators working in 46 self-access centres in five countries, concerning their beliefs about learner autonomy in relation to self-access learning. Sadly, their chapter paints a grim view of the lot of teachers working in these centres. Reinders and Lázaro conclude that the challenges that educators face have a negative impact on their motivation and identities as educators. As an implication of their study, they cite the need for pre-service training for self-access workers and ongoing support as they assume the role of facilitators. Interestingly, Benson (2007: 25) notes that in the past decade, 'the importance of self-access within the literature on autonomy has diminished somewhat'. Perhaps this is indicative of current problems in the area and, coupled with Reinders and Lazaro's findings, suggests the need for a renewed self-access language learning research agenda that will hopefully result in administrators and policymakers taking a more favourable view of this mode of learning.

A salient feature of self-access centres has been the promotion of pop culture in language learning. Several of the studies in this collection point to the importance of incorporating pop culture into the curriculum. In their life history inquiry of learners in Hong Kong and Berlin, Chik and Breidbach illustrate how engaging with popular culture can encompass the cultivation of identity, motivation and autonomy. In other studies where pop culture was not the predominant theme, the researchers nonetheless note the role it played in the participants' language learning. For example, Dico in Lamb's chapter and the young Brazilian in Sade's chapter both developed their English proficiency through music and participation in rock bands. Sade recommends that teachers bring pop culture into their classes because this could help create 'identification positions' between learners and target language speakers. As Sade's comments suggest, pop culture materials can provide an opening for students to engage their transportable identities in the language classroom. In his chapter, Murray calls for the use of pop culture materials because of their potential to support learners' motivation and identity construction by enhancing their visions of possible L2 selves and the communities they might one day participate in. In short, these studies present strong evidence to suggest that promoting the use of pop culture materials can support learners' motivation, identity construction and autonomy.

A number of the chapters explore the role that visions of a future L2 self play in the motivation to learn a language. However, as Dörnyei (2009) points out, for a future L2 self to be effective as a motivator, the vision needs to be accompanied by an action plan. According to Dörnyei, an effective action plan will incorporate a goal-setting component with individualised study plans and 'instructional avenues'. This puts the onus on the classroom teacher to discover what form these avenues might take and to implement individualised study plans into what is most likely a traditional textbook-centred curriculum. In his chapter, Murray explores an approach that blends self-access learning with classroom-based instruction. With the guidance and support of the instructor, learners set their language learning goals and devise their own study plans. Taking an in-depth look at three students in the course, Murray illustrates how this particular learning structure enabled the students to 'operationalise their visions' (cf. Dörnyei, 2009) of an L2 self participating in imagined target language communities. However, for teachers, adjusting their practice in this way could present the additional challenge of questioning their beliefs about teaching and learning.

Some of the studies in this collection illustrate the need for teachers to be continuously vigilant and reflexive (Schön, 1986) concerning their beliefs and how these beliefs influence their practice. For example, Cowie and Sakui effectively illustrate the close relationship between teachers' beliefs concerning motivation and their classroom practices. Reinders and Lázaro remind teachers that questioning their beliefs can prevent them from imposing their notions of 'good teaching and good learning' on students when there may be alternatives more suitable for the learners. Malcolm cautions teachers about the dangers of being too quick to form beliefs about learners' potential. In their chapter, Ryan and Mercer provide an example of how teachers, when promoting study abroad, might inadvertently reinforce certain student-held beliefs that could be detrimental to their learning and the development of an identity as an autonomous language learner. These studies indicate the need for teachers to be aware of their beliefs, their students' beliefs and the impact these beliefs can have on learner autonomy, motivation and identity.

Teachers also need to be aware that for many foreign language learners the stakes are high. The construction of L2 identities is serious business. For many learners, their future lives are at risk. This comes across very poignantly in Huang's account of Chinese pre-service teachers preparing for their final examinations. Similarly, in Gao and Zhang's chapter illustrating a young Chinese woman's exercise of agency and metacognitive development, the reader is made acutely aware that the choices she makes are determining her future and the identities she will develop. In another part of the world, young Middle Eastern men must learn English in order to pursue their medical degrees. Malcolm portrays how their future selves and the hopes and dreams of their families depend on their successful language acquisition. These stories serve to remind us that as language teachers, the work we engage in has serious, life-altering consequences for many people, and can significantly influence their motivation, identity construction and development as autonomous learners.

Directions for Future Research

In addition to yielding insights to guide theory development and practice, the chapters also suggest a number of directions for future research. Nearly all of the chapters concluded with suggestions related to their specific line of inquiry. What follows is a consideration of possible trends and areas of investigation that emerge from a reflection on the chapters as a whole.

Teachers' perspectives on motivation

Cowie and Sakui (this volume) observe that a voice rarely heard in the literature on motivation in language learning is that of the teacher. Acknowledging the value of theoretical models, Cowie and Sakui call for motivational research, which provides explanations that can directly inform classroom practice. To this end, they suggest that future inquiries include teachers' perspectives. An interesting aspect of Cowie and Sakui's study was that teachers referred to components of learner autonomy, but stopped short of making explicit references to autonomy or suggesting that it be promoted as a means of enhancing learner motivation. Therefore, future research exploring teachers' perspectives on motivation might also examine their views on the role of learner autonomy and identity, especially 'transportable identities', in relation to classroom pedagogy.

Teacher motivation

Dörnyei (2005) notes that few research studies have explored teachers' motivation. Reinders and Lázaro's chapter draws attention to the importance of this issue through their exploration of how teachers' beliefs can conflict with the actual challenges of working in the area of self-access language learning, and the impact these conflicts can have on their teacher identities and motivation. Future research might explore teacher motivation in both classroom and self-access settings, and include a focus on the role that teacher autonomy plays in the evolution of their identities and motivation.

Cultural variations in the conceptualisation of self

MacIntyre *et al.* (2009) caution researchers to consider cultural variation in the conception of self in studies exploring the motivational potential of the L2 self. While it is commonly accepted that 'people define themselves using the concepts, terms, values, and ideologies provided by their cultural and social environments' (Cross & Gore, 2003: 536), a consideration of cultural variation raises a number of issues. First of all, it implies the comparison of cultures on a macro level; e.g. contrasting western independent conceptions of the self with East Asian interdependent notions of the self (see Cross & Gore, 2003, for a review of this literature). The search for cultural variations on this level can lead to sweeping generalisations that can unduly influence educators' interpretations of learners' experiences in particular contexts. For example, in the area of learner autonomy, such generalisations have led to a debate concerning the appropriateness of autonomy - a construct with its roots in 'western' moral and political philosophy - for learners of other cultural backgrounds, specifically Asian. Reinders and Lázaro's (this volume) study, which crossed several cultural boundaries, illustrates the need to be weary of such notions when interpreting data. In their study, they found that a pervasive complaint among teachers involved in self-access learning was that students do not see the value in developing autonomy and tend to lack the skills necessary for independent learning. While one might explain this phenomenon in terms of cultural variation, Reinders and Lázaro's data pointed to a lack of educational experience on the part of the learners rather than cultural differences. They concluded that the students were simply not familiar with the concept of taking responsibility for their learning. Viewing the situation in this light opens up the possibility of engaging students in appropriate pedagogical interventions. Their conclusion draws attention to the importance of looking beyond cultural variations in order to focus analyses on the experiences of individual learners operating within a particular context - a strategy that was prevalent in the studies collected in this volume.

Other issues to be explored in relation to the culturally mediated self pertain to notions that foreign language learning involves inter-cultural learning and challenges 'culturally-conditioned conceptions of the self' (Benson, 2007: 25). In their review of the literature on the bicultural and multicultural self, Cross and Gore (2003: 554) confirm that 'engagement in new cultural contexts can result in a change in self-concept as individuals receive feedback that is discrepant with their world views'. Moreover, they note that there is 'mounting evidence [which] indicates that individuals with exposure to two cultures can develop separate, culturally derived self representations'; in other words, 'multiple internalized cultures are not necessarily blended' (Cross & Gore, 2003: 554). These findings support the suggestion arising from Castillo Zaragoza's (this volume) study that plurilingual learners develop separate L2 selves for each language they are learning. Future research will need to explore this possibility and other issues related to culture change and the self from an SLA perspective.

Study abroad

Benson (2007) observes that although one would expect autonomy to figure prominently in work investigating learners' overseas language learning experiences, this is not the case. Discussing agency in study abroad contexts, Ryan and Mercer (this volume) warn that a reliance on the learning environment, i.e. immersion in the target language and culture, or natural ability, rather than on purposeful learning behaviour might impede the development of an autonomous language learning identity, which could subsequently hamper gains in language proficiency. They propose a research agenda that examines learners' mindsets and their influence on learners' agency, motivation and identity in various language learning contexts. Clearly, the study abroad context provides fertile ground for the exploration of the interplay of these constructs.

Support for the emergence and realisation of an L2 self

In Lamb's chapter exploring the long-term development of learners' L2 selves and motivation in Indonesia, he observes that one of a school teacher's greatest challenges in a foreign language context will be to provide students with opportunities to 'authenticate' their possible selves through actual communication both in and out of the classroom. He further notes that motivating many of the learners will be a challenge because it means helping them acquire visions of themselves as L2 speakers. Researchers will have to come to the aid of teachers in identifying effective means of supporting the emergence and realisation of L2 selves in formal educational settings. In many instances, teachers themselves will be best situated to carry out this work, which could take the form of action research projects. In view of Dörnyei's (2009) tacit suggestion that potential 'instructional avenues' will need to incorporate elements associated with autonomous learning, i.e. goal setting and individual study plans, educators in the area of learner autonomy appear to be well positioned to take the lead in this endeavour.

Pop culture

As demonstrated in the chapters by Chik and Briedbach, Murray, and Sade, pop culture materials can fuel learners' imaginations, which can enable them to experience a sense of belonging to imagined communities (cf. Wenger, 1998). However, pop culture materials can also serve as a conduit for another mode of belonging to communities: alignment. Wenger (1998: 179) writes that 'alignment bridges time and space to form broader enterprises so that participants become connected through the coordination of their energies, actions and practices. Through alignment, we become part of something big because we do what it takes to play our part'. He later adds that 'imagination helps build a picture of how our part fits' (Wenger, 1998: 180). To clarify the distinction between imagination and alignment as modes of belonging, it may be helpful to consider the situation of Mandy, the Chinese female video gamer in Chik and Breidbach's study (this volume). Through her imagination, Mandy had a sense of active engagement in the fictional worlds created by the computer games she played; however, through alignment, she experienced a sense of belonging to a wide community of video gamers who enjoyed the game in English.

Wenger (1998: 183) notes that 'most of what we do involves a combination of the three modes of belonging: engagement, imagination, and alignment'. Discussing the relationship between imagination and alignment, Norton (2001) explains that imagination does not necessarily lead to action whereas alignment does. Dörnyei (2005) points out the need for an increased understanding of how imagination and alignment interact in order to move learners to take action leading to the realisation of ideal self images. Further inquiries similar to those done by Chik and Briedbach and Murray, which focus on the role of pop culture, and by Sade, which view pop culture as a means of creating 'identification positions' between learners and target language speakers, could shed light on the interaction between imagination and alignment.

Agency, and identity, motivation and autonomy

Future research will have to broaden our understanding of what is meant by agency in language learning and its relationship to identity, motivation and autonomy. The chapters by Huang and Gao and Zhang raise several questions that these inquiries might address. Huang indicates that the degree of control that learners are able to exercise in a given context might serve to distinguish agency from autonomy. Giddens (1984: 14) remarks that 'an agent ceases to be such if he or she loses the capability to "make a difference", that is, to exercise some sort of power'. Therefore, what role do power and control play in determining, distinguishing or linking agency and autonomy? Here, the role of the learning context needs to be investigated since, according to Giddens (1984: 169), the structure, 'defined as rules and resources', of an environment can both enable and constrain the exercise of agency, as it can autonomy. Huang's findings point to a non-linear interaction among identity, agency and autonomy, which is embedded in the learning context. His conclusions suggest the need to explore current understandings of context and the extent to which learners can be viewed as part of the context. Questions of another nature are raised by Gao and Zhang, such as, can metacognition and agency, in fact, be conceptualised as prerequisites for autonomous learning? Or, could it be that they are co-emergent? Are they perhaps smaller systems within a larger complex system? These are just some of the questions that might be addressed as researchers examine agency and its relationship to identity, motivation and autonomy.

Research methodology

While studies of motivation in language education have often been large-scale inquiries relying on psychometric approaches, studies in the area of learner autonomy have often been small-scale qualitative inquiries focusing on individual learners in a specific context. Ushioda's (2009, this volume) call for a theoretical perspective that takes a person-in-context relational view of motivation carries with it the suggestion that future research will need to adopt methods enabling researchers to focus on people as individuals within the various contexts that constitute their daily lives. In this regard, it is noteworthy that half of the studies reported in this collection rely on narrative inquiry or a combination of narratives and interviews. In most cases, these interviews could be described as life history interviews in that their focus is on understanding 'the complex interaction between individuals' lives and the institutional and societal contexts within which they are lived' (Cole & Knowles, 2001: 126). These studies illustrate the potential of various forms of narrative inquiry and life history interviews to explore an individual's identities and sense of self within the multiple contexts that comprise his or her world.

However, as MacIntyre *et al.* (2009) caution in their discussion of theoretical issues pertaining to motivation and the self, we must not throw out the baby with the bathwater. Just as theoretical perspectives on motivation need not be mutually exclusive, neither do research paradigms. For example, Lamb (this volume) cites the need for 'larger-scale investigations' of the L2 motivational self system in early adolescence. Although large-scale projects are often quantitative in design, perhaps inquiries, such as the one suggested by Lamb, would be well served by a blended methods approach. Researchers conducting future inquiries into identity, motivation and autonomy might wish to explore the possibility of employing imaginative designs that integrate quantitative and qualitative methods rather than ones that relegate qualitative inquiry to exploratory studies viewed as precursors to the 'actual' study, and are designed to provide data that can enable researchers to contextualise the findings suggested by their statistical analyses. Clearly, future inquiries into identity, motivation and autonomy will require researchers to experiment with all the methodological resources at their disposal and to extend the boundaries of their theoretical perspectives and research paradigms.

Conclusion

This final chapter has attempted to draw readers' attention to the richness of the chapters in this volume in terms of their potential to inform theory, practice and future research directions. Noels (2009: 310) observes that at this time we cannot rely on any one theory to explain motivation in language learning; rather, we must continue to 'test the limits of our theories, and stretch beyond their boundaries'. The same can be said for work on autonomy, identity and their interplay with motivation. Through their exploration of the links between these three constructs from a variety of theoretical and methodological perspectives, the authors of the chapters in this volume are testing theories and pushing against their current boundaries. Their work has raised important questions and offered insights related to theory, pedagogical practice and future research directions. Perhaps, most importantly, these chapters have revealed the potential of taking an approach that sees identity, motivation and autonomy as interrelated constructs.

References

Ahearn, L.M. (2001) Language and agency. *Annual Review of Anthropology* 30, 109–137.

Benson, P. (2007) Autonomy in language teaching and learning. *Language Teaching* 40, 21–40.

Benson, P. (2008) Teachers' and learners' perspectives on autonomy. In T. Lamb and H. Reinders (eds) *Learner and Teacher Autonomy: Concepts, Realities, and Responses* (pp. 15–32). Amsterdam: John Benjamin.

Biesta, G. and Tedder, M. (2006) How is agency possible? Towards an ecological understanding of agency-as-achievement. *Working Paper 5, Learning Lives: Learning, Development and Agency in the Life Course.* University of Exeter: Teaching and Learning Research Programme. On WWW at http://www.tlrp.org/project%20sites/LearningLives/papers/working_papers/Working_paper_5_Exeter_Feb_06.pdf. Accessed 7.17.08.

Cole, A.L. and Knowles, J.G. (2001) *Lives in Context: The Art of Life History Research.* Walnut Creek, CA: Altamira.

Cross, S.E. and Gore, J.S. (2003) Cultural models of the self. In M.R. Leary and J. Price Tangney (eds) *Handbook of Self and Identity* (pp. 536–564). New York: Guilford.

Csizér, K. and Kormos, J. (2009) Learning experiences, selves, and motivated learning behaviour: A comparative analysis of structural models for Hungarian secondary and university learners of English. In Z. Dörnyei and E. Ushioda (eds) *Motivation, Language Identity and the L2 Self* (pp. 98–119). Bristol: Multilingual Matters.

Dörnyei, Z. (2005) *The Psychology of the Language Learner: Individual Differences in Second Language Acquisition.* Mahwah, NJ: Lawrence Erlbaum.

Dörnyei, Z. (2009) The L2 Motivational Self System. In Z. Dörnyei and E. Ushioda (eds) *Motivation, Language Identity and the L2 Self* (pp. 9–42). Bristol: Multilingual Matters.

Dörnyei, Z. and Ushioda, E. (eds) (2009) *Motivation, Language Identity and the L2 Self.* Bristol. Multilingual Matters.

Giddens, A. (1984) *The Constitution of Society: Outline of the Theory of Structuration.* Berkeley and Los Angeles: University of California Press.

Holec, H. (1981) *Autonomy in Foreign Language Learning.* Oxford: Pergamon.

Holec, H. (2009) Autonomy in language learning: A single pedagogical paradigm or two? In F. Kjisik, P. Voller, N. Aoki and Y. Nakata (eds) *Mapping the Terrain of Learner Autonomy: Learning Environments, Learning Communities, and Identities* (pp. 21–47). Tampere: University of Tampere Press.

Kaplan, A. and Flum, H. (2009) Motivation and identity: The relations of action and development in educational contexts - An introduction to the special issue. *Educational Psychologist* 44 (2), 73–77.

Kramsch, C. (2002) *Language Acquisition and Language Socialization.* London: Continuum.

Larsen-Freeman, D. and Cameron, L. (2008) *Complex Systems and Applied Linguistics.* Oxford: Oxford University Press.

Little, D. (1991) *Learner Autonomy 1: Definitions, Issues and Problems.* Dublin: Authentik.

Little, D. (2007a) Language learner autonomy: Some fundamental considerations revisited. *Innovations in Language Learning and Teaching* 1 (1), 14–29.

Little, D. (2007b) Introduction: Restructuring learner and teacher autonomy in language education. In A. Barfield and S.H. Brown (eds) *Restructuring Autonomy in Language Education: Inquiry and Innovation* (pp. 1–12). Basingstoke: Palgrave Macmillan.

MacIntyre, P., MacKinnon, S. and Clément, R. (2009) The baby, the bathwater and the future of language learning motivation research. In Z. Dörnyei and E. Ushioda (eds) *Motivation, Language Identity and the L2 Self* (pp. 43–65). Bristol: Multilingual Matters.

Noels, K.A. (2009) The internalisation of language learning into the self and social identity. In Z. Dörnyei and E. Ushioda (eds) *Motivation, Language Identity and the L2 Self* (pp. 295–313). Bristol: Multilingual Matters.

Norton, B. (2000) *Identity and Language Learning: Gender, Ethnicity and Educational Change.* London: Longman/Pearson Education.

Norton, B. (2001) Non-participation, imagined communities and the language classroom. In M.P. Breen (ed.) *Learner Contributions to Language Learning: New Directions in Research* (pp. 159–171). Harlow: Longman.

Paiva, V.L.M.O. (2006) Autonomia e complexidade. *Linguagem e Ensino* 9 (1), 77–127.

Richards, K. (2006) 'Being the teacher': Identity and classroom conversation. *Applied Linguistics* 27 (1), 51–77.

Ryan, R.M. and Deci, E.L. (2003) On assimilating identities to the self: A self-determination theory perspective on internalization and integrity within cultures. In M.R. Leary and J. Price Tangney (eds) *Handbook of Self and Identity* (pp. 253–272). New York: Guilford.

Schön, D.A. (1983) *The Reflective Practitioner: How Professionals Think in Action.* New York: Basic.

Van Lier, L. (2004) *The Ecology and Semiotics of Language Learning: A Sociocultural Perspective.* Boston, MA: Kluwer Academic.

Wenger, E. (1998) *Communities of Practice: Learning, Meaning and Identity.* Cambridge: Cambridge University Press.

Index